£9.99

AQA Mathematics

Unit 2 Higher

New GCSE

Series Editor
Paul Metcalf

Series Advisor
Andy Darbourne

Lead Authors
Sandra Burns
Shaun Procter-Green
Margaret Thornton

Authors
Tony Fisher
June Haighton
Anne Haworth
Gill Hewlett
Andrew Manning
Ginette McManus
Howard Prior
David Pritchard
Dave Ridgway
Paul Winters

Nelson Thornes

Published in 2010 by:
Nelson Thornes Ltd
Delta Place
27 Bath Road
CHELTENHAM
GL53 7TH
United Kingdom

10 11 12 13 14 / 10 9 8 7 6 5 4 3 2 1

A catalogue record for this book is available from the British Library

ISBN 978 1 4085 0626 4

Cover photograph: PureStock/Photolibrary
Illustrations by Rupert Besley, Roger Penwill and Tech-Set Limited
Page make-up by Tech-Set Limited, Gateshead

Printed and bound in Spain by GraphyCems

Photograph acknowledgements:
Fotolia: 1.3; 3.7; 6.1; 8.8; 9.2; 13.1; C1.2; C1.4; C1.5; C1.6; C1.7; C1.8; C1.12.
iStockphoto: 1.1; 1.2; 2.1; 3.6; 8.1; 8.9; 8.10; 10.1; 11.12; 13.3a&b; C1.13.
Photolibrary: 3LH-B&W / 5.1.
Wikipedia: Plimpton 322 / 12.1.

Contents

Nelson Thornes and AQA

Nelson Thornes has worked in partnership with AQA to ensure that this book and the accompanying online resources offer you the best support for your GCSE course.

All AQA endorsed resources undergo a thorough quality assurance process to ensure that their contents closely match the AQA specification. You can be confident that the content of materials branded with AQA's 'Exclusively Endorsed' logo have been written, checked and approved by AQA senior examiners, in order to achieve AQA's exclusive endorsement.

The print and online resources together unlock blended learning; this means that the links between the activities in the book and the activities online blend together to maximise your understanding of a topic and help you achieve your potential.

These online resources are available on *kerboodle!* which can be accessed via the internet at **www.kerboodle.com/live**, anytime, anywhere.

If your school or college subscribes to *kerboodle!* you will be provided with your own personal login details. Once logged in, access your course and locate the required activity.

For more information and help on how to use *kerboodle!* visit **www.kerboodle.com**.

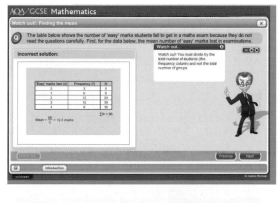

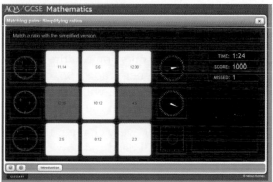

How to use this book

To help you unlock blended learning, we have referenced the activities in this book that have additional online coverage in *kerboodle!* by using this icon: **k!**

The icons in this book show you the online resources available from the start of the new specification and will always be relevant.

In addition, to keep the blend up-to-date and engaging, we review customer feedback and may add new content onto *kerboodle!* after publication!

Welcome to GCSE Mathematics

This book has been written by teachers and examiners who not only want you to get the best grade you can in your GCSE exam, but also to enjoy maths. It covers all the material you will need to know for AQA GCSE Mathematics Unit 2 Higher. This unit does not allow you to use a calculator, so you will not be able to use this most of the time throughout this book. Look out for calculator or non-calculator symbols (shown below) which may tell you whether to use a calculator or not.

In the exam, you will be tested on the Assessment Objectives (AOs) below. Ask your teacher if you need help to understand what these mean.

AO1 recall and use your knowledge of the prescribed content

AO2 select and apply mathematical methods in a range of contexts

AO3 interpret and analyse problems and generate strategies to solve them.

Each chapter is made up of the following features:

Objectives

The objectives at the start of the chapter give you an idea of what you need to do to get each grade. Remember that the examiners expect you to do well at the lower grade questions on the exam paper in order to get the higher grades. So, even if you are aiming for a Grade A you will still need to do well on the Grade D questions on the exam paper.

On the first page of every chapter, there are also words that you will need to know or understand, called Key Terms. The box called 'You should already know' describes the maths that you will have learned before studying this chapter. There is also an interesting fact at the beginning of each chapter which tells you about maths in real life.

The Learn sections give you the key information and examples to show how to do each topic. There are several Learn sections in each chapter.

Practise...

Questions that allow you to practise what you have just learned.

D The bars that run alongside questions in the exercises show you what grade the question is aimed at. This will give you an idea of what grade you're working at. Don't forget, even if you are aiming at a Grade A, you will still need to do well on the Grades D–B questions.

⚠ These questions are harder questions.

⚙ These questions are Functional Maths type questions, which show how maths can be used in real life.

❓ These questions are problem solving questions, which will require you to think carefully about how best to answer.

▦ These questions should be attempted **with** a calculator.

☒ These questions should be attempted **without** using a calculator.

Assess

End of chapter questions written by examiners. Some chapters feature additional questions taken from real past papers to further your understanding.

Hint

These are tips for you to remember whilst learning the maths or answering questions.

AQA Examiner's tip

These are tips from the people who will mark your exams, giving you advice on things to remember and watch out for.

Bump up your grade

These are tips from the people who will mark your exams, giving you help on how to boost your grade, especially aimed at getting a Grade C.

Consolidation

The consolidation chapter allows you to practise what you have learned in previous chapters. The questions in these chapters can cover any of the topics you have already seen.

1 Prime factors

Objectives

Examiners would normally expect students who get these grades to be able to:

C

find the least common multiple (LCM) of two simple numbers

find the highest common factor (HCF) of two simple numbers

write a number as a product of prime factors

B

find the least common multiple (LCM) of two or more numbers

find the highest common factor (HCF) of two or more numbers.

Did you know?

Padlocked

Did you know that **prime numbers** are used to keep credit card numbers secret when people buy things on the internet?

The system works a bit like a padlock and key. The seller sends the buyer a 'padlock' (the product of two very large prime numbers), but keeps the 'key' (the two prime numbers themselves). The buyer uses the padlock to 'lock up' their credit card number and send it to the seller. The seller is the only person who has the key to unlock the padlock. This system is very safe because it is extremely difficult to find two large prime numbers that multiply to give a particular product. Can you find two prime numbers whose product is 817?

The **product** is the result when you multiply numbers.

Those used for internet shopping are much larger than 817.

Key terms

prime number
product
factor
common factor
highest common factor (HCF)
multiple
least common multiple (LCM)
index

You should already know:

✔ how to apply the four rules, +, −, × and ÷, to integers

✔ about place value

✔ how to recognise even and odd numbers

✔ the meaning of 'sum', 'difference' and 'product'

Learn... 1.1 Factors and multiples 🔑

A **factor** is a positive whole number that divides exactly into another number.

For example, the factors of 16 are: 1   2   4   8   16

A factor is sometimes called a divisor.

Factors usually occur in pairs:
$1 \times 16 = 16, 2 \times 8 = 16, 4 \times 4 = 16$

To find all the factors of a number, look for factor pairs.

For example, $20 = 1 \times 20$ so 1 and 20 are factors of 20

               $20 = 2 \times 10$ so 2 and 10 are factors of 20

               $20 = 4 \times 5$ so 4 and 5 are factors of 20

> AQA **Examiner's tip**
>
> Be systematic so you don't lose any factors.

The factors of 20 are 1, 2, 4, 5, 10, 20.

The **common factors** of two or more numbers are the factors that are the same for all the numbers.

The **highest common factor (HCF)** of two or more numbers is the highest factor that is the same for all the numbers.

The **multiples** of a number are the products in its multiplication table.

For example, $1 \times 3 = \mathbf{3}, 2 \times 3 = \mathbf{6}, 3 \times 3 = \mathbf{9}, \dots$ The answers 3, 6, 9, ... are the multiples of 3.

So the multiples of 3 are   3   6   9   12   15   18   21,   ... (goes on forever)

The **least common multiple (LCM)** of two or more numbers is the least multiple that is the same for all the numbers.

Example: Find the highest common factor (HCF) of 20 and 24.

> AQA **Examiner's tip**
>
> Remember 1 is a factor of all numbers.

Solution: A factor of a number is something that divides exactly into the number.

               The factors of 20 are **1, 2, 4,** 5, 10, 20

               The factors of 24 are **1, 2,** 3, **4,** 6, 8, 12, 24

               The common factors are the numbers that are in both lists.

               The common factors are **1, 2, 4.**

               The highest common factor is **4.**

Example: Find the least common multiple (LCM) of 6, 8 and 12.

Solution: A multiple of a number is something that the number divides into.

               The multiples of 6 are   6, 12, 18, **24,** 30, 36, 42, **48,** 54, 60, 66, **72,** ...

               The multiples of 8 are   8, 16, **24,** 32, 40, **48,** 56, 64, **72,** ...

               The multiples of 12 are 12, **24,** 36, **48,** 60, **72,** ...

               The common multiples are the numbers that are in all lists.

               The common multiples are **24, 48, 72,** ...

               The least common multiple is **24.**

> **Bump up your grade**
>
> For a Grade C, you must be able to find the highest common factor and the least common multiple.

Practise...   1.1 Factors and multiples *k!*   D C B A A*

1 **a** Write down the first 12 multiples of 9. Then find their digit sums. What do you notice?

b Here is a list of numbers.
153   207   378   452   574   3789
Which of these do you think are multiples of 9?

c Check your answers to part **b** by dividing by 9.

d How can you tell whether a number is a multiple of 9?

e How can you tell whether a number is a multiple of 18? Explain your answer.

2 Sam is finding factors of 627.
Here are his results so far.

627 ÷	1	3		
gives	627	209		

a Explain why Sam does not need to try dividing by 4 and 5.

b Sam works out 627 ÷ 7 and gets 89.5…
How does this show that 7 is not a factor?

c Copy and complete Sam's table of factors.

d Explain how you know that there are no other factors.

3 Find the common factors of the following pairs of numbers.

a 9 and 12   **c** 14 and 35   **e** 15 and 35

b 8 and 28   **d** 24 and 36   **f** 12 and 30

4 Which of these statements are true? Which are false? Explain your answers.

a 16 is a common factor of 32 and 80.

b 16 is a common multiple of 32 and 80.

c The smallest common factor of 12 and 20 is 2.

d The highest common factor of 12 and 20 is 4.

5 Find the common factors of 42 and 70 and write down the highest common factor.

6 Find the factors then the highest common factors of the following sets of numbers.

a 12 and 18   **d** 75 and 100

b 24 and 32   **e** 8, 10 and 12

c 48 and 60

7 **a** The highest common factor of two numbers is 7. Give a possible pair of numbers.

b The highest common factor of three numbers is 15. Give a possible set of three numbers.

8 Find the least common multiple of the following sets of numbers.

a 6 and 8   **d** 2, 3 and 5

b 5 and 9   **e** 6, 18 and 24

c 12 and 20   **f** 3, 4 and 7

C

9 Tracy says that the least common multiple of 24 and 60 is 12.

Is she correct? Explain your answer.

B

10 Find the least common multiple of the following sets of numbers.

a 6, 8 and 32

b 15, 20 and 25

c 50, 75 and 100

11 Ahmed says that the least common multiple of any two numbers is the same as their product.

He gives the example that the least common multiple of 4 and 5 is 4 × 5 = 20

Give an example to shows that Ahmed is not correct.

12 Find the highest common factor of:

a 36, 45 and 54

b 14, 56 and 84

c 60, 75 and 90.

13 **a** Find the least common multiple of:

i 12 and 13

ii 12 and 14.

b Explain why the LCM of 12 and 13 is the same as their product, but the LCM of 12 and 14 is not the same as their product.

14 **a** One common factor of 48 and 60 is an odd number. What is it?

b A common multiple of 2 and 7 lies between 30 and 50. What is it?

15 John sets his watch using the kitchen clock. But the kitchen clock loses one hour a day.

How long will it be until John's watch next shows the same time as the kitchen clock?

16 Mark is trying to find 'perfect' numbers.

	Definition	Example
Perfect	A number whose factors (not including itself) have a sum that is **equal** to the number itself.	6 (factors 1, 2, 3, 6) because 1 + 2 + 3 = 6
Deficient	A number whose factors (not including itself) have a sum that is **smaller than** the number itself.	9 (factors 1, 3, 9) because 1 + 3 = 4 which is smaller than 9
Abundant	A number whose factors (not including itself) have a sum that is **greater than** the number itself.	12 (factors 1, 2, 3, 4, 6, 12) because 1 + 2 + 3 + 4 + 6 = 16 which is greater than 12

a Find the next perfect number after 6.

b List the deficient and abundant numbers that lie between 6 and your answer to part **a**.

c Explain why all prime numbers are deficient.

Learn... 1.2 Prime numbers and prime factors 🄺

A prime number is a positive whole number that has **exactly two factors**.

The first seven prime numbers are:

2	3	5	7	11	13	17
Factors	Factors	Factors	Factors	Factors	Factors	Factors
1 & 2	1 & 3	1 & 5	1 & 7	1 & 11	1 & 13	1 & 17

1 is not a prime number because it has only one factor.

2 is the only even prime number. All other even numbers have 1, themselves and 2 as factors, and may have other factors as well.

All the missing odd numbers have three or more factors.
For example, the factors of 15 are 1, 3, 5 and 15.

Index form

Prime numbers are the 'building blocks' of mathematics. All other numbers can be written as products of prime numbers.

index

For example, $12 = 2 \times 2 \times 3 = 2^2 \times 3$

This is called index form or **index** notation.

product   index

and $81 = 9 \times 9 = 3 \times 3 \times 3 \times 3 = 3^4$

Sometimes the **prime factor decomposition** of more difficult numbers can be found from that of easier numbers.

For example, $120 = 12 \times 10 = 2^2 \times 3 \times 2 \times 5 = 2^3 \times 3 \times 5$

Multiplying by 10 raises the power of 2 by 1 and gives an extra factor 5.

12   10

The following example shows another way of finding prime factors, called the **tree method**.

Example: Write 280 as a product of its prime factors in index form.

Solution: Two 'trees' are shown below. The first starts by splitting 280 into 28×10.

The numbers are then split again and again until you get to prime numbers.

The second tree starts by splitting 280 into 2×140.

This shows that whichever tree you use, you end with three 2s, a 5 and a 7.

This is sometimes called prime factor decomposition.

Keep splitting up until you reach prime numbers.

Can you see why you stop when you get prime numbers?

280 written as a product of its prime factors is $2 \times 2 \times 2 \times 5 \times 7$

In index form, $280 = 2^3 \times 5 \times 7$

$2^3 = 2 \times 2 \times 2$

Bump up your grade

For a Grade C, you must be able to write a number as a product of its prime factors.

Example: **a** Write each of these numbers as a product of prime factors in index form.

  i 280 **ii** 300

  b Find the highest common factor (HCF) of 280 and 300.

  c Find the least common multiple (LCM) of 280 and 300.

Solution: **a** The ladder method is a systematic way of writing a number as a product of its prime factors.

> **AQA** *Examiner's tip*
> Remember 1 is NOT a prime number.

2	280
2	140
2	70
5	35
7	7
	1

Try the next prime number to see if it is a factor:

2 then 3, 5, 7, 11, …

Sometimes you can divide by a factor more than once.

2	300
2	150
3	75
5	25
5	5
	1

280 written as a product of its prime factors is $2 \times 2 \times 2 \times 5 \times 7$

In index form, $280 = 2^3 \times 5 \times 7$

$300 = 2 \times 2 \times 3 \times 5 \times 5$
$= 2^2 \times 3 \times 5^2$

  b Compare $280 = 2 \times 2 \times 2 \times 5 \times 7$
  with $300 = 2 \times 2 \times 3 \times 5 \times 5$

  To find the HCF of 280 and 300, multiply all the factors they have in common.
  The HCF of 280 and 300 = $2 \times 2 \times 5 = $ **20**

  c The LCM must contain all the factors of both numbers.
  The LCM of 280 and 300 = $2 \times 2 \times 2 \times 3 \times 5 \times 5 \times 7$
  This has the same factors as 300 with an extra 2 and 7.
  So the LCM of 280 and 300 is $300 \times 14 = $ **4200**

Practise... 1.2 Prime numbers and prime factors ⒦ D C B A A*

1 Write down all the prime numbers between 20 and 40.

2 Which of these numbers are **not** prime numbers?

  51 53 55 57 59

  Explain your answers.

3 Two prime numbers lie between 80 and 90. Find:

  a their sum **b** their difference.

> **Hint**
> Add to find the sum.
> Subtract to find the difference.

4 Write each number as the product of two prime factors.

  a 14 **b** 33 **c** 65 **d** 91

5 Write each number as a product of prime factors. Use index notation.

  a 24 **c** 84 **e** 132 **g** 216

  b 36 **d** 96 **f** 144 **h** 520

6　**a**　Write 30 as a product of prime factors.

　　b　Use your answer to part **a** to write these numbers as products of prime factors in index form.

　　　i　60　　　**ii**　90　　　**iii**　210　　　**iv**　300　　　**v**　750

7　**a**　Write each number as a product of prime factors, using index notation.

　　　i　270　　　**ii**　450

　　b　Use your answers to part **a** to find:

　　　i　the highest common factor of 270 and 450

　　　ii　the least common multiple of 270 and 450.

8　**a**　Write each number as a product of prime factors, using index notation.

　　　i　42　　　**ii**　60　　　**iii**　72

　　b　Use your answers to part **a** to find:

　　　i　the highest common factor of 42, 60 and 72

　　　ii　the least common multiple of 42, 60 and 72.

9　A Mersenne number is one less than a power of 2. This can be written as $2^n - 1$.

　　For example, when n is 3, $2^3 - 1 = 8 - 1 = 7$. So 7 is a Mersenne number.

　　a　Copy and complete this table of Mersenne numbers.

n	1	2	3	4	5	6	7	8	9	10
$2^n - 1$			7							

　　b　Which of these Mersenne numbers are prime?

10　Which of these numbers **cannot** be prime?

　　　1895　　　2356　　　3457　　　5739

　　Give a reason for your answers.

11　**a**　Write each of these numbers in the form $2^a \times 3^b \times 5^c$.

　　　i　1080　　　**ii**　1800　　　**iii**　8100

　　b　Write the HCF and LCM of these three numbers in the form $2^a \times 3^b \times 5^c$.

12　The prime factorisation of a number is $2^3 \times 3^2$. What is the number?

13　The product of two prime numbers is sometimes used as a security device.
　　To 'break the code' you need to find two prime numbers that give a particular product.

　　a　Find two prime numbers that multiply to give:

　　　i　111　　　**ii**　221　　　**iii**　319　　　**iv**　437　　　**v**　767

　　b　Why are even numbers not very useful in this situation?

　　c　What advice can you give someone who is trying to find two prime numbers that multiply to give a particular product?

14   Work out what each number is.

a   It is a prime number. It is a factor of 35. It is not a factor of 25.

b   It is less than 50. It is a multiple of 3. It is also a multiple of 5.
The sum of its digits is a prime number.

c   It is a prime number less than 100.
It is one more than a multiple of 8 and its digits add up to 10.

d   Make up number descriptions of your own. Ask a friend to find the numbers.

15   Any even number greater than 4 can be written as the sum of two odd prime numbers, sometimes in more than one way.

For example, 22 = 3 + 19 or 5 + 17 or 11 + 11

a   Find two odd prime numbers that add up to:

i   8   **ii**   20   **iii**   42   **iv**   60

b   Any number greater than 7 can be written as the sum of three prime numbers.
Find three prime numbers that add up to:

i   12   **ii**   25   **iii**   48   **iv**   99

Can you explain why this is true?

Assess

C

1   Write down all the factors of 36 which are also factors of 48.

2   **a**   Write down a 2-digit number that is a factor of 105 and a multiple of 7.

b   What is the next prime number after 89?

3   Find:

a   the highest common factor of 16 and 24

b   the least common multiple of 16 and 24.

4   Write 392 as a product of its prime factors in index form.

5   Here are three numbers.

    36   42   49

Give a reason why each number could be the odd one out.

B

6   **a**   Express 120 as the product of its prime factors.
Write your answer in index form.

b   Find the highest common factor of 84 and 120.

7   Helen is training for a triathlon.
She plans to run every 2 days, swim every 4 days and cycle every 5 days.
Today she ran, swam and cycled.

How many days will it be before she next runs, swims and cycles on the same day?

B

8 James races two model cars around a track.
The first car takes 42 seconds to complete each circuit.
The second car takes 1 minute to complete each circuit.
The cars start together from the starting line.

How long will it be before they are together on the starting line again?

9 **a** You are given that $54 = 2 \times 3^3$
Write each of the following as the product of prime factors in index form.

i 108 **ii** 216 **iii** 540

b What is the highest common factor of 54 and 84?

c What is the least common multiple of 54 and 84?

10 Sara says that the value of the expression $n^2 + n + 41$, where $n = 0, 1, 2, 3, \ldots$ always gives prime numbers.

a Show this is true for $n = 0$ to 6.

b Without any calculation, name one value of n that disproves Sara's theory.

AQA Examination-style questions 🔾

1 Polly Parrot squawks every 12 seconds. Mr Toad croaks every 21 seconds.
They both make a noise at the same time.
After how many seconds will they next make a noise at the same time? *(2 marks)*

AQA 2007

2 Work out the highest common factor (HCF) of 63 and 105. *(2 marks)*

AQA 2008

3 $N = a^2b$ is a formula where a and b are prime numbers.

a Find N when $a = 5$ and $b = 3$ *(1 mark)*

b When $a = b$, what sort of number is N? Choose from the options below.
PRIME SQUARE CUBE *(1 mark)*

c Find the values of a and b when $N = 2009$ *(3 marks)*

AQA 2009

2 Sequences

Objectives

Examiners would normally expect students who get these grades to be able to:

D

write the terms of a sequence or a series of diagrams given the nth term

C

write the nth term of a linear sequence or a series of diagrams.

Did you know?

Sequences in nature

Have you ever wondered why four-leaf clovers are so rare? It's because four isn't a number in the Fibonacci sequence.

The Fibonacci sequence 0, 1, 1, 2, 3, 5, 8, 13, … is well known in nature and can be applied to seashell shapes, branching plants, flower petals, pine cones and pineapples.

If you count the number of petals on a daisy, you are most likely to find 13, 21, 34, 55 or 89 petals… all numbers in the Fibonacci sequence.

You should already know:

✔ how to continue a sequence of numbers or diagrams

✔ how to write terms in a sequence of numbers or diagrams

✔ how to write the term-to-term rule in a sequence of numbers or diagrams.

Key terms

sequence
term-to-term
nth term
linear sequence

Learn... 2.1 The *n*th term of a sequence (k!)

A **sequence** is a set of patterns or numbers with a given rule.

▭ ▭▭ ▭▭▭ … is a sequence of patterns.

2, 4, 6, 8, 10, … is a sequence of numbers.

A linear sequence is one where the differences between the terms are all the same.

  5, 10, 15, 20, …

5,   10,   15,   20, …

+5   +5   +5   The **term-to-term** rule is +5.

To find the **nth term** of a **linear sequence**, you can use the formula:

*n*th term = difference × *n* + (first term − difference)

   = $dn + (a - d)$

For 7, 10, 13, 16, …   *d* is the difference = + 3

   a is the first term = 7

*n*th term = difference × *n* + (first term − difference)

   = $dn + (a - d)$

   = $3n + (7 - 3)$

   = $3n + 4$

You can check this as follows.

1st term = 3 × 1 + 4 = 7

2nd term = 3 × 2 + 4 = 10

3rd term = 3 × 3 + 4 = 13

Example: The first four terms of a sequence are 3, 7, 11, 15.

Find the *n*th term.

Solution: 1st   2nd   3rd   4th
   term   term   term   term

   3,   7,   11,   15,

   +4   +4   +4

The term to term rule is +4.

The sequence goes up in 4's, just like the 4 times table, so the rule begins 4 × *n* (4*n*, for short).

> AQA *Examiner's tip*
>
> The *n*th term is sometimes called the general term.

This tells you that the rule is of the form 4*n* + …

1st term = 4 × 1 + … = 3

2nd term = 4 × 2 + … = 7

3rd term = 4 × 3 + … = 11

4th term = 4 × 4 + … = 15

This method only works for linear sequences.

From the above you can see that the *n*th term is 4*n* − 1.

> *Bump up your grade*
>
> You need to be confident in finding the *n*th term for a Grade C.

D

Practise... 2.1 The *n*th term of a sequence *k!* | D | C | B | A | A* |

1 Write down the term-to-term rule for the following sequences.

a   0, 3, 6, 9, ...   e   25, 20, 15, 10, ...

b   3, 7, 11, 15, ...   f   2, 3, 4.5, 6.25, ...

c   1, 2, 4, 8, 16, ...   g   54, 18, 6, 2, ...

d   3, 4.5, 6, 7.5, ...   h   0.01, 0.1, 1, 10, ...

2 The term-to-term rule is +6.

Write down five different sequences which fit this rule.

> **AQA** *Examiner's tip*
>
> Always check your *n*th term to see that it works for the sequence.

3 Write down the first five terms of the sequence whose *n*th term is:

a $n + 3$ e $n^2 - 5$

b $n + \frac{1}{2}$ f $4n^2$

c $5n - 3$ g $\frac{n}{n + 11}$

d $n^2 + 3$

4 Aisha writes down the sequence 2, 6, 10, 14, ...

She says that the *n*th term is $n + 4$.

Is she correct? Give a reason for your answer.

5 The *n*th term of a sequence is $3n - 1$.

a   Colin says that 31 is a number in this sequence.
Is Colin correct? Give a reason for your answer.

b   Diane says the 20th term is double the 10th term.
Is Diane correct? Give a reason for your answer.

6 Copy and complete the following table.

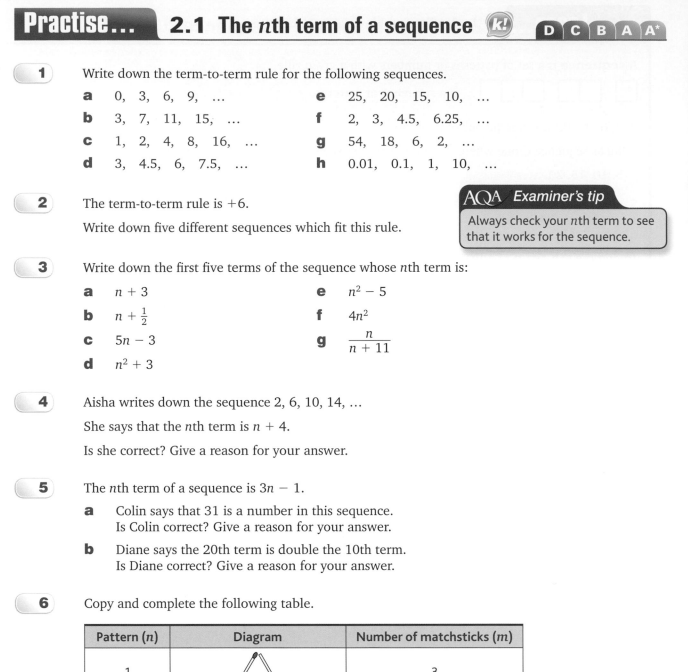

Pattern (*n*)	Diagram	Number of matchsticks (*m*)
1		3
2		5
3		7
4		
5		

a   What do you notice about the pattern of matchsticks?

b   Write down the formula for the number of matchsticks *m* in the *n*th pattern.

c   How many matchsticks will there be in the 10th pattern? Check your answer by drawing the 10th pattern and counting the number of matchsticks.

d   There are 41 matchsticks in the 20th pattern. How many matchsticks are there in the 21st pattern? Give a reason for your answer.

7 Write down the *n*th term in the following sequences.

a 3, 6, 9, 12, ...

b 0, 5, 10, 15, ...

c 8, 14, 20, 26, ...

d $\frac{1}{5}$, $\frac{2}{7}$, $\frac{3}{9}$, $\frac{4}{11}$, ...

e 23, 21, 19, 17, ...

f 105, 100, 95, 90, ...

g −5, −1, 3, 7, ...

h 4, 6.5, 9, 11.5, ...

i −5, 3, 11, 19, ...

j $\frac{2}{7}$, $\frac{4}{13}$, $\frac{6}{19}$, $\frac{8}{25}$, ...

8 Write down the formula for the number of squares in the *n*th pattern.

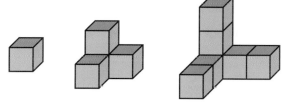

9 Stuart says that the number of cubes in the 100th pattern is 300.

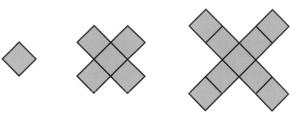

How can you tell that Stuart is wrong? Give a reason for your answer.

10 Jacob is exploring number patterns.

He writes down the following products in a table.

1 × 1	1
11 × 11	121
111 × 111	12 321
1111 × 1111	1 234 321
11 111 × 11 111	
111 111 × 111 111	

Copy and complete the next two rows for the table.

Jacob says he can use the table to work out 1 111 111 111 × 1 111 111 111

Is he correct? Give a reason for your answer.

11 Write down the *n*th term in the following non-linear sequences.

a 1, 4, 9, 16, ...

b 2, 5, 10, 17, ...

c 2, 8, 18, 32, ...

d 1, 8, 27, 64, 125, ...

e 0, 7, 26, 63, 124, ...

f 10, 100, 1000, ...

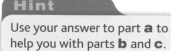

> **Hint**
>
> Use your answer to part **a** to help you with parts **b** and **c**.

12 Write down the *n*th term in the following sequences.

a 1 × 2, 2 × 3, 3 × 4, ...

b $\frac{2}{3}$, $\frac{3}{4}$, $\frac{4}{5}$, $\frac{5}{6}$ ...

c 1 × 2 × 5, 2 × 3 × 6, 3 × 4 × 7, 4 × 5 × 8, ...

d 0.1, 0.2, 0.3, 0.4, ...

e 0.11, 0.22, 0.33, 0.44, ...

⚠ **13**

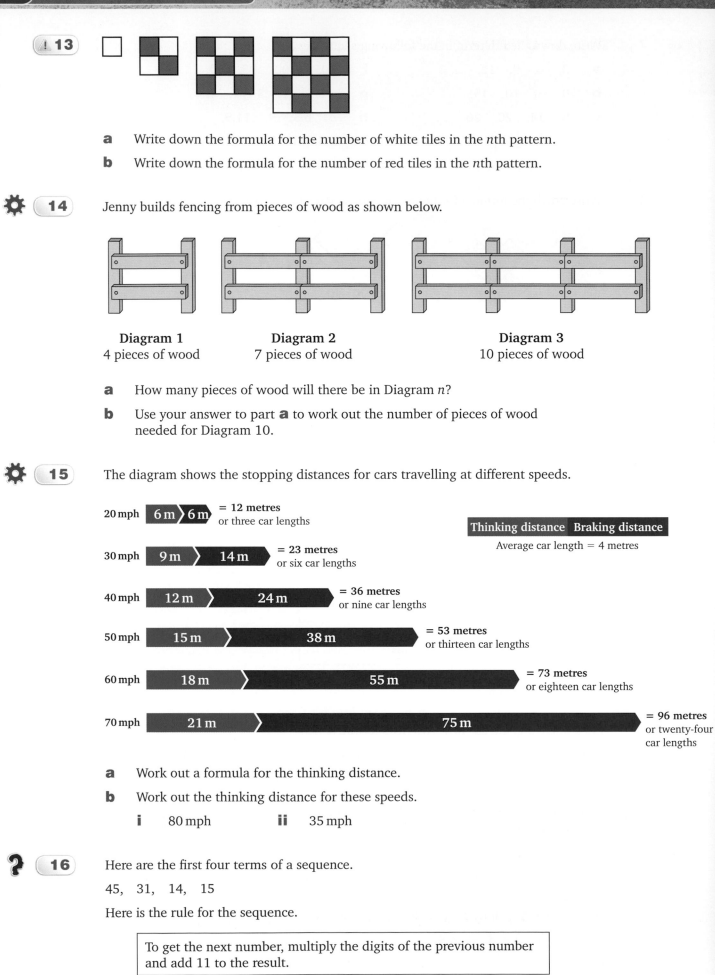

a   Write down the formula for the number of white tiles in the nth pattern.

b   Write down the formula for the number of red tiles in the nth pattern.

⚙ **14**   Jenny builds fencing from pieces of wood as shown below.

Diagram 1
4 pieces of wood

Diagram 2
7 pieces of wood

Diagram 3
10 pieces of wood

a   How many pieces of wood will there be in Diagram n?

b   Use your answer to part **a** to work out the number of pieces of wood needed for Diagram 10.

⚙ **15**   The diagram shows the stopping distances for cars travelling at different speeds.

20 mph   6 m   6 m   = 12 metres or three car lengths

30 mph   9 m   14 m   = 23 metres or six car lengths

40 mph   12 m   24 m   = 36 metres or nine car lengths

50 mph   15 m   38 m   = 53 metres or thirteen car lengths

60 mph   18 m   55 m   = 73 metres or eighteen car lengths

70 mph   21 m   75 m   = 96 metres or twenty-four car lengths

Thinking distance	Braking distance

Average car length = 4 metres

a   Work out a formula for the thinking distance.

b   Work out the thinking distance for these speeds.

   i   80 mph   **ii**   35 mph

❓ **16**   Here are the first four terms of a sequence.

45,   31,   14,   15

Here is the rule for the sequence.

> To get the next number, multiply the digits of the previous number and add 11 to the result.

Work out the 100th number of the sequence.

2 Assess

1 Write down the first three terms, then the 5th, 25th and 50th terms of the sequences that have the nth term:

a $2n + 1$ **b** $5n - 2$ **c** $n^2 + 1$

2 The nth term of a sequence is $3n + 15$.

a Work out the 5th term.

b Show that every term of the sequence is a multiple of 3.

3 The nth term of a sequence is $36 - 2n$.

a Work out the first four terms.

b Explain why one of the terms of the sequence will be zero.

4 Information about some squares is shown.

Side of square (cm)	1	2	3	4	n
Area of square (cm²)	1	4	9	16	

Copy and complete the table.

5 The sequence 3, 7, 11, 15, ... has nth term $4n - 1$

a What is the nth term of this sequence?

$\frac{1}{3}, \frac{2}{7}, \frac{3}{11}, \frac{4}{15}, \ldots$

b Here is another sequence.

$2 \times 3, \quad 4 \times 7, \quad 6 \times 11, \quad 8 \times 15, \ldots$

Explain why the nth term is $8n^2 - 2n$.

6 The diagrams show a quadrilateral, a pentagon and a hexagon with all possible diagonals drawn in.

a Draw figures with seven and eight sides and fill in all the possible diagonals.

b Copy and complete the table.

Number of sides	4	5	6	7	8
Number of diagonals	2				

c Use your table to predict the number of diagonals in polygons having:

i 9 sides **ii** 10 sides **iii** 11 sides **iv** 12 sides.

d Use your answers to find the formula which gives the number of diagonals for a polygon with n sides.

e Use your formula to predict the number of diagonals in polygons with:

i 15 sides **ii** 20 sides **iii** 50 sides **iv** 100 sides.

D

D
C

C

C

7 The nth term of a sequence is $4n - 5$.

The nth term of a different sequence is $8 + 2n$.

Jo says that there are no numbers that are in both sequences.

Show that Jo is correct.

8 Write down a linear sequence where the 4th term is twice the 2nd term.

Scotty says that this is always true if the first term is equal to the difference.

Is Scotty correct?

Give a reason for your answer.

C
B

9 Here is a sequence.

1000,   100,   10,   1,   ...

a Write the terms of the sequence as powers of 10.

b Write the next term of the sequence.
Give your answer as a fraction.

? **10** Four numbers add up to 80.

The numbers form part of a sequence.

Each number in the sequence is three times the number before it.

Work out the largest number in the sequence.

AQA Examination-style questions 🔘

1 In a sequence, the next term is made by taking the last term, subtracting 1 and then squaring the result.
Here are two adjacent terms in the sequence.
p, $(p - 1)^2$

a Show that the next term in the sequence can be simplified to:
$[p(p - 2)]^2$ *(3 marks)*

b Find an expression for the term that precedes p in the sequence. *(2 marks)*

AQA 2009

$$\cfrac{1}{1 + \cfrac{1}{1 + \cfrac{1}{1 + 1}}}$$

Objectives

Examiners would normally expect students who get these grades to be able to:

D
- find one quantity as a fraction of another
- solve problems involving fractions
- divide a quantity in a given ratio
- solve simple ratio and proportion problems, such as finding the ratio of teachers to students in a school
- add and subtract fractions and decimals
- multiply and divide decimals

C
- add and subtract mixed numbers
- multiply and divide fractions and mixed numbers
- find the reciprocal of a number
- convert fractions to decimals
- solve more complex ratio and proportion problems
- solve ratio and proportion problems using the unitary method
- round numbers to different degrees of accuracy, decimal places and significant figures
- recognise that recurring decimals are exact fractions and that some exact fractions are recurring decimals
- understand the effect of multiplying and dividing by numbers between 0 and 1

B
- convert recurring decimals to fractions.

Key terms

denominator
improper fraction
mixed number
numerator
reciprocal
terminating decimal

recurring decimal
equivalent fraction
ratio
unitary method
significant figure

Did you know?

Continuing fractions

The word fraction comes from the Latin word *frangere* meaning 'to break into pieces'.

Here's an amazing fraction! 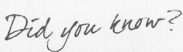 $\cfrac{1}{1 + \cfrac{1}{1 + \cfrac{1}{1 + 1}}}$

It is part of a series of fractions that starts:

$$1, \quad \frac{1}{1+1}, \quad \cfrac{1}{1 + \cfrac{1}{1 + 1}}, \quad \cfrac{1}{1 + \cfrac{1}{1 + \cfrac{1}{1 + 1}}}, \quad \cfrac{1}{1 + \cfrac{1}{1 + \cfrac{1}{1 + \cfrac{1}{1 + 1}}}}$$

This is a sequence of what are called continuing fractions. Can you see how the sequence could continue?

The fractions in the sequence simplify to $1, \frac{1}{2}, \frac{2}{3}, \frac{3}{5}, \frac{5}{8}, \ldots$ Can you continue this sequence?

Have you seen these numbers before?

You may not be able to do hard fractions yet but by the end of the chapter perhaps you will!

You should already know:

- ✔ how to add, subtract, multiply and divide simple numbers without a calculator
- ✔ the meaning of 'sum', 'difference' and 'product'
- ✔ how to find equivalent fractions
- ✔ how to simplify ratios and fractions
- ✔ how to add and subtract simple fractions
- ✔ how to calculate fractions of quantities
- ✔ how to express simple decimals and percentages as fractions.

Learn... 3.1 Adding and subtracting fractions

To add fractions with different **denominators** you first have to change them so that they have the same denominator.

To find the sum of three-quarters and two-thirds you have to change the fractions to twelfths, because 12 is the smallest number that is a multiple of both 3 and 4.

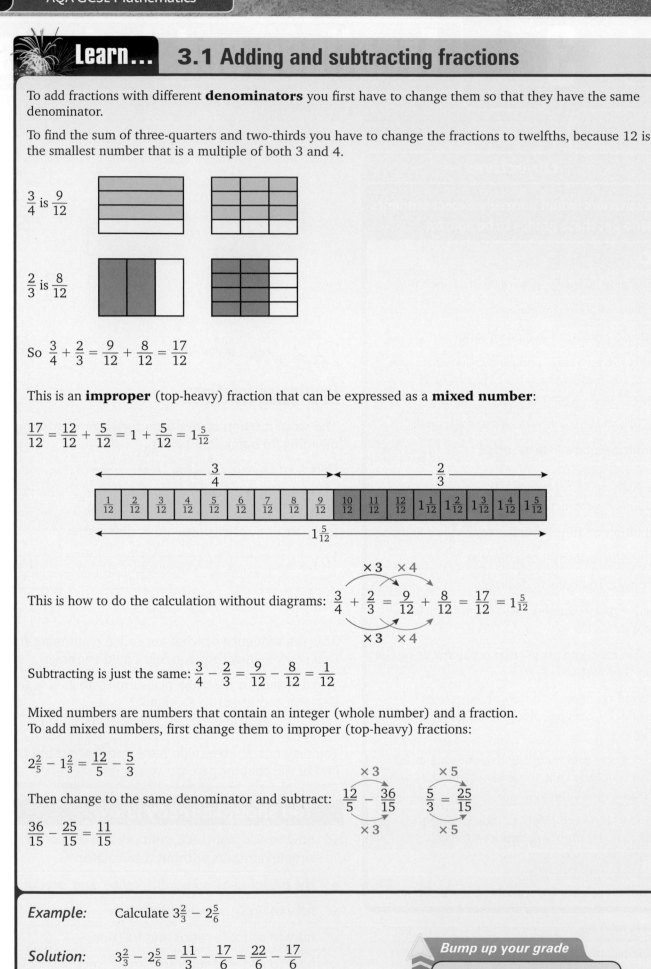

$\frac{3}{4}$ is $\frac{9}{12}$

$\frac{2}{3}$ is $\frac{8}{12}$

So $\frac{3}{4} + \frac{2}{3} = \frac{9}{12} + \frac{8}{12} = \frac{17}{12}$

This is an **improper** (top-heavy) fraction that can be expressed as a **mixed number**:

$$\frac{17}{12} = \frac{12}{12} + \frac{5}{12} = 1 + \frac{5}{12} = 1\frac{5}{12}$$

This is how to do the calculation without diagrams: $\frac{3}{4} + \frac{2}{3} = \frac{9}{12} + \frac{8}{12} = \frac{17}{12} = 1\frac{5}{12}$

Subtracting is just the same: $\frac{3}{4} - \frac{2}{3} = \frac{9}{12} - \frac{8}{12} = \frac{1}{12}$

Mixed numbers are numbers that contain an integer (whole number) and a fraction.
To add mixed numbers, first change them to improper (top-heavy) fractions:

$$2\frac{2}{5} - 1\frac{2}{3} = \frac{12}{5} - \frac{5}{3}$$

Then change to the same denominator and subtract: $\frac{12}{5} - \frac{36}{15} \qquad \frac{5}{3} = \frac{25}{15}$

$$\frac{36}{15} - \frac{25}{15} = \frac{11}{15}$$

Example: Calculate $3\frac{2}{3} - 2\frac{5}{6}$

Solution: $3\frac{2}{3} - 2\frac{5}{6} = \frac{11}{3} - \frac{17}{6} = \frac{22}{6} - \frac{17}{6}$

$$= \frac{5}{6}$$

Bump up your grade

To get a Grade C you have to be able to add and subtract mixed numbers.

Practise... **3.1 Adding and subtracting fractions** 🅺! D C B A A*

1 Work out:

a $\frac{4}{5} + \frac{3}{4}$ b $\frac{4}{5} - \frac{3}{4}$ c $\frac{5}{8} + \frac{1}{3}$ d $\frac{5}{8} - \frac{1}{3}$

2 Fran says that:

$$\frac{1}{2} + \frac{1}{2} = \frac{1+1}{2+2} = \frac{2}{4} = \frac{1}{2}$$

What has Fran done wrong?

3 Two fractions add up to $\frac{9}{10}$. One fraction is $\frac{17}{20}$.

What is the other fraction?

4 Four of these calculations give the same answer and one gives a different answer.

Which is the odd one out?

A $\frac{1}{2} + \frac{1}{3} + \frac{1}{6}$

B $\frac{1}{2} + \frac{1}{2}$

C $\frac{2}{3} + \frac{1}{4} + \frac{1}{12}$

D $\frac{3}{4} + \frac{1}{8} + \frac{1}{16}$

E $\frac{3}{5} + \frac{1}{3} + \frac{1}{15}$

5 Work out:

a $\frac{3}{4} + \frac{3}{4}$ c $\frac{3}{4} + \frac{3}{4} + \frac{3}{4} + \frac{3}{4}$

b $\frac{3}{4} + \frac{3}{4} + \frac{3}{4}$ d $\frac{3}{4} + \frac{3}{4} + \frac{3}{4} + \frac{3}{4} + \frac{3}{4}$

6 Work out:

a $3\frac{3}{4} + 1\frac{4}{5}$

b $3\frac{3}{4} - 1\frac{4}{5}$

c $2\frac{2}{3} - 1\frac{5}{6}$

d $4\frac{1}{4} + 3\frac{1}{3}$

e $4\frac{3}{5} - 2\frac{3}{10}$

⚠ 7 The fraction $\frac{1+3}{2+4}$ is between the fractions $\frac{1}{2}$ and $\frac{3}{4}$

Make other fractions like this from two others.
Is the result always between the two?

⚙ 8 a Anne's recipe needs $\frac{2}{3}$ of a cup of sugar. She has $\frac{3}{4}$ of a cup.
How much will she have left?

b June's recipe needs $1\frac{1}{2}$ cups of sugar and $1\frac{2}{3}$ cups of sugar.
How much sugar does June need altogether?

⚙ 9 A pair of trousers needs $1\frac{1}{2}$ yards of fabric and a jacket needs $2\frac{3}{8}$ yards.

How much fabric is needed in total?

Learn... 3.2 Multiplying and dividing fractions

Multiplying fractions

You can find the area of a rectangle by multiplying: $2 \times 3 = 6$

You can multiply fractions to find areas too.

The diagram shows that three-quarters times two-thirds

is six-twelfths, which is a half: $\dfrac{3}{4} \times \dfrac{2}{3} = \dfrac{6}{12} = \dfrac{1}{2}$

The diagram shows why the answer is smaller than both three-quarters and two-thirds.

The 6 in the six-twelfths comes from the shaded area.
It is 3 units across and 2 units down, so contains 6 squares.

The 12 in the answer comes from the whole area.
It is 4 units across and 3 units down, so contains 12 squares.

6 out of 12 squares are shaded, so the answer is $\dfrac{6}{12}$, which simplifies to $\dfrac{1}{2}$

multiply numerators

This is how to do it without the diagram: $\dfrac{3}{4} \times \dfrac{2}{3} = \dfrac{3 \times 2}{4 \times 3} = \dfrac{6}{12} = \dfrac{1}{2}$

multiply denominators

AQA Examiner's tip

Be careful not to mix up the method for adding fractions with the method for multiplying them.

The working can be reduced by dividing the **numerator** and denominator of $\dfrac{3 \times 2}{4 \times 3}$ by 3 and by 2 to

simplify the fraction: $\dfrac{3}{4} \times \dfrac{2}{3} = \dfrac{{}^1\cancel{3} \times \cancel{2}^1}{{}_2\cancel{4} \times \cancel{3}_1} = \dfrac{1 \times 1}{2 \times 1} = \dfrac{1}{2}$

What about calculations such as $1\frac{3}{4} \times 2\frac{2}{3}$?

To multiply mixed numbers you convert them to improper fractions:

$$1\tfrac{3}{4} \times 2\tfrac{2}{3} = \tfrac{7}{4} \times \tfrac{8}{3}$$

Then simplify if possible and multiply to get the answer.

$$1\tfrac{3}{4} \times 2\tfrac{2}{3} = \dfrac{7}{{}_1\cancel{4}} \times \dfrac{\cancel{8}^2}{3} = \dfrac{7}{1} \times \dfrac{2}{3} = \dfrac{14}{3} = 4\tfrac{2}{3}$$

Example: Work out $3\frac{1}{2} \times 2\frac{5}{6}$

Solution: Change the mixed numbers to improper fractions, then multiply numerators and denominators.

$$3\tfrac{1}{2} \times 2\tfrac{5}{6} = \dfrac{7}{2} \times \dfrac{17}{6} = \dfrac{119}{12} = 9\tfrac{11}{12}$$

Reciprocals and division of fractions

To divide by a fraction, you multiply by its **reciprocal**.

Any number multiplied by its reciprocal gives 1.
1 divided by a number gives the reciprocal of the number.
So the reciprocal of 2 is $\frac{1}{2}$ and the reciprocal of $\frac{1}{2}$ is 2.

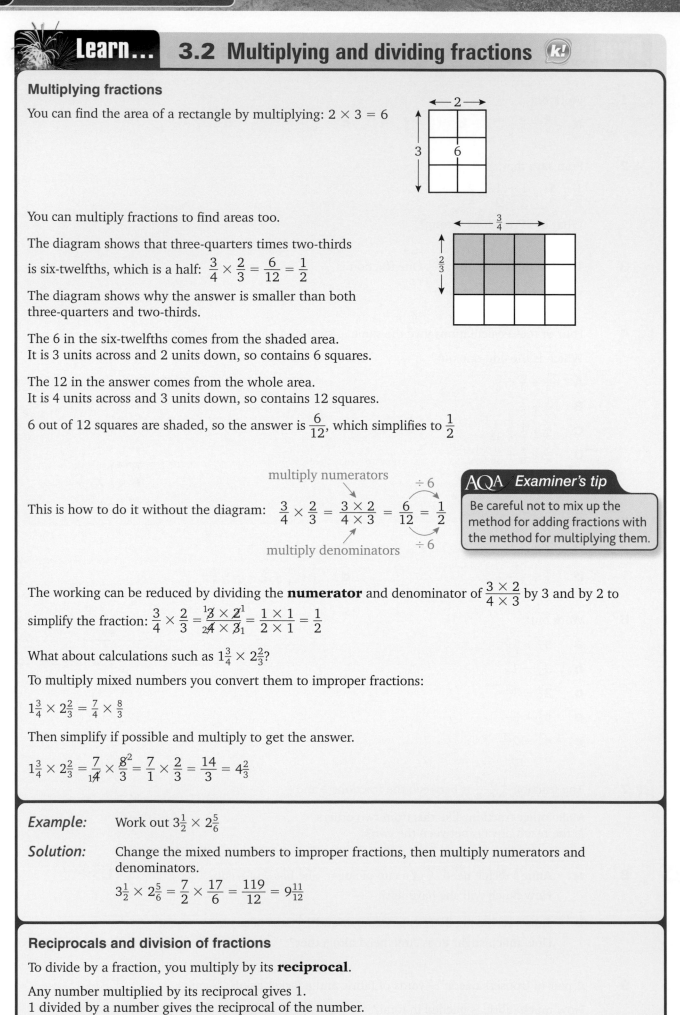

Example: What are the reciprocals of these numbers?

    a 4   **b** $\frac{1}{6}$ **c** 0.7   **d** $2\frac{2}{3}$ **e** -2

Solution: **a** Reciprocal is $1 \div 4 = \frac{1}{4}$

> **Hint**
>
> To find the reciprocal of a fraction, turn it upside down. This works because $\frac{a}{b} \times \frac{b}{a} = 1$

        b Reciprocal is $\frac{6}{1} = \mathbf{6}$

        c 0.7 is equal to $\frac{7}{10}$, so its reciprocal $= \frac{10}{7} = \mathbf{1\frac{3}{7}}$ ← Write a decimal as a fraction first.

        d $2\frac{2}{3}$ is equal to $\frac{8}{3}$, so its reciprocal is $\frac{3}{8}$ ← Write a mixed number as an improper fraction first.

        e Reciprocal is $\frac{1}{-2} = -\frac{1}{2}$

> **AQA** *Examiner's tip*
>
> You can check these by multiplying:
>
> $4 \times \frac{1}{4} = 1$ $\frac{8}{3} \times \frac{3}{8} = 1$
>
> $\frac{1}{6} \times 6 = 1$ $-2 \times -\frac{1}{2} = 1$
>
> $\frac{7}{10} \times \frac{10}{7} = 1$

> **Bump up your grade**
>
> To get a Grade C you need to be able to find reciprocals.

Dividing fractions

To divide by $\frac{3}{4}$, multiply by the reciprocal of $\frac{3}{4}$, which is $\frac{4}{3}$:

$$\frac{2}{3} \div \frac{3}{4} = \frac{2}{3} \times \frac{4}{3} = \frac{8}{9}$$

For mixed numbers, change them to improper fractions first:

$$1\frac{3}{4} : 2\frac{2}{3} = \frac{7}{4} \div \frac{8}{3} = \frac{7}{4} \times \frac{3}{8} = \frac{21}{32}$$

> **AQA** *Examiner's tip*
>
> Only the fraction you are dividing by gets turned upside down. The fraction you are dividing into does not change.

> **Bump up your grade**
>
> To get a Grade C you have to be able to multiply and divide mixed numbers.

Example: Work out $3\frac{1}{2} \div 2\frac{5}{6}$

Solution: Change the mixed numbers into improper fractions, change dividing to multiplying by the reciprocal, then multiply numerators and denominators.

$$3\frac{1}{2} \div 2\frac{5}{6} = \frac{7}{2} \div \frac{17}{6} = \frac{7}{2} \times \frac{6}{17} = \frac{42}{34} = 1\frac{4}{17}$$

Practise... 3.2 Multiplying and dividing fractions 🄚 D C B A A*

1 Work out: **D**

    a $\frac{4}{5} \times \frac{3}{4}$ **c** $\frac{5}{8} \times \frac{1}{3}$ **e** $12\frac{1}{2} \times \frac{3}{5}$ **g** $(2\frac{1}{2})^2$

    b $\frac{4}{5} \div \frac{3}{4}$ **d** $\frac{5}{8} \div \frac{1}{3}$ **f** $12\frac{1}{2} \div \frac{3}{5}$ **h** $(1\frac{1}{2})^3$

2 These calculations can all be done very easily. How?

    a $3\frac{2}{5} \div 3\frac{2}{5}$ **b** $1\frac{1}{2} \times \frac{2}{3} \div \frac{2}{3}$ **c** $1\frac{1}{2} \times \frac{2}{3} \times \frac{3}{2}$

C

3 Work out:

a **i** $\frac{2}{5} \div \frac{1}{3}$ **ii** $\frac{1}{3} \div \frac{2}{5}$

b What do you notice about the answers?

c Try another pair of fractions and compare answers.

d Does the same thing happen with $5 \div 3$ and $3 \div 5$?

4 **a** Write down the reciprocal of: **i** 5   **ii** 8   **iii** 10   **iv** 20   **v** 100

     b Write down the reciprocal of: **i** $\frac{1}{3}$ **ii** $\frac{1}{7}$ **iii** $\frac{1}{9}$ **iv** $\frac{1}{15}$ **v** $\frac{1}{50}$

     c Write down the reciprocal of: **i** $\frac{2}{3}$ **ii** $\frac{4}{5}$ **iii** $\frac{5}{8}$ **iv** $\frac{3}{10}$ **v** $\frac{4}{25}$

     d Find the reciprocal of: **i** 0.1   **ii** 0.6   **iii** 0.9   **iv** 0.03   **v** 0.15

     e Find the reciprocal of: **i** $1\frac{1}{5}$ **ii** $2\frac{3}{5}$ **iii** $3\frac{5}{8}$ **iv** 1.2   **v** 2.8

     f Find the reciprocal of: **i** -1 **ii** -3 **iii** $-\frac{1}{4}$ **iv** $-\frac{2}{5}$ **v** $-4\frac{2}{7}$

5 Work out:

a $\left(1\frac{1}{4}\right)^2$ **b** $\frac{3}{4} + 2\frac{1}{2} \times 1\frac{1}{2}$ **c** $\left(\frac{3}{4} + 2\frac{1}{2}\right) \times 1\frac{1}{2}$

6 **a** Which is bigger: $\frac{5}{6} \times \frac{2}{7}$ or $\frac{5}{6} + \frac{2}{7}$? Explain how you got your answer.

     b Which is bigger: $\frac{5}{6} \times \frac{2}{7}$ or $\frac{5}{6} \div \frac{2}{7}$? Explain how you got your answer.

     c Which is bigger: $2\frac{1}{2} \times 1\frac{1}{4}$ or $2\frac{1}{2} + 1\frac{1}{4}$? Explain how you got your answer.

     d Which is bigger: $2\frac{1}{2} \times 1\frac{1}{4}$ or $2\frac{1}{2} \div 1\frac{1}{4}$? Explain how you got your answer.

7 A sequence of fractions starts $\frac{1}{2}$, $\frac{3}{4}$, ...

Find the next term by adding 1 to the last term and dividing the result by the term before. Continue the sequence until you can see what has happened.

Do you get the same result with other starting numbers?

8 A recipe for 16 biscuits needs $\frac{2}{3}$ of a cup of flour.
How much flour is needed for 48 biscuits?

9 Jack fills three jugs with water.
Each jug contains $2\frac{3}{4}$ litres of water.

How much water is this altogether?

10 One kilogram is approximately $2\frac{1}{4}$ pounds.

How many pounds is 6 kilograms?

11 Seema makes tops for her friends.
Each top uses one and three quarter yards of fabric.

How many tops can she make from 6 yards of fabric and how much fabric is left?

12 Copy these calculations and find the missing numbers.

$\frac{1}{2} \times \boxed{} = 1$

$\frac{1}{2} \div \boxed{} = 1$

$2\frac{1}{2} \times \boxed{} = 4$

$\boxed{} \div \frac{3}{4} = 6$

Learn... 3.3 One quantity as a fraction of another

To work out one quantity as a fraction of another, change both quantities to the same units if necessary. Write the first quantity as the numerator and the second quantity as the denominator and then simplify the fraction.

Example: What fraction of £5 is 25p?

Solution: Change £5 to 500p.

The fraction is $\frac{25}{500}$.

The fraction in its simplified form is $\frac{1}{20}$

Simplify the fraction by dividing the numerator and the denominator both by the common factor, 25.

Example: Some patients are taking part in a medical trial.

Drug A is given to 150 of them with a disease and 102 of them get better.

Drug B is given to 120 of them and 80 of them get better.

Find the fraction of patients who get better with each drug and simplify the fractions.

Solution: The fraction of patients who get better with Drug A is:
$$\overset{\div 2 \quad \div 3}{\frac{102}{150} = \frac{51}{75} = \frac{17}{25}}_{\div 2 \quad \div 3}$$

The fraction of patients who get better with Drug B is:
$$\overset{\div 10 \quad \div 4}{\frac{80}{120} = \frac{8}{12} = \frac{2}{3}}_{\div 10 \quad \div 4}$$

(Note: In real life, doctors need to compare the fractions to see which drug seems to be more effective. They would change the fractions to decimals or percentages.)

AQA *Examiner's tip*

Simplify your fractions whenever possible.

Practise... 3.3 One quantity as a fraction of another 🔊 D C B A A*

Give all fractions in their simplest form.

1 Work out the first number or quantity as a fraction of the second.

    a 150, 250

    b 50p, £4.50

    c 800 g, 2 kg

    d 75 cm, 120 m

    e 15 minutes, one hour

    f 25 minutes, $2\frac{1}{2}$ hours

D

2 At a football match, the crowd was 15 000. There were 10 500 home supporters.

    a What fraction of the crowd was this?

    b What fraction of the crowd were not home supporters?

D

3 a Mr Howes is marking 35 Year 11 books.
What fraction has he still left to do when he has marked 14 books?

b Miss Jones has marked 12 books out of 32.
Who is further ahead with their marking, Miss Jones or Mr Howes?

C

4 Kate earns two and a half times as much as Andy.
What fraction is Andy's salary of Kate's salary?

⚠ 5 A rectangle has an area of bh cm² and a perimeter of $2(b + h)$ cm.
It is enlarged so that its area is $4bh$ cm² and its perimeter is $4(b + h)$ cm.

a What fraction is the old area of the new area?

b What fraction is the old perimeter of the new perimeter?

⚙ 6 Sara's mark in one spelling test is 15 out of 20. In the next test, her mark is 20 out of 25.
Which mark is better?

⚙ 7 In Class 9Y, 18 out of 20 passed a maths test. In Class 9X, 25 out of 30 passed the same test.
Which class did better?

⚙ 8 In Kate's house, 16 of her 20 light bulbs are low-energy. In Jane's house, 20 out of her 24 bulbs are low-energy.

a Who has the higher fraction of low-energy bulbs?

b There are 30 bulbs in Dipak's house.
How many low-energy bulbs does Dipak need so that he has at least the same fraction as Jane?

Learn... 3.4 Fractions as decimals 🔑

To be able to convert fractions to decimals, remember that fractions are also divisions.

For example, if 7 pizzas are shared by 10 people each person would get $\frac{7}{10}$ of a pizza.
The fraction $\frac{7}{10}$ is the same as $7 \div 10$. You should already know that $7 \div 10$ is 0.7

To work out $\frac{5}{8}$ as a decimal, for example, calculate $5 \div 8$

$$\begin{array}{r} 0.\,6\,2\,5 \\ 8\overline{)5.\,^5 0\,^2 0\,^4 0} \end{array}$$

> **AQA** *Examiner's tip*
> Make sure you divide 5 by 8 not the other way round!

$\frac{5}{8}$ is an example of a fraction that converts to a **terminating decimal**.

Not all fractions terminate. For example, $\frac{4}{11} = 4 \div 11 = 0.36363636...$ which is a **recurring decimal**.

This can be written as $0.\dot{3}\dot{6}$ showing that the number sequence 36 repeats forever.

For use in practical situations, recurring decimals have to be rounded to an appropriate degree of accuracy (see Learn 3.6).

Example: Here are some fractions: $\frac{1}{3}$, $\frac{2}{5}$, $\frac{5}{6}$, $\frac{7}{8}$

a Change the fractions to decimals.

b Which of these fractions convert to terminating decimals and which convert to recurring decimals?

Solution: **a**   In each case, divide the numerator by the denominator until the division stops or recurs.

$1 \div 3 = 0.333333...$ (or $0.\dot{3}$)

$2 \div 5 = 0.4$

$5 \div 6 = 0.83333...$ (or $0.8\dot{3}$)

$7 \div 8 = 0.875$

   b   The fractions that terminate are $\frac{2}{5}$ and $\frac{7}{8}$.
The ones that recur are $\frac{1}{3}$ and $\frac{5}{6}$.

> AQA **Examiner's tip**
>
> If you have never learnt how to do division without a calculator now is the time to do so!

Expressing a terminating decimal as a fraction

Write the decimal as a fraction with a denominator of 1. Then change it to an **equivalent fraction** with a whole number numerator by multiplying numerator and denominator by 10, or 100, or 1000, ... as necessary. Simplify the fraction if possible.

Example: Express 0.225 as a fraction.

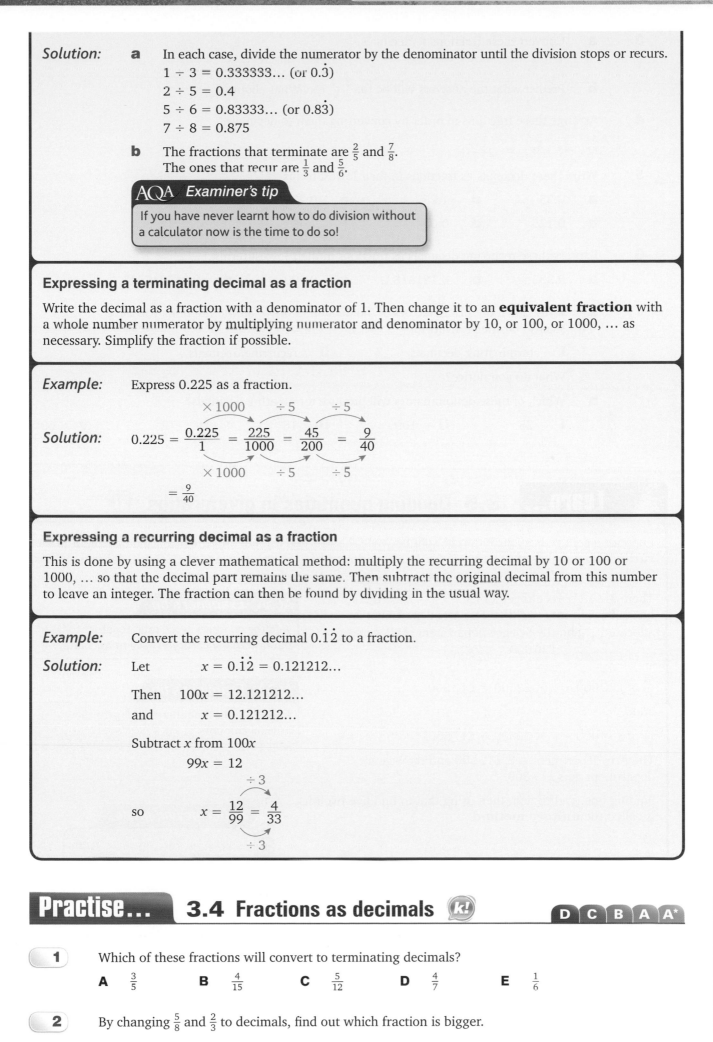

Solution: $0.225 = \dfrac{0.225}{1} = \dfrac{225}{1000} = \dfrac{45}{200} = \dfrac{9}{40}$

$= \dfrac{9}{40}$

Expressing a recurring decimal as a fraction

This is done by using a clever mathematical method: multiply the recurring decimal by 10 or 100 or 1000, ... so that the decimal part remains the same. Then subtract the original decimal from this number to leave an integer. The fraction can then be found by dividing in the usual way.

Example: Convert the recurring decimal $0.\dot{1}\dot{2}$ to a fraction.

Solution: Let $x = 0.\dot{1}\dot{2} = 0.121212...$

Then $100x = 12.121212...$

and $x = 0.121212...$

Subtract x from $100x$

$99x = 12$

so $x = \dfrac{12}{99} = \dfrac{4}{33}$

Practise...   3.4 Fractions as decimals   🄚   D C B A A*   C

1   Which of these fractions will convert to terminating decimals?

   A $\frac{3}{5}$ **B** $\frac{4}{15}$ **C** $\frac{5}{12}$ **D** $\frac{4}{7}$ **E** $\frac{1}{6}$

2   By changing $\frac{5}{8}$ and $\frac{2}{3}$ to decimals, find out which fraction is bigger.

C

3 **a** Convert these fractions to decimals.

$\frac{1}{9}$, $\frac{2}{9}$, $\frac{3}{9}$

   b Predict what the answers will be for $\frac{4}{9}$, $\frac{5}{9}$, etc. What about $\frac{9}{9}$?

4 Arrange these fractions in order by converting them to decimals.

$\frac{3}{4}$, $\frac{5}{8}$, $\frac{2}{3}$, $\frac{7}{9}$, $\frac{3}{5}$

5 Write these decimals as fractions in their lowest terms.

   a 0.35   **c** 1.25   **e** 0.225

   b 0.125   **d** 0.004   **f** 2.45

B

6 Express these recurring decimals as fractions in their lowest terms.

   a 0.333...   **b** 0.181818...   **c** 0.999...   **d** 0.315315315...

7 **a** Write down the prime factors of the denominators of all the fractions you have seen so far that convert to:

   i terminating decimals   **ii** recurring decimals.

   What do you notice?

   b Which of these denominators will produce terminating decimals?

   i 25   **ii** 100   **iii** 18   **iv** 12   **v** 60

Learn... 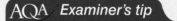 **3.5 Dividing quantities in given ratios** **k!**

Suppose a college has £30 000 to be split between the Arts department and the Science department in the **ratio** of the number of students. If the Arts department has 250 students and the Science department has 350 students, the ratio of the numbers is 250 : 350 = 25 : 35 = 5 : 7

There are 12 parts altogether (5 + 7 = 12) so the money has to be split into twelfths. The Arts department is allocated $\frac{5}{12}$ and the Science department is allocated $\frac{7}{12}$.

$\frac{1}{12}$ of £30 000 = $\frac{£30\,000}{12}$ = £2500

$\frac{5}{12}$ of £30 000 = 5 × £2500 = £12 500

and

$\frac{7}{12}$ of £30 000 = 7 × £2500 = £17 500

The Arts department gets £12 500 and the Science department gets £17 500.

Finding one-twelfth first, then using that to find five-twelfths, is called the **unitary method**.

> **AQA** *Examiner's tip*
> Add the numbers in the ratio together to find out how many parts you have to calculate.

> **AQA** *Examiner's tip*
> Make sure that the shares add up to the original amount.

> *Bump up your grade*
> To get a Grade C you have to be able to use the unitary method.

Example: A mix of concrete is made from cement, sand and gravel in the ratio 2 : 3 : 5
What is the volume of cement in 500 litres of concrete?

Solution: The total number of parts required is 2 + 3 + 5 = 10

$\frac{1}{10}$ of 500 litres is 50 litres.

So the volume of cement is 2 × 50 litres = 100 litres

Practise...   **3.5 Dividing quantities in given ratios** 🔊 D C B A A*

D

1   £5500 is shared between the Drama and Art departments in the ratio of the number of students who take GCSEs in each of those subjects.

45 students take GCSE drama and 65 take GCSE art.

Work out how much each subject receives.

2   **a**   Split £100 in the following ratios.
i	$1:1$	**iii**	$1:3$	**v**	$1:5$
ii	$1:2$	**iv**	$1:4$		

Round your answers to the nearest penny if necessary.

b   Explain why some of these were easier to do than others.

3   Divide £100 in these ratios.

a $2:3:5$ **b** $1:4:5$

4   What ratio, in its simplest form, is used to divide £150 to be split between two people so that the first person gets:

a   £20   **b**   £13   **c**   £x?

5   £6000 is shared between two people so that the first person receives twice as much as the second. How much does the second person receive?

6   A mix of concrete has cement, sand and gravel in the ratio $1:2:1$

a   How much sand is needed for 30 kg of concrete?

b   A builder has only 20 kg of gravel, but plenty of cement and sand.
How much concrete can he make?

7   In a typical group of people, the ratio of the number of right-handed people to the number of left-handed people is $9:1$

a   How many left-handed students would you expect in a class of 30?

b   How many would you expect in a school of 1200 students?

c   Which of your answers is more likely to be correct (assuming you have worked out the numbers accurately)? Explain your answer.

Learn...   **3.6 Rounding**

If 9635 people were at a concert, it would be correct to say that the number attending was approximately 10 000. The number 9635 is rounded to the nearest thousand to give a good idea of the number of people at the concert.

Rounding to the nearest 10, 100, 1000

The number 9635 is between 9000 and 10 000 but nearer to 10 000 than to 9000.

```
9000              9635              10 000
```

So 9635 to the nearest 1000 is 10 000.

What is 9635 to the nearest hundred?

The number 9635 is between 9600 and 9700 but nearer to 9600.

```
  9600                9635                    9700
```

So 9635 correct to the nearest hundred is 9600.

The number 9635 is exactly halfway between 9630 and 9640. The usual rule is that numbers exactly halfway are rounded upwards.

So 9635 to the nearest ten is 9640.

```
            Any number in this range rounds to 9640
  9630          9635          9640          9645
```

The smallest number that rounds to 9640 is 9635.

The biggest integer that rounds to 9640 is 9644.

The biggest non-integer number that rounds to 9640 is 9644.9999…

So 9645 rounds up to 9650.   (Note: $9644.\dot{9} = 9645$, which rounds to 9650)

So, if n is a number that rounds to 9640 to the nearest ten, $9635 \leqslant n < 9645$. This means that 9635 is less than or equal to any number that rounds to 9640 ($9635 \leqslant n$) and any number that rounds to 9640 is less than 9645 ($n < 9645$).

If n is a number that rounds to 9600 to the nearest hundred, $9550 \leqslant n < 9650$

Example: Round these numbers to the nearest 100.

    a   77 530   **b**   48 967   **c**   145 235   **d**   398 684

Solution: **a**   77 500   **b**   49 000   **c**   145 200   **d**   398 700

Rounding to decimal places

Decimal numbers can be rounded to the nearest integer, to one decimal place, two decimal places and so on. You still have to consider numbers on either side.

Consider the number 9.635

```
  9.6               9.635                    9.7
```

The number 9.635 is between 9.6 and 9.7 but nearer to 9.6 than to 9.7

So 9.635 correct to one decimal place is 9.6

When rounding 9635 to the nearest 100, you need zeros to show that the rounded answer is 9600 not 96. You do not need zeros to show that 9.635 to one decimal place is 9.6

So 9.635 correct to two decimal places is 9.64

> **Hint**
> For the numbers 12 000 and 13 000, zeros are needed to show the place value of the other digits. For 1.2 and 1.3 this is not necessary.

Example: **a**   Round these numbers to two decimal places.

     i   7.3654   **ii**   35.689   **iii**   0.5637   **iv**   0.0673254

     b   Round the same numbers to the nearest integer.

Solution: **a**   **i**   7.37   **ii**   35.69   **iii**   0.56   **iv**   0.07

            b   **i**   7   **ii**   36   **iii**   1   **iv**   0

Rounding to significant figures

You can also round to different numbers of **significant figures**.

The number 9635 rounds to 9600 and 9.635 rounds to 9.6

So 9600 is rounded to the nearest 100 and 9.6 to one decimal place, but they are both rounded to two significant figures. Each rounded answer has two significant figures, 9 and 6. (The zeros in 9600 indicate the place value of the 9 and the 6. They are not necessary in 9.6 and are not 'significant'.)

Zeros can be significant figures. 7.0235 rounded to two significant figures is 7.0; the zero is significant and shows that 7.0235 is nearer to 7.0 than it is to 7.1

Example:	Round these numbers to three significant figures.

	a	9674	**b**	0.9674	**c**	342 960	**d**	0.3998	**e**	1.6784

Solution:	**a**	9670	**b**	0.967	**c**	343 000	**d**	0.400	**e**	1.68

Note that zeros can sometimes be significant figures.

Bump up your grade

To get a Grade C you have to be able to round to different numbers of significant figures.

AQA **Examiner's tip**

Be sure you understand the difference between figures that are significant and those that are not.

Practise... 3.6 Rounding

D C B A A*

1 Round these numbers to two decimal places.

    a 12.567   **c** 67.895   **e** 0.00482

    b 0.00385   **d** 0.568

2 **a** Vida says that 456 736 rounded to one significant figure is 5.
        Is she correct? Explain your answer.

    b Arif says that 15.602 rounded to three significant figures is 15.60
        Is he correct? Explain your answer.

3 Round these numbers to one significant figure.

    a 86   **c** 17.5   **e** 0.55

    b 950   **d** 0.175

4 Round these numbers to one significant figure and write down mental estimates of the answer to each calculation.

    a 56 × 4.45   **b** 0.55 × 124   **c** 27 × 956   **d** 12.9 ÷ 2.2

5 Round these numbers to three significant figures.

    a 1946   **b** 24.567   **c** 129.25   **d** 0.00953

6 Round the numbers in Question 1 to two significant figures.
Which of the numbers is the same when rounded to two decimal places and two significant figures?

7 Find three numbers that are the same when rounded to one significant figure as when rounded to one decimal place.

C

8 To the nearest ten, a number rounds to 150.

    a What is the biggest number it could be?

    b What is the smallest number it could be?

9 Write down three different numbers that are 0.01 when rounded to one significant figure.

⚠ 10 Copy the diagram and then find one number to put in each of the three regions.

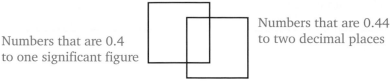

Numbers that are 0.4 to one significant figure

Numbers that are 0.44 to two decimal places

❓ 11 Think about the number 367.174

What would be sensible rounding of the number if it is:

    a an amount of money in pounds

    b the length of a field in metres

    c the answer to a calculation where the numbers were correct to three significant figures?

Learn... 3.7 Decimal calculations

You should already know how to add, subtract, multiply and divide whole numbers without a calculator. Calculating with decimals is very similar.

Addition and subtraction of decimals

To add and subtract decimals, write the numbers in columns with the decimal points in line and add or subtract the numbers in the columns just as you do for whole numbers.

$$
\begin{array}{r}
5\ \cancel{4}^{3}.\ \cancel{2}^{11}\cancel{0}^{1} \\
-\ \ 0\ .\ 6\ 7 \\
\hline
5\ 3\ .\ 5\ 3
\end{array}
$$

    Line up all the decimal points

Multiplying decimals

Any standard method of multiplying whole numbers, such as the grid method, works for decimals. The digits in the answer are just the same as for the whole number calculation. Use estimation to find where to place the decimal point in the answer.

So, if you need to multiply 0.63 by 4.7, remember that the digits in the answer will be the same as for the calculation 63 × 47.

So 63 × 47 = 2400 + 120 + 420 + 21 = 2961

Now estimate the answer to 0.63 × 4.7

0.63 × 4.7 is roughly $\frac{1}{2}$ × 5, which is 2.5

63 × 47 = 2961 so 0.63 × 4.7 = 2.961

×	60	3
40	2400	120
7	420	21

The decimal point is placed so that the answer is close to the estimate of 2.5

You can also find the position of the decimal point by finding the total number of figures after the decimal points in the question, then making the answer have the same total number. As there are two numbers after the decimal point in 0.63 and one in 4.7, there should be three numbers after the decimal point in the answer. So the answer is 2.961

Division

To divide by a decimal number, write the division as a fraction and change the fraction to an **equivalent fraction** with an integer denominator, then divide as normal.

$$135.2 \div 0.5 = \frac{135.2}{0.5} = \frac{135.2 \times 10}{0.5 \times 10} = \frac{1352}{5}$$

Multiply by 10 to change 0.5 to an integer

So $135.2 \div 0.5 = 1352 \div 5 = 270.4$

$$\begin{array}{r} 2\,7\,0.\,4 \\ 5\overline{)1^13^35\;2.^20} \end{array}$$

Example: Work out $15.3 \div 0.12$

Solution: $15.3 \div 0.12 = \dfrac{15.3}{0.12} = \dfrac{15.3 \times 100}{0.12 \times 100} = \dfrac{1530}{12} = 1530 \div 12 = 127.5$

$$\begin{array}{r} 1\,2\,7.\,5 \\ 12\overline{)15^33^90.^60} \end{array}$$

AQA *Examiner's tip*

Dividing a number by something less than 1 gives an answer bigger than the original number.

Practise... 3.7 Decimal calculations (k!)   D C B A A*

AQA *Examiner's tip*

Check that the answers you get are reasonable by estimating what they should be.

1   Work out:

   a 84×0.5 **b** $103.2 + 0.56$ **c** $15 \div 1.5$ **d** $67.5 - 29.8$

2   Work out:

   a 3.6×2.2 **b** 3.56×1.5 **c** $15 \div 2.5$ **d** $7.3 \div 25$

3   **a**   Work out:

     i $150 \div 100$ **iii** $150 \div 1$ **v** $150 \div 0.01$

     ii $150 \div 10$ **iv** $150 \div 0.1$

   b   What is happening to the divisors?

   c   What is happening to the answers? Why?

4   **a**   Work out:

     i 150×100 **iii** 150×1 **v** 150×0.01

     ii 150×10 **iv** 150×0.1

   b   What is happening to the multipliers?

   c   What is happening to the answers? Why?

D

C

C

5 $82.1 \times 5.6 = 459.76$

Using the same digits in the same order, write down a multiplication sum with the answer:

a 45.976 **b** 4.5976 **c** 0.45976 **d** 0.045976

6 $42.6 \div 4 = 10.65$

Using the same digits in the same order, write down a division sum with the answer:

a 1.065 **b** 106.5 **c** 1065 **d** 10650

7 Rob's employer pays him mileage expenses of 40p per mile.
He drives 15.2 miles one day and 17.9 miles the next.
How much will he be paid in total?

8 Sue is paid £1.50 for every exam paper she marks.
How many papers has she marked if she is paid £967.50?

9 Hafsa has £250 to spend on a carpet for her living room. She needs 17.6 square metres.
The carpet she likes costs £14.25 a square metre.
Does Hafsa have enough money to buy this carpet?

3 Assess

D

1 Work out the first quantity as a fraction of the second.

a 24, 36 **b** £2, £4.50 **c** 10 cm, 1 m **d** 150 g, 1.5 kg

2 Work out $\frac{7}{8} - \frac{3}{5}$

C

3 The reciprocal of a fraction is $3\frac{7}{8}$
What is the fraction?

4 Paula makes trousers for her twin toddlers.
Each pair of trousers needs three-eighths of a yard of fabric.
How much fabric is needed for four pairs of trousers?

5 Which is bigger, $2\frac{3}{5} \times 1\frac{1}{2}$ or $2\frac{3}{5} \div 1\frac{1}{2}$? Explain how you found the answer.

6 Convert these fractions to decimals and then arrange them in order of size, starting with the smallest.

$\frac{3}{4}, \frac{8}{9}, \frac{2}{3}, \frac{3}{5}, \frac{9}{10}$

7 Which of these fractions will convert to recurring decimals?

A $\frac{4}{7}$ **B** $\frac{7}{20}$ **C** $\frac{1}{12}$ **D** $\frac{3}{11}$ **E** $\frac{7}{80}$

8 Find the reciprocal of:

a 8 **b** −3 **c** $\frac{2}{5}$ **d** −0.5 **e** $2\frac{1}{4}$

9 One litre is approximately one and three quarter pints.
How many pints are there in 6.5 litres?

10 The ratio of the number of people with 'attached' earlobes to the number of people with 'unattached' earlobes is approximately 3 : 7
How many students with 'attached' earlobes would you expect in a school with 950 students?

11 A sum of money is divided between two people in the ratio 4 : 5
If the first person gets £18, what does the second person get?

12 A number is 0.05 correct to one significant figure.
Which of these numbers could it **not** be?

A 0.045 **B** 0.0525 **C** 0.049999 **D** 0.055 **E** 0.0476

13 Manish drove for 3.5 hours and covered 215 miles.
Calculate how far he would go in one hour at the same rate, rounding your answer to an appropriate degree of accuracy.

14 Jane's car travels an average of 7.6 miles per litre of fuel.
How far can she travel if she has 22 litres of fuel?

15 Express these decimals as fractions in their lowest terms.

a 0.245 **b** 1.205 **c** 2.795 **d** 5.572 **e** 17.4545

16 **a** What is the only number that is the same as its reciprocal?

b What is the only number that does not have a reciprocal?

Explain your answers.

17 Say whether each of these statements is true or false.

a $25 \div 0.35$ is less than 25

b 25×0.35 is less than 25

c $25 + 0.35$ is less than 25

d $25 - 0.35$ is less than 25

e $25 - -0.35$ is less than 25

18 Express these recurring decimals as fractions in their lowest terms.

a 0.555... **d** 1.272727...

b 0.404040... **e** 2.123123123...

c 0.624624624...

AQA Examination-style questions

1 A box of coloured counters contains only red, white and blue counters.
$\frac{1}{3}$ of the counters are red.
$\frac{1}{4}$ of the counters are white.
100 counters are blue.
How many counters are in the box? *(4 marks)*

AQA 2008

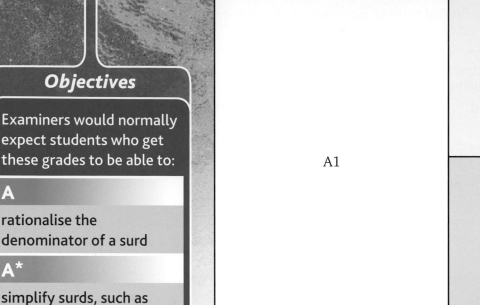

Examiners would normally expect students who get these grades to be able to:

A

rationalise the denominator of a surd

A*

simplify surds, such as write $(3 - \sqrt{5})^2$ in the form $a + b\sqrt{5}$

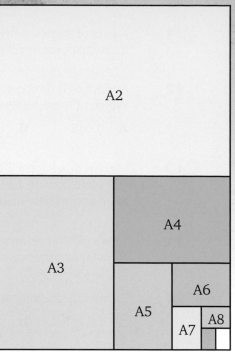

Did you know?

Surds

Take a piece of A4 paper and carefully measure the length and the width. Use your answers to calculate the length ÷ width.

What do you notice?

What has this got to do with surds?

Try this out for a sheet of A3 paper or a sheet of A5 paper.

What do you notice?

What has this got to do with surds?

Does this work for all sizes of paper?

You should already know:

✔ how to multiply fractions, and convert fractions to decimals and vice versa

✔ the squares of numbers up to 15

✔ the meaning of $\sqrt{2}$

✔ how to find prime factors

✔ how to multiply out two brackets.

Key terms

rational number
irrational number
surd

Learn... 4.1 Simplifying surds

Irrational and rational numbers

Rational numbers are numbers that **can** be expressed in the form $\frac{p}{q}$ where p and q are both integers.

Irrational numbers are numbers that **cannot** be expressed in the form $\frac{p}{q}$ where p and q are both integers.

Rational numbers, written as decimals, either terminate or recur.

Irrational numbers, written as decimals, continue forever without recurring.

$\sqrt{2}, \sqrt{3}, \sqrt{5}, \sqrt{6}, \sqrt{7}, \sqrt{8}, \sqrt{10}, \sqrt{11}, \sqrt{12}, \sqrt{13}, \sqrt{14}, \sqrt{15}$ are all irrational numbers because they cannot be written as fractions. If you write them as decimals they continue forever without recurring.

π is another example of an irrational number because it cannot be written as a fraction. If you write π as a decimal it will continue forever without recurring.

$\sqrt{1}, \sqrt{4}, \sqrt{9}, \sqrt{16}$ are all rational numbers because they can be written as fractions:

$\sqrt{1} = \frac{1}{1}, \sqrt{4} = \frac{2}{1}, \sqrt{9} = \frac{3}{1}, \sqrt{16} = \frac{4}{1}$

Example: Decide whether these are rational or irrational.

    a $\sqrt{16}$ **b** $\sqrt{17}$ **c** $\sqrt{225}$ **d** $\frac{\pi}{2}$

Solution: **a** $\sqrt{16} = 4$ so it is rational because 4 can be written $\frac{4}{1}$ All integers are rational.

    b $\sqrt{17}$ is irrational because it cannot be written in the form $\frac{p}{q}$

    c $\sqrt{225} = 15$ so it is rational because 15 can be written $\frac{15}{1}$

    d $\frac{\pi}{2}$ is irrational because π is irrational and all multiples of irrational numbers are irrational.

> ### AQA Examiner's tip
> Remember that you must know your squares up to 15^2. This means you should also know the associated square roots.

Surds

A **surd** is a square root that cannot be written in the form $\frac{p}{q}$

The following rules apply to surds:

$\sqrt{ab} = \sqrt{a} \times \sqrt{b}$ $a\sqrt{c} + b\sqrt{c} = (a + b)\sqrt{c}$

$\sqrt{\frac{a}{b}} = \frac{\sqrt{a}}{\sqrt{b}}$ $a\sqrt{c} - b\sqrt{c} = (a - b)\sqrt{c}$

Example: Simplify:

    a $\sqrt{20}$ **b** $\sqrt{3} \times \sqrt{24}$ **c** $3\sqrt{3} + \sqrt{12}$ **d** $\frac{\sqrt{75}}{\sqrt{3}}$

Solution: **a** To simplify $\sqrt{20}$ consider the factors of 20.

    You need to find a factor which is a square number (but not 1).

    $\sqrt{20} = \sqrt{1 \times 20}$

    $\sqrt{20} = \sqrt{2 \times 10}$

    $\sqrt{20} = \sqrt{4 \times 5}$

    Choosing the pair of factors where one factor is a square number:

    $\sqrt{20} = \sqrt{4 \times 5}$

    $= \sqrt{4} \times \sqrt{5}$ ⟵ $\sqrt{ab} = \sqrt{a} \times \sqrt{b}$

    $= 2 \times \sqrt{5}$

    $= 2\sqrt{5}$

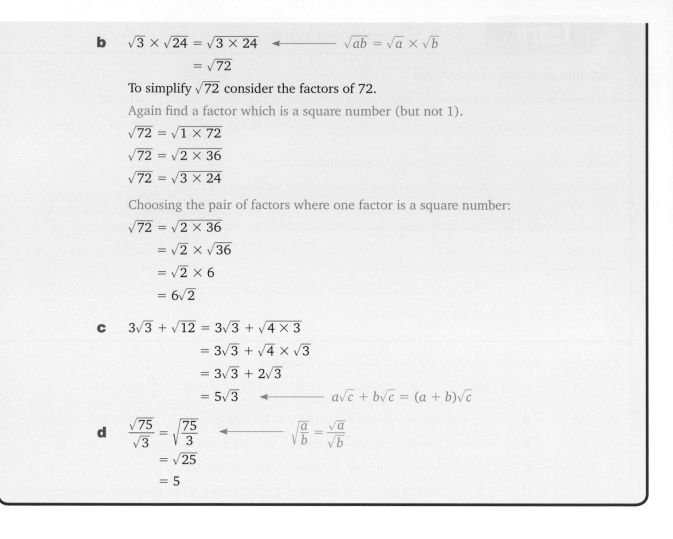

b $\sqrt{3} \times \sqrt{24} = \sqrt{3 \times 24}$ ⟵ $\sqrt{ab} = \sqrt{a} \times \sqrt{b}$

$\qquad = \sqrt{72}$

To simplify $\sqrt{72}$ consider the factors of 72.

Again find a factor which is a square number (but not 1).

$\sqrt{72} = \sqrt{1 \times 72}$

$\sqrt{72} = \sqrt{2 \times 36}$

$\sqrt{72} = \sqrt{3 \times 24}$

Choosing the pair of factors where one factor is a square number:

$\sqrt{72} = \sqrt{2 \times 36}$

$\qquad = \sqrt{2} \times \sqrt{36}$

$\qquad = \sqrt{2} \times 6$

$\qquad = 6\sqrt{2}$

c $3\sqrt{3} + \sqrt{12} = 3\sqrt{3} + \sqrt{4 \times 3}$

$\qquad = 3\sqrt{3} + \sqrt{4} \times \sqrt{3}$

$\qquad = 3\sqrt{3} + 2\sqrt{3}$

$\qquad = 5\sqrt{3}$ ⟵ $a\sqrt{c} + b\sqrt{c} = (a + b)\sqrt{c}$

d $\dfrac{\sqrt{75}}{\sqrt{3}} = \sqrt{\dfrac{75}{3}}$ ⟵ $\sqrt{\dfrac{a}{b}} = \dfrac{\sqrt{a}}{\sqrt{b}}$

$\qquad = \sqrt{25}$

$\qquad = 5$

Practise... 4.1 Simplifying surds 🆗   D C B A A*

B

1 Which of these numbers are irrational, and which are rational?

Give a reason for each answer.

a $\sqrt{32}$ **d** $\dfrac{\sqrt{4}}{11}$ **g** $\sqrt{8} \times \sqrt{8}$ **j** $\sqrt{3} \times 3$ **m** $(\sqrt{7})^2$

b $\sqrt{16}$ **e** $\dfrac{4}{\sqrt{11}}$ **h** $8 \times \sqrt{8}$ **k** $\sqrt{3} \times \sqrt{3}$

c $\dfrac{3}{17}$ **f** $\sqrt{8}$ **i** $\sqrt{3}$ **l** $\sqrt{3} \times \sqrt{12}$

2 Jill and Jack are having an argument about square roots.

Jill says that $\sqrt{90}$ must be irrational because all square roots are irrational.

Jack says she is wrong: $\sqrt{9} = 3$, so $\sqrt{90} = 30$

Who is wrong? How do you know?

A

3 Simplify the following.

a $\sqrt{40}$ **e** $7\sqrt{5} - 2\sqrt{5}$ **i** $\sqrt{3} \times \sqrt{27}$ **m** $\dfrac{\sqrt{88}}{2}$

b $\sqrt{90}$ **f** $\sqrt{20} + \sqrt{5}$ **j** $4\sqrt{3} \times \sqrt{6}$ **n** $\dfrac{3\sqrt{12}}{\sqrt{3}}$

c $\sqrt{98}$ **g** $\sqrt{72} + \sqrt{18}$ **k** $2\sqrt{5} \times \sqrt{10}$

d $5\sqrt{3} + 3\sqrt{3}$ **h** $\sqrt{8} + 3\sqrt{2} - \sqrt{50}$ **l** $\dfrac{\sqrt{27}}{\sqrt{3}}$

4 Marc says $\sqrt{10} + \sqrt{15} = \sqrt{25} = 5$

Tanya works it out differently, but gets the same answer.

She says $\sqrt{10} + \sqrt{15} = \sqrt{2} \times \sqrt{5} + \sqrt{3} \times \sqrt{5} = (\sqrt{2} + \sqrt{3}) \times \sqrt{5} = \sqrt{5} \times \sqrt{5} = 5$

a What did Marc do wrong?

b Where did Tanya go wrong?

! 5 Write down three irrational numbers between 1 and 2.

! 6 Show that:

$\sqrt{2} \times \sqrt{3} \times \sqrt{4} \times \sqrt{5} \times \sqrt{6} = 12\sqrt{5}$

7 A company makes wall tiles. The company makes two different sizes of square tile (purple and yellow) and one size rectangle (blue), to fit together as shown.
The yellow square tile has an area of 30 cm² and the purple square tile has an area of 15 cm².

a What are the exact dimensions (length and width) of the rectangular blue tile?

b What is the area of the rectangular blue tile?

Give your answers as surds in their simplest form.

8 **a** Can you find two irrational numbers that multiply together to make a rational number?

b Can you find two irrational numbers that, when divided, give an answer of 2?

9 Write $\sqrt{5} \times \sqrt{35}$ in the form $p\sqrt{q}$, where p and q are both prime numbers.

10 **a** You are given that $A = \sqrt{a} + \sqrt{b}$ and $B = \sqrt{a} - \sqrt{b}$
Prove that $A^2 + B^2 = 30$ when $a = 12$ and $b = 3$.

b Find a different pair of values of a and b where $(\sqrt{a} + \sqrt{b})^2 + (\sqrt{a} - \sqrt{b})^2$ is a rational number.

Learn... 4.2 Rationalising the denominator k!

One way to simplify expressions involving surds is to rationalise the denominator.
This means removing the square root from the denominator.
Rationalising the denominator involves multiplying the numerator and denominator by fractions.

For example:

If the denominator is $\sqrt{a}$ then multiply the numerator and denominator by $\sqrt{a}$.
This leaves a in the denominator.

Using the fact that $\sqrt{a} \times \sqrt{a} = a$ since $\sqrt{a} \times \sqrt{a} = \sqrt{a \times a} = \sqrt{a^2} = a$

If the denominator is $b + \sqrt{c}$ then multiply the numerator and denominator by $b - \sqrt{c}$

Using the fact that $(b + \sqrt{c})(b - \sqrt{c}) = b^2 - c$ since $(b + \sqrt{c})(b - \sqrt{c}) = b^2 - b\sqrt{c} + b\sqrt{c} - c = b^2 - c$

Example: Rationalise the denominator of the following.

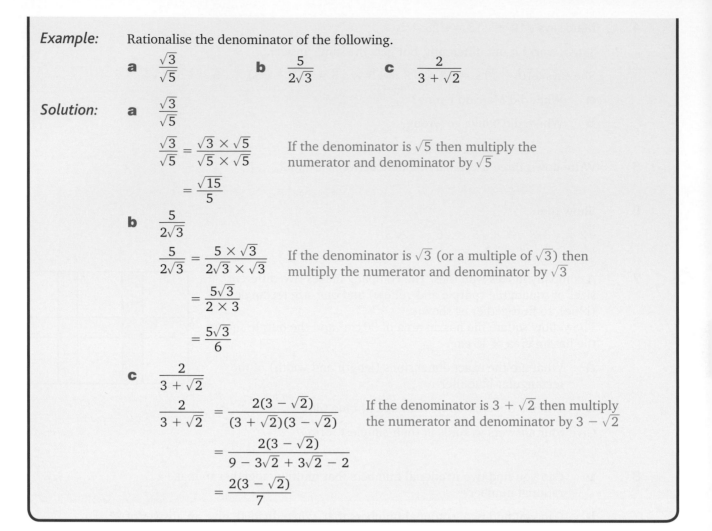

a $\dfrac{\sqrt{3}}{\sqrt{5}}$ **b** $\dfrac{5}{2\sqrt{3}}$ **c** $\dfrac{2}{3 + \sqrt{2}}$

Solution: **a** $\dfrac{\sqrt{3}}{\sqrt{5}}$

$$\dfrac{\sqrt{3}}{\sqrt{5}} = \dfrac{\sqrt{3} \times \sqrt{5}}{\sqrt{5} \times \sqrt{5}}$$ If the denominator is $\sqrt{5}$ then multiply the numerator and denominator by $\sqrt{5}$

$$= \dfrac{\sqrt{15}}{5}$$

b $\dfrac{5}{2\sqrt{3}}$

$$\dfrac{5}{2\sqrt{3}} = \dfrac{5 \times \sqrt{3}}{2\sqrt{3} \times \sqrt{3}}$$ If the denominator is $\sqrt{3}$ (or a multiple of $\sqrt{3}$) then multiply the numerator and denominator by $\sqrt{3}$

$$= \dfrac{5\sqrt{3}}{2 \times 3}$$

$$= \dfrac{5\sqrt{3}}{6}$$

c $\dfrac{2}{3 + \sqrt{2}}$

$$\dfrac{2}{3 + \sqrt{2}} = \dfrac{2(3 - \sqrt{2})}{(3 + \sqrt{2})(3 - \sqrt{2})}$$ If the denominator is $3 + \sqrt{2}$ then multiply the numerator and denominator by $3 - \sqrt{2}$

$$= \dfrac{2(3 - \sqrt{2})}{9 - 3\sqrt{2} + 3\sqrt{2} - 2}$$

$$= \dfrac{2(3 - \sqrt{2})}{7}$$

Practise...   4.2 Rationalising the denominator   🅚   D C B A A*

A

1   Rationalise the denominators of these fractions.

a $\dfrac{\sqrt{7}}{\sqrt{3}}$ **d** $\dfrac{\sqrt{5}}{\sqrt{35}}$ **g** $\dfrac{5}{\sqrt{10}}$ **j** $\dfrac{30}{\sqrt{15}}$

b $\dfrac{3}{2\sqrt{3}}$ **e** $\dfrac{7}{4\sqrt{7}}$ **h** $\dfrac{4}{2 + \sqrt{3}}$ **k** $\dfrac{5}{2 - \sqrt{3}}$

c $\dfrac{7}{5 + \sqrt{7}}$ **f** $\dfrac{3}{3 - \sqrt{3}}$ **i** $\dfrac{\sqrt{3}}{3 - \sqrt{3}}$ **l** $\dfrac{\sqrt{2}}{2 + \sqrt{2}}$

2   Angela says $\sqrt{\dfrac{6}{18}} = \sqrt{\dfrac{1}{3}} = \sqrt{\dfrac{1 \times \sqrt{3}}{3 \times \sqrt{3}}} = \dfrac{\sqrt{3}}{3\sqrt{3}} = \dfrac{1}{3}$

Marco says $\sqrt{\dfrac{6}{18}} = \dfrac{\sqrt{6}}{\sqrt{18}} = \dfrac{\sqrt{6}}{\sqrt{9} \times \sqrt{2}} = \dfrac{\sqrt{6}}{3\sqrt{2}} = \dfrac{\sqrt{2}}{\sqrt{2}} = 1$

a   Find Angela's mistake.

b   Find Marco's mistake.

c   Work out the correct answer.

3   Show that $\dfrac{2}{3 + \sqrt{5}} = \dfrac{3 - \sqrt{5}}{2}$

4   A room has a length which is exactly $\sqrt{2}$ times its width. The length is 10 m.

a   What is the width? Give your answer as a surd (with a rational denominator).

b   What is the area of the room?

5 Simplify the following.

a $\dfrac{1}{2} + \dfrac{3}{\sqrt{5}}$

b $\dfrac{3}{2\sqrt{3}} - \dfrac{2}{3\sqrt{2}}$

6 Write $(3 - \sqrt{5})^2$ in the form $a + b\sqrt{5}$

⚠ 7 If $x = \sqrt{2} + \sqrt{3}$

a find x^2

b show that $x^4 - 10x^2 + 1 = 0$

⚠ 8 In his homework, Manesh had to rationalise the denominator of a fraction. He can remember that the denominator was $(2 - \sqrt{3})$, but he can't remember the numerator. He knows that the answer is $3(2 + \sqrt{3})$.

What was the numerator?

? 9 Prove that $\dfrac{\sqrt{20} - 10}{\sqrt{5}} = 2(1 - \sqrt{5})$

4 Assess

1 Which of the following numbers are rational and which are irrational? How can you tell?

a $\sqrt{7}$
b $\sqrt{16}$
c $\dfrac{\sqrt{16}}{7}$
d $\sqrt{\dfrac{16}{7}}$
e $\dfrac{\sqrt{63}}{\sqrt{7}}$

2 Write these in their simplest form.

a $\sqrt{8}$
b $\sqrt{63}$
c $\sqrt{98}$
d $4\sqrt{27}$
e $2\sqrt{50}$

3 Express each of these as a square root of a single number.

a $2\sqrt{3}$
b $4\sqrt{5}$
c $5\sqrt{7}$
d $2\sqrt{11}$
e $10\sqrt{2}$

4 Rationalise the following expressions.

a $\dfrac{2}{\sqrt{2}}$
b $\dfrac{3}{\sqrt{7}}$
c $\dfrac{4}{2\sqrt{5}}$
d $\dfrac{5}{\sqrt{2} + 1}$
e $\dfrac{7}{\sqrt{3} - \sqrt{2}}$
f $\dfrac{\sqrt{2}}{\sqrt{3} + \sqrt{6}}$

5 Write the following in the form $a + b\sqrt{c}$

a $(\sqrt{2} + 3)^2$
c $(1 + \sqrt{2})(2 - \sqrt{2})$
e $(2\sqrt{5} + 3\sqrt{7})(2\sqrt{5} - 3\sqrt{7})$

b $(\sqrt{5} - 3)^2$
d $(\sqrt{3} + \sqrt{5})(\sqrt{3} - \sqrt{5})$

6 Given that $a = \sqrt{2}$, $b = \sqrt{8}$ and $c = \sqrt{12}$, work out the value of $\dfrac{c}{a - b}$

Give your answer in its simplest form.

AQA Examination-style questions 🎮

1 The formula to find the volume of a cylinder is

$$\text{volume} = \pi \times \text{radius}^2 \times \text{height}$$

A cylinder has radius $= 2\sqrt{3}$ metres and height $= \dfrac{1}{\sqrt{2}}$ metres.

Work out the volume of the cylinder in terms of π.
Rationalise the denominator and give your answer in its simplest form.

(5 marks)

AQA 2008

2 Find the value of x if $\dfrac{\sqrt{x} \times 50}{\sqrt{5}} = 4\sqrt{5}$

(4 marks)

AQA 2008

Working with symbols

Examiners would normally expect students who get these grades to be able to:

D

expand brackets such as $4(x - 3)$

factorise an expression such as $6x + 8$

C

expand and simplify an expression such as $3(3x - 7) - 2(3x + 1)$

B

expand and simplify two brackets such as $(x - 3)(x + 5)$

expand and simplify two brackets such as $(3x + 1)(2x - 3)$

simplify fractions such as $\dfrac{x}{3} + \dfrac{x}{5}$ and $\dfrac{2(x - 1)^2}{x - 1}$

Did you know?

$$E = mc^2$$

This is probably the most famous piece of algebra ever written down. It is a formula written by the scientist Albert Einstein in 1905 to explain the relationship between matter and energy.

In April 2008, the American singer Mariah Carey had a number one hit in the United States with her album called $E = mc^2$

You should already know:

✔ number operations and BIDMAS

✔ how to add and subtract negative numbers

✔ how to multiply and divide negative numbers

✔ how to find common factors

✔ how to add and subtract fractions

✔ the meaning of indices

✔ how to collect like terms.

Key terms

expand
simplify
factorise
quadratic expression

Learn... 5.1 Expanding brackets and collecting like terms

When you **expand** brackets, **all** the terms inside the brackets must be multiplied by the term outside the brackets.

You will usually be given the instruction **expand** or multiply out.

When you **simplify** an expression, you collect like terms.

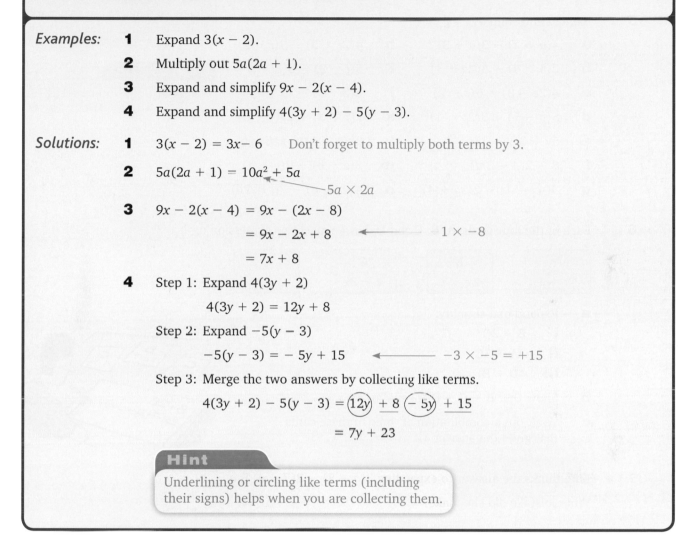

Examples: **1** Expand $3(x - 2)$.

2 Multiply out $5a(2a + 1)$.

3 Expand and simplify $9x - 2(x - 4)$.

4 Expand and simplify $4(3y + 2) - 5(y - 3)$.

Solutions: **1** $3(x - 2) = 3x - 6$ Don't forget to multiply both terms by 3.

2 $5a(2a + 1) = 10a^2 + 5a$
$5a \times 2a$

3 $9x - 2(x - 4) = 9x - (2x - 8)$

$= 9x - 2x + 8$ 1×-8

$= 7x + 8$

4 Step 1: Expand $4(3y + 2)$

$4(3y + 2) = 12y + 8$

Step 2: Expand $-5(y - 3)$

$-5(y - 3) = -5y + 15$ $-3 \times -5 = +15$

Step 3: Merge the two answers by collecting like terms.

$4(3y + 2) - 5(y - 3) = 12y + 8 - 5y + 15$

$= 7y + 23$

Hint

Underlining or circling like terms (including their signs) helps when you are collecting them.

Practise... 5.1 Expanding brackets and collecting like terms k!

D C B A A*

1 Multiply out:

a $2(a + 3)$ **d** $5(d + e)$ **g** $3x(2x - 3)$

b $4(b - 1)$ **e** $2(3f - 2)$ **h** $5m(1 - 2n)$

c $3(2c + 3)$ **f** $4(p + 2q)$ **i** $2pq(p - 3q)$

2 The answer to an expansion is $3x + 6y$

What was the expression before it was expanded?

3 The answer to an expansion is $pq - pr$

What was the expression before it was expanded?

D

D

4
Joe says the expansion of $4ab(2c - d)$ is $8abc - d$

Kevin says it is $4abc - 4abd$

Liam's answer is $8ab - abd$

All their answers are incorrect.

Explain their mistakes and write down the correct answer.

> **Bump up your grade**
>
> To get a Grade C you need to be able to expand and simplify the same expression.

C

5
Expand and simplify:

a $4(a + 2) + 3(a + 3)$ **h** $4(2r + 5) - 3(r - 2)$

b $2(b - 4) + 3(2b + 1)$ **i** $5(t - 3) - 3(2 - t)$

c $4(2c - 3) + 5(c - 2)$ **j** $6(2 - x) - (3 - x)$

d $5(p - 1) + 3(2p - 1)$ **k** $y(y + 5) + 2y(y - 3)$

e $5y - 3(y - 1)$ **l** $3k(1 + k) - k(k + 6)$

f $8 - 2(4 - 3m)$ **m** $3(a + b) + 2(a - b)$

g $3(4q - 1) - 2(3q + 4)$ **n** $4(2c - d) - 7(c - 2d)$

> **AQA** *Examiner's tip*
>
> Set out the steps of your working clearly so that you can gain marks even if your final answer is wrong.

> **Hint**
>
> Think of $-(3 - x)$ as $-1(3 - x)$

⚠ 6
Each of the four cards, **A**, **B**, **C** and **D**, has an algebraic expression on it.

A	**B**	**C**	**D**
$5x + 1$	$2x - 7$	$4 - 3x$	$x + 3$

a   Expand and simplify:

   i   **B + 2C**

   ii   **2A + 3C**

   iii   **4D + B**

b   Show that **B + C + D** is equal to zero.

c   Work out a combination of three of these cards that gives the answer 12.

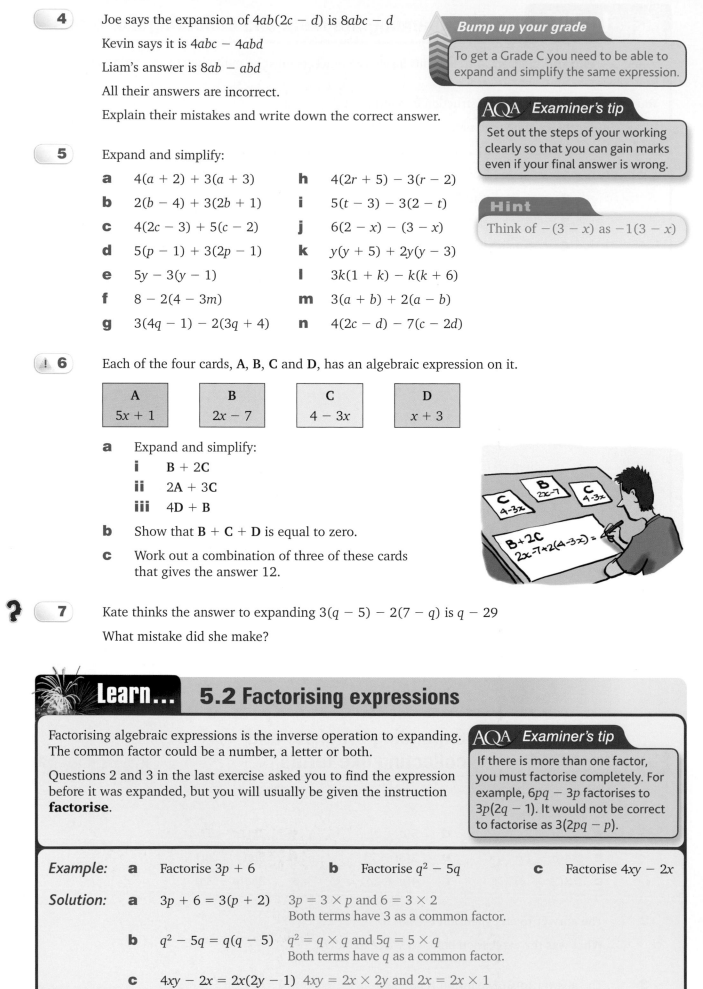

?   7
Kate thinks the answer to expanding $3(q - 5) - 2(7 - q)$ is $q - 29$

What mistake did she make?

Learn... 5.2 Factorising expressions

Factorising algebraic expressions is the inverse operation to expanding. The common factor could be a number, a letter or both.

Questions 2 and 3 in the last exercise asked you to find the expression before it was expanded, but you will usually be given the instruction **factorise**.

> **AQA** *Examiner's tip*
>
> If there is more than one factor, you must factorise completely. For example, $6pq - 3p$ factorises to $3p(2q - 1)$. It would not be correct to factorise as $3(2pq - p)$.

Example: **a**   Factorise $3p + 6$ **b**   Factorise $q^2 - 5q$ **c**   Factorise $4xy - 2x$

Solution: **a** $3p + 6 = 3(p + 2)$ $3p = 3 \times p$ and $6 = 3 \times 2$
                                         Both terms have 3 as a common factor.

      b $q^2 - 5q = q(q - 5)$ $q^2 = q \times q$ and $5q = 5 \times q$
                                           Both terms have q as a common factor.

      c $4xy - 2x = 2x(2y - 1)$ $4xy = 2x \times 2y$ and $2x = 2x \times 1$
                                           Both terms have $2x$ as a common factor.

Practise... 5.2 Factorising expressions

1 Match each expression with the correct factors.

Expression	Factors
$8a + 10b$	$2(4a - 5b)$
$10b - 8a$	$2(5a - 4b)$
$8a - 10b$	$2(4a + 5b)$
$10a + 8b$	$2(5b - 4a)$
$10a - 8b$	$2(5a + 4b)$

2 Factorise:

a
- **i** $2a + 4$
- **ii** $3b + 15$
- **iii** $5c - 10$
- **iv** $7d - 21$
- **v** $4e + 6$
- **vi** $12 - 2f$
- **vii** $g^2 + 6g$
- **viii** $8j - 2k$
- **ix** $2x + 4y - 6z$
- **x** $22m - 11n - 33p$
- **xi** $pq + pr - pt$
- **xii** $x^2 - 7x$

b
- **i** $y^2 + y$
- **ii** $3z^2 + 4z$
- **iii** $2a - 3a^2$
- **iv** $4c^2 - 6c$
- **v** $2d^2 + 8d$
- **vi** $5e + 20e^2$
- **vii** $2w^2 - 6w + 10$
- **viii** $6y^2 - 3xy + 9y$
- **ix** $5xyz - xyt$
- **x** $2ab + 4a^2b$
- **xi** $c^3 - 2c^2$
- **xii** $3mn^2 + 9m^2n$

3 Explain why the expression $5x + 11y$ cannot be factorised.

4 Lisa says that $7p + 2q$ can be factorised as $2(3\frac{1}{2}p + q)$.

Is she correct?

Explain your answer.

5 Factorise each set of expressions to find the odd one out.

a $3x + 12$ $2x - 8$ $4x + x^2$

b $3 - 3y^2$ $2y - 2y^2$ $5 - 5y$

c $6p^2 + 4q^2$ $6p + 4q$ $3p^2 + 2pq$

6
a Show that $2(x + 3) + 6(x + 1) = 4(2x + 3)$

b Show that $3(y - 5) - 2(3 - 2y) = 7(y - 3)$

c Show that $4(2t + 1) - 3(t - 2) = 5(t + 2)$

Learn... 5.3 Multiplying two brackets together

When you multiply two brackets together, you have to multiply each term in the second bracket by each term in the first bracket.

$$(x + 2)(x + 4) = x(x + 4) + 2(x + 4)$$
$$= x^2 + 4x + 2x + 8$$
$$= x^2 + 6x + 8$$

$x^2 + 6x + 8$ is a **quadratic expression**, because it contains a term in x^2, but no higher power of x.

The multiplication can be worked out in a table:

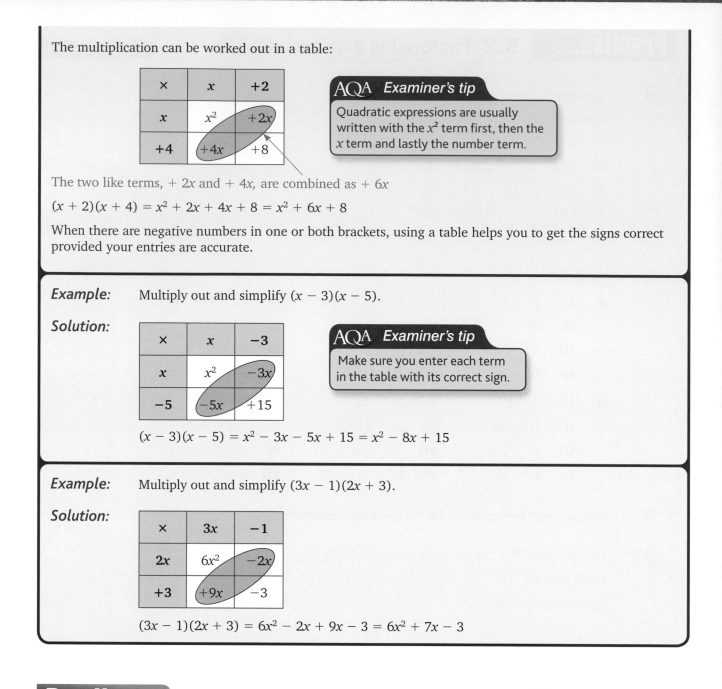

×	x	+2
x	x^2	+2x
+4	+4x	+8

AQA *Examiner's tip*

Quadratic expressions are usually written with the x^2 term first, then the x term and lastly the number term.

The two like terms, $+2x$ and $+4x$, are combined as $+6x$

$(x + 2)(x + 4) = x^2 + 2x + 4x + 8 = x^2 + 6x + 8$

When there are negative numbers in one or both brackets, using a table helps you to get the signs correct provided your entries are accurate.

Example: Multiply out and simplify $(x - 3)(x - 5)$.

Solution:

×	x	−3
x	x^2	−3x
−5	−5x	+15

AQA *Examiner's tip*

Make sure you enter each term in the table with its correct sign.

$(x - 3)(x - 5) = x^2 - 3x - 5x + 15 = x^2 - 8x + 15$

Example: Multiply out and simplify $(3x - 1)(2x + 3)$.

Solution:

×	3x	−1
2x	6x^2	−2x
+3	+9x	−3

$(3x - 1)(2x + 3) = 6x^2 - 2x + 9x - 3 = 6x^2 + 7x - 3$

Practise... 5.3 Multiplying two brackets together (k!) D C B A A*

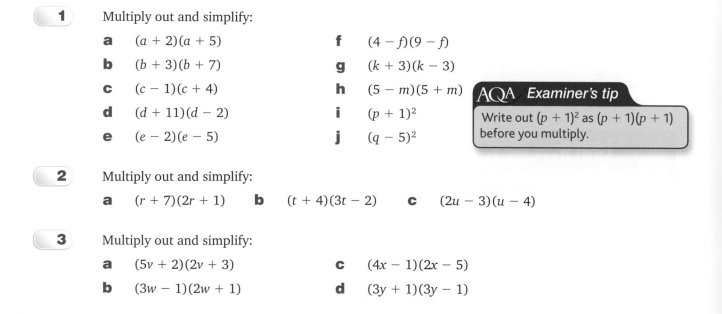

B

1 Multiply out and simplify:

a $(a + 2)(a + 5)$ **f** $(4 - f)(9 - f)$

b $(b + 3)(b + 7)$ **g** $(k + 3)(k - 3)$

c $(c - 1)(c + 4)$ **h** $(5 - m)(5 + m)$

d $(d + 11)(d - 2)$ **i** $(p + 1)^2$

e $(e - 2)(e - 5)$ **j** $(q - 5)^2$

AQA *Examiner's tip*

Write out $(p + 1)^2$ as $(p + 1)(p + 1)$ before you multiply.

2 Multiply out and simplify:

a $(r + 7)(2r + 1)$ **b** $(t + 4)(3t - 2)$ **c** $(2u - 3)(u - 4)$

3 Multiply out and simplify:

a $(5v + 2)(2v + 3)$ **c** $(4x - 1)(2x - 5)$

b $(3w - 1)(2w + 1)$ **d** $(3y + 1)(3y - 1)$

B

4 Multiply out and simplify:

    a $(5 - 2z)(5 + 2z)$ **b** $(3p + 1)^2$ **c** $(2q - 5)^2$

5 Show that $(4x + 3)(x - 1) - (x - 3)(4x + 1) = 10x$

! 6 Multiply out and simplify:

    a $(5a + b)(a - 3b)$ **d** $(2x - 3y)^2$

    b $(2c - 7d)(c - 2d)$ **e** $(m + 7n)(m - 7n)$

    c $(4p - q)(4p + q)$ **f** $(3e + 2f)(2e - 3f)$

! 7 **a** Write down the areas of each of these rectangles.

        i *ABED*

        i *BCFE*

        iii *DEHG*

        iv *EFIH*

   b Add your results to find the area of the rectangle *ACIG*.

? 8 Louise says that $(3x + 1)^2 = 9x^2 + 1$

Why is she wrong?

? 9 Ed multiplies $(2y \quad 7)$ by $(3y \quad 1)$.

His answer is $6y^2 + 23y + 7$

How can you tell, **without multiplying the brackets**, that he has made a mistake?

Learn...   5.4 Simplifying algebraic fractions   *k!*

Algebraic fractions obey the same rules as ordinary fractions.

Multiplying fractions

$$\frac{3}{4} \times \frac{2}{5}$$
    Multiply numerators together.
    Multiply denominators together.

$$\frac{3}{\cancel{4}} \times \frac{2}{5} = \frac{\cancel{6}}{\cancel{20}} = \frac{3}{10}$$
    Divide top and bottom by the common factor.

$$\frac{a}{bc} \times \frac{cd}{e}$$

$$\frac{a}{bc} \times \frac{cd}{e} = \frac{a\cancel{c}d}{b\cancel{c}e} = \frac{ad}{be}$$
    Divide top and bottom by the common factor.

Adding fractions

$$\frac{1}{3} + \frac{2}{5} = \frac{5}{15} + \frac{6}{15}$$
    Use the lowest common denominator 15.

$$= \frac{11}{15}$$
    Add the numerators.

$$\overset{\times 5}{\frac{x}{3} = \frac{5x}{15}} \quad \overset{\times 3}{\frac{2x}{3} = \frac{6x}{15}} \quad \frac{x}{3} + \frac{2x}{5} = \frac{5x}{15} + \frac{6x}{15}$$

$$= \frac{11x}{15}$$

To simplify algebraic fractions, you should factorise the numerator and/or the denominator.

Then divide the numerator and denominator by common factors.

Example: Simplify $\dfrac{4x + 6}{6x - 18}$

Solution: Factorise the numerator $\quad 4x + 6 = 2(2x + 3)$

Factorise the denominator $\quad 6x - 18 = 6(x - 3)$

Rewrite the fraction as $\quad \dfrac{2(2x + 3)}{6(x - 3)}$

Divide top and bottom by the common factor which is 2 $\quad \dfrac{{}^{1}\cancel{2}(2x + 3)}{{}^{3}\cancel{6}(x - 3)} = \dfrac{2x + 3}{3(x - 3)}$

AQA **Examiner's tip**

If there is no common factor in a question like this you are likely to have made an error.

Practise... 5.4 Simplifying algebraic fractions k! D C B A A*

B

1 Simplify:

a $\dfrac{ab}{4a}$

b $\dfrac{6cd}{8d^2}$

c $\dfrac{12e}{3f}$

d $\dfrac{3(x + 1)}{6x}$

e $\dfrac{5yz}{y(t - 4)}$

f $\dfrac{pqrs}{q^2r}$

g $\dfrac{a - 5}{3a - 15}$

h $\dfrac{10 + 5b}{b + 2}$

2 Simplify:

a $\dfrac{a}{2} + \dfrac{3a}{8}$

b $\dfrac{2b}{3} + \dfrac{b}{6}$

c $\dfrac{3c}{8} + \dfrac{3c}{16}$

d $\dfrac{3d}{5} - \dfrac{d}{2}$

e $\dfrac{e}{3} - \dfrac{e}{9}$

f $\dfrac{5f}{8} - \dfrac{f}{4}$

g $\dfrac{11x}{12} - \dfrac{5x}{6}$

h $\dfrac{2y}{5} + \dfrac{y}{6}$

i $\dfrac{4z}{9} + \dfrac{5z}{6}$

3 Simplify:

a $\dfrac{3p}{5} + \dfrac{p}{4} - \dfrac{7p}{10}$

b $\dfrac{7t}{8} - \dfrac{5t}{6} + \dfrac{t}{12}$

c $\dfrac{4m}{15} + \dfrac{m}{6} - \dfrac{2m}{5}$

Simplify:

⚠ 4 $\dfrac{3}{8x} + \dfrac{1}{2x}$

⚠ 5 $\dfrac{3}{4y} - \dfrac{5}{16y}$

⚠ 6 $\dfrac{3}{5t} + \dfrac{2}{3t} - \dfrac{9}{10t}$

⚠ 7 $\dfrac{1}{x} + \dfrac{4}{2 - x}$

5 Assess

D

1 Multiply out:

a $7(a - 2)$

b $3(2b - 1)$

c $4(c + d)$

d $5(e - 3f)$

e $2m(n + 2p)$

f $3t(2u - 3v)$

g $x(x + 2)$

h $y(3 - y)$

i $5z(z - 1)$

2 Factorise:

a $3a - 12$

b $2b + 10$

c $9 - 6c$

d $14 - 7d$

e $4p - 2q + 8r$

f $12x + 6y - 4z$

g $x^2 - 4x$

h $yz + z^2$

i $w^2 + vw - 3w$

3 Expand and simplify:

a $3(a + 2) + 2(a - 1)$ f $8(w - 1) + 2(4 + 2w)$

b $3(b - 2) + 3(b + 5)$ g $2(x + y) + 5(2x + y)$

c $2(3c + 4) - 3(c - 4)$ h $3(4p - q) + 2(p - 3q)$

d $5(x + 1) + 6(x + 7)$ i $5(2a + 3b) - 2(3a + 4b)$

e $6(2y - 3) - 4(3y - 2)$ j $4(m - 3n) - (3m - 5n)$

4 Show that $5(x + 1) + 2(5 - x) = 3(x + 5)$

5 Multiply out and simplify:

a $(a + 1)(a + 3)$ e $(e - 4)^2$ i $(2x + 1)(x + 4)$ m $(2w + 3)^2$

b $(b - 2)(b + 8)$ f $(f + 2)(f - 1)$ j $(3y + 4)(y - 2)$

c $(c - 6)(c + 6)$ g $(h - 9)(h - 2)$ k $(5z - 3)(z + 1)$

d $(d - 7)(d - 4)$ h $(m + 2)(m - 2)$ l $(2l + 3)(3t - 2)$

6 Simplify:

a $\dfrac{3xy}{6x}$ c $\dfrac{6t}{2t - 4}$ e $\dfrac{y^2 - 3y}{5y}$ g $\dfrac{(z + 5)(z - 7)}{(z - 1)(z + 5)}$

b $\dfrac{pqr}{qr^2}$ d $\dfrac{v + 5}{2v + 10}$ f $\dfrac{3c - 9}{2c - 6}$

7 Simplify:

a $\dfrac{x}{8} + \dfrac{3x}{4}$ c $\dfrac{2z}{9} + \dfrac{z}{6}$ e $\dfrac{9a}{10} - \dfrac{8a}{15}$

b $\dfrac{5y}{8} - \dfrac{y}{4}$ d $\dfrac{t}{2} - \dfrac{3t}{16}$ f $\dfrac{7c}{12} + \dfrac{4c}{9}$

AQA Examination-style questions

1 a Simplify $y + 2 \times y \times y$ *(1 mark)*

   b Factorise $15y + 25$ *(1 mark)*

   c Factorise $z^2 + 8z$ *(1 mark)*

   d Expand and simplify $(2n - 1)(n + 1)$ *(1 mark)*

AQA 2008

Graphs of linear functions

Objectives

Examiners would normally expect students who get these grades to be able to:

D

draw the graph of a line, such as $y = 3x - 5$, without being given a table of values

solve problems such as finding where the line $y = 3x - 5$ crosses the line $y = 4$

C

find the gradients of straight-line graphs

find the midpoint of a line segment such as the line from $A(1, 5)$ to $B(3, 7)$

B

find the gradient and equation of a line through two points such as $(0, 3)$ and $(5, 13)$

find the equation of a line parallel to another line, such as $y = 3x - 5$, passing through a given point.

Did you know?

Rollercoaster

The design of a rollercoaster has to have a long slope with a chain lift to drag the rollercoaster car to the top. This gives it enough energy to reach the end of the track. The slope needs to be high enough so that the car will roll along to the end of the track. The designer has to choose a gradient for the first slope. If it is too steep, it could be unsafe. If it is too shallow, there may not be enough room within the area available for the rollercoaster in the theme park. Choosing the proper gradient is very important.

You should already know:

✔ how to plot points in all four quadrants

✔ how to recognise lines such as $y = 4$ or $x = -3$

Key terms

linear
gradient
variables
coefficient
intercept
constant

Learn... 6.1 Drawing straight-line graphs k!

An equation such as $y = 3x - 5$ can be shown on a graph.

The graph will be a straight line and $y = 3x - 5$ is called a **linear** equation.

A linear equation does not contain any powers of x or y.

To draw the graph you need to work out the coordinates of three points on the line.

Choose any three values of x that lie within the range you have been given.

Work out the corresponding y-values, using the equation of the line.

Plot the points and then draw the line through them.

> **AQA Examiner's tip**
>
> It is a good idea to use zero as one of your x-values because it is easy to substitute.

Example: Draw the graph of $y = 3x - 5$ for values of x from -2 to 4.

Solution: Choose $x = -2, 0, 4$

Work out the y-values and put them in a table.

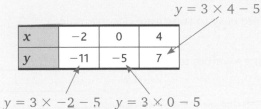

$y = 3 \times 4 - 5$

x	-2	0	4
y	-11	-5	7

$y = 3 \times -2 - 5$ $y = 3 \times 0 - 5$

> **AQA Examiner's tip**
>
> Always use three plots, not just two. They should be in a straight line. If they are not, you have made a mistake in working out one of the y-values, so check and correct the values.

Plot the points. (In the exam the axes will be drawn for you.)

Draw the line through your plots.

It must go all the way from $x = -2$ to $x = 4$

This straight-line graph has been drawn using the same scales on both axes.

This makes it easy to plot the points.

The range of y-values is large so the graph is tall and narrow.

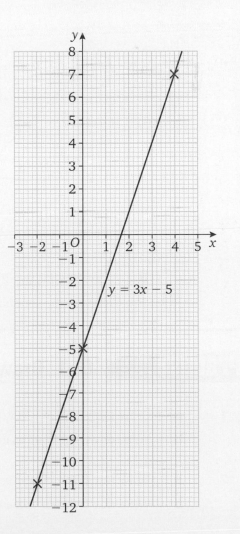

This is the same straight-line graph but using a different scale on the y-axis.

This makes it a little harder to plot the points, but the graph is not so tall.

You may be given axes with different scales to use in the exam, so you need to be able to plot against axes with different scales.

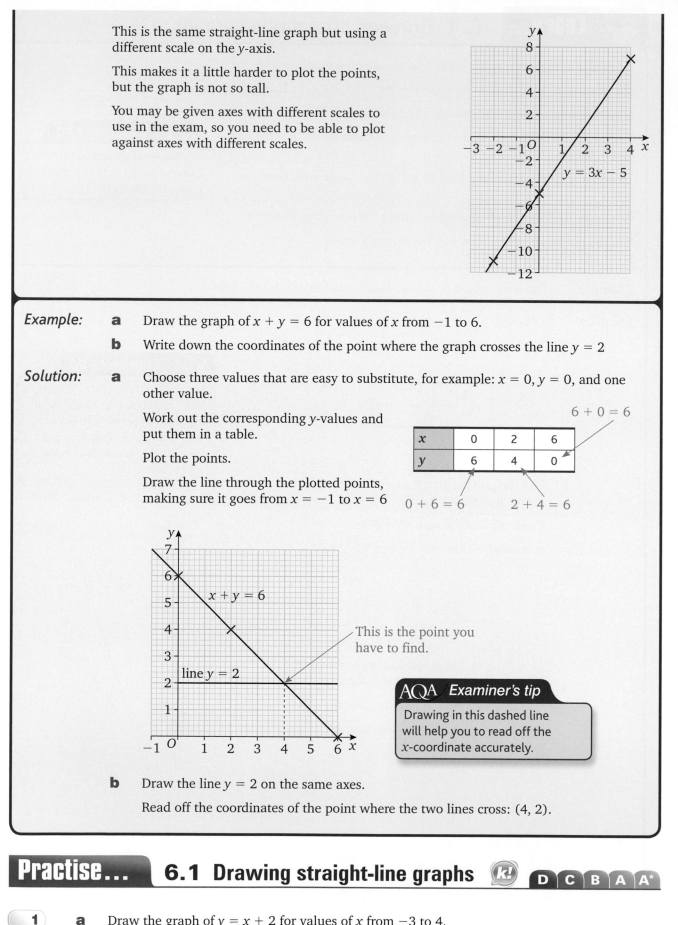

Example: **a** Draw the graph of $x + y = 6$ for values of x from -1 to 6.

b Write down the coordinates of the point where the graph crosses the line $y = 2$

Solution: **a** Choose three values that are easy to substitute, for example: $x = 0$, $y = 0$, and one other value.

Work out the corresponding y-values and put them in a table.

Plot the points.

$6 + 0 = 6$

x	0	2	6
y	6	4	0

Draw the line through the plotted points, making sure it goes from $x = -1$ to $x = 6$

$0 + 6 = 6$ $2 + 4 = 6$

This is the point you have to find.

AQA **Examiner's tip**

Drawing in this dashed line will help you to read off the x-coordinate accurately.

b Draw the line $y = 2$ on the same axes.

Read off the coordinates of the point where the two lines cross: (4, 2).

Practise... 6.1 Drawing straight-line graphs k! D C B A A*

D

1 **a** Draw the graph of $y = x + 2$ for values of x from -3 to 4.

b Write down the coordinates of the point where this graph crosses the y-axis.

2 **a** Draw the graph of $y = 3x - 1$ for values of x from -3 to 3.

b Write down the coordinates of the point where this graph crosses the line $y = -3$

3   **a**   Draw the graph of $y = \frac{1}{2}x$ for values of x from -4 to 4.
　　b   If this line was extended, would it go through the point $(7, 4)$?
　　　　Explain your answer.

4   **a**   Draw the graph of $y = 2x$ for values of x from -3 to 3.
　　b   On the same axes, draw the graph of $y = x$ for values of x from -3 to 3.
　　c   Your two graphs go through the same point.
　　　　What is this point?

5   **a**   Draw the graph of $y = 2x + 1$ for values of x from -3 to 3.
　　b   On the same axes, draw the graph of $y = 1 \quad 3x$ for values of x from -3 to 3.
　　c   Write down the coordinates of the point where these two lines cross.

6   **a**   Draw the graph of $x + 2y = 9$ for values of x from -2 to 5.
　　b   Write down the coordinates of the point where your graph crosses the line $x = 4$

7   **a**   Draw the graph of $x - 2y = 1$ for values of x from -3 to 3.
　　b   Write down the coordinates of the point where your graph crosses the line $y = \frac{1}{2}$

⚠ 8   Which of these points lie on the line $3x + 2y = 12$?
　　A $(0, 4)$ **B** $(2, 3)$ **C** $(3, 2)$ **D** $(1, 4\frac{1}{2})$ **E** $(0, 6)$ **F** $(6, -3)$ **G** $(-2, 8)$
　　Show how you found your answers.

9 $P(-3, 6)$, $Q(0, 0)$ and $R(2, -4)$ are three points on a straight line.
　　Which of these is the equation of the line?
　　$y = x + 9 \quad\quad x + y = 3 \quad\quad y + 2x = 0$
　　Show how you found your answer.

10   Each of the following points lies on one or more of the given lines.
　　Match the points to their lines.
　　Points: $A(-2, 7)$ $B(0, 0)$ $C(1, 4)$ $D(2, 5)$ $E(3, 3)$ $F(4, 1)$
　　Lines: $y = 4x \quad 2x + y = 9 \quad x + y = 5 \quad y = 6x - 7$

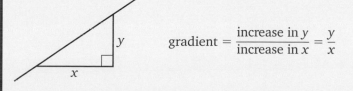

Learn...   **6.2 Gradients of straight-line graphs** 🔑

The **gradient** of a straight-line graph is a measure of how steep it is.

The **gradient** can be found from the graph of the line as shown below.

A line that slopes from top right to bottom left has a positive gradient because y increases as x increases.

To find the gradient, draw a line parallel to the x-axis and a line parallel to the y-axis to make a right-angled triangle on the graph. The triangle can be anywhere on the graph.

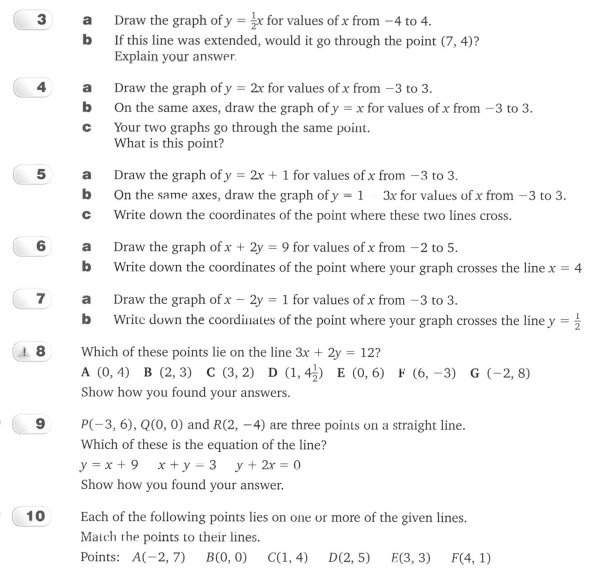

$$\text{gradient} = \frac{\text{increase in } y}{\text{increase in } x} = \frac{y}{x}$$

AQA *Examiner's tip*

Take a careful note of the scales on the graph. They might be different on the x- and the y-axes.

A line that slopes from top left to bottom right has a negative gradient because y decreases as x increases.

$$\text{gradient} = -\frac{y}{x}$$

Here is an example of finding the gradient from the graph:

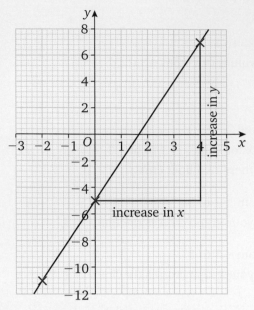

Increase in y from -5 to $7 = 12$

Increase in x from 0 to $4 = 4$

Gradient $= \dfrac{12}{4} = 3$

The **gradient** can also be found from the equation of the line.

To find the gradient, write the equation of the line in the form $y = mx + c$

y and x are the **variables** in the equation.

m (the **coefficient** of x) is the **gradient** of the line.

The **intercept** is the point where the line crosses the y-axis.

In the form $y = mx + c$, c is the **constant** and the intercept is at $(0, c)$.

For example:

The line $y = 2x - 1$ has a gradient equal to 2 and the intercept is at $(0, -1)$.

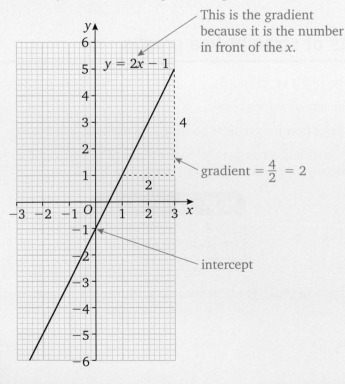

This is the gradient because it is the number in front of the x.

gradient $= \dfrac{4}{2} = 2$

intercept

Example: Find the gradient and intercept of:

    a $y = 5x - 2$ **b** $y = 3 - 2x$ **c** $x + y = 5$

Solution: **a** $y = 5x - 2$
        $m = 5$ so the gradient is 5
        $c = -2$ so the intercept is at $(0, -2)$

        b $y = 3 - 2x$
        $m = -2$ so the gradient is -2
        $c = 3$ so the intercept is at $(0, 3)$

        c $x + y = 5$
        You have to start rearranging the equation to read as $y = \ldots$
        $x + y = 5$
        $x + y \left(- x\right) = 5 \left(- x\right)$ Subtract x from both sides.
        $y = 5 - x$

        $m = -1$ so the gradient is -1
        $c = 5$ so the intercept is at $(0, 5)$

Practise...   6.2 Gradients of straight-line graphs   k!   D C B A A*

1   Write down the gradient and intercept of each line.   **C**

a

b

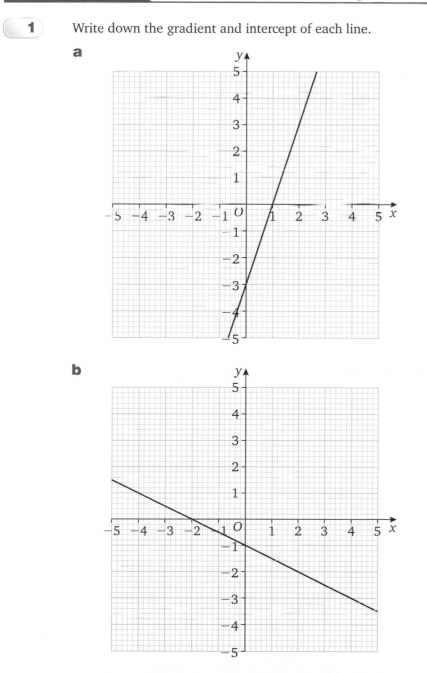

C

2 Jo says that the lines whose equations are $y = 5 - 2x$ and $y = 5 - 4x$ have the same gradient. Explain why Jo is wrong.

3 Look at these lines.

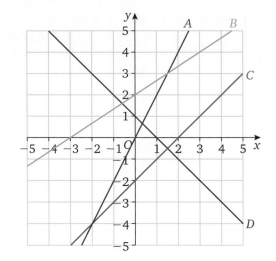

    a Which line has a gradient of 2?
How do you know?

    b Which line has a gradient of 1?
How do you know?

    c Which line or lines have a negative gradient?
How do you know?

4 Write down the gradient of each graph.

Hint
Read the vertical scale carefully because it is not the same as the horizontal scale.

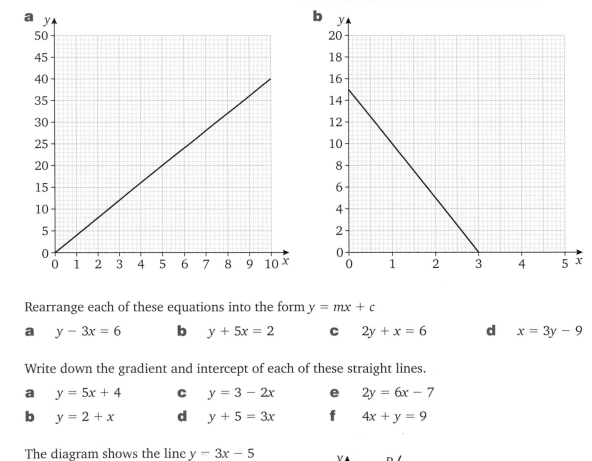

5 Rearrange each of these equations into the form $y = mx + c$

    a $y - 3x = 6$ **b** $y + 5x = 2$ **c** $2y + x = 6$ **d** $x = 3y - 9$

6 Write down the gradient and intercept of each of these straight lines.

    a $y = 5x + 4$ **c** $y = 3 - 2x$ **e** $2y = 6x - 7$

    b $y = 2 + x$ **d** $y + 5 = 3x$ **f** $4x + y = 9$

7 The diagram shows the line $y = 3x - 5$

$RQ = 3$ units

What is the length of PQ?
Show your working.

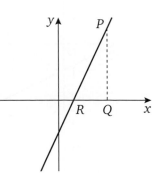

8 Show that the lines $5x + 2y = 9$ and $4y = 3 - 10x$ have the same gradient.

C

⚠ 9 On the same axes, draw the graphs of $y = 2x$, $y = 2x + 4$ and $y = 2x - 5$ for values of x from -4 to 4.

What do you notice?

? 10 Use your knowledge of gradients and intercepts to match the equations to the sketch graphs.

i $y = 3x$ **ii** $y = -2x$ **iii** $x + y = 4$ **iv** $y = 3x + 8$

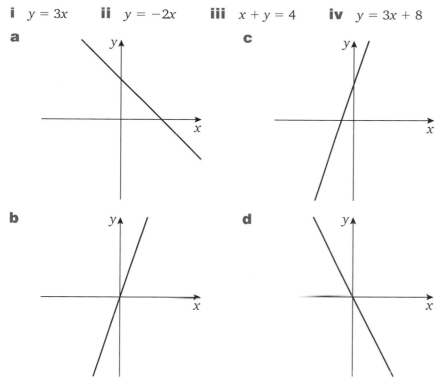

a

c

b

d

Learn... **6.3 The midpoint of a line segment** *k!*

A line segment is the part of a line joining two points.
There are two ways to find the midpoint of a line segment.

Method 1:
Measure halfway along the line.

Method 2:
Find the mean of the coordinates of the end points.

Remember, a mean is calculated by adding terms together and then dividing by the number of terms.

Example: A line segment has been drawn from $A(-4, 1)$ to $B(2, 3)$.

Find the midpoint of AB.

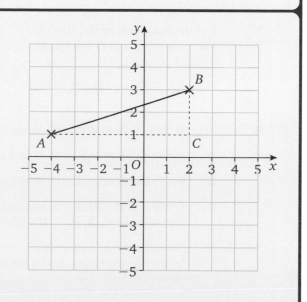

Solution:

Method 1

Measure halfway along the line.

The midpoint of the line is at $(-1, 2)$.

Method 2

Find the mean of the coordinates of the end points.

x-coordinate of the midpoint: $\dfrac{-4 + 2}{2} = -1$ Add the two x-coordinates and divide by 2.

y-coordinate of the midpoint: $\dfrac{1 + 3}{2} = 2$ Add the two y-coordinates and divide by 2.

The midpoint of the line is at $(-1, 2)$.

Practise... 6.3 The midpoint of a line segment 🗨️ D C B A A*

1 **a** Work out the coordinates of the midpoint of the line from $(2, 5)$ to $(-4, 1)$.

   b Draw a grid with the x-axis and the y-axis labelled from -5 to 5.
   Plot the points $(2, 5)$ and $(-4, 1)$.
   Use your diagram to check your answer to part **a**.

2 Work out the coordinates of the midpoint of the line from $(0, 4)$ to $(2, 6)$.

3 Joe says that the point $(1, 2\frac{1}{2})$ is halfway between $(-4, 3)$ and $(6, -8)$.

   Is he correct?

   Give a reason for your answer.

4 A is the point $(3, -1)$ and B is the point $(-5, -5)$.

   a Work out the coordinates of the midpoint of the line AB.

   b Find the gradient of the line AB.

> **AQA Examiner's tip**
>
> It often helps to sketch a diagram and put the points on it. This also gives you a quick check on your calculations.

5 R is the midpoint of the line PQ.
   The coordinates of Q are $(3, 2)$.
   R is the point $(1, 1)$.

   What are the coordinates of P?

6 $A(2, 5)$, $B(5, -2)$ and $C(-2, 2)$ are the vertices of a triangle.

   a Find the coordinates of M, the midpoint of AB.

   b Find the coordinates of N, the midpoint of BC.

   c Draw a grid with the x-axis and y-axis labelled from -3 to 6.
   Plot the points A, B, C, M and N.

   d Draw the lines MN and AC.
   What do you notice about them?

7 A quadrilateral *PQRS* has these coordinates.

$P(0, 4)$ $Q(6, 2)$ $R(1, -3)$ $S(-5, -1)$

a Find the gradient of the line *SP*.

b Find the gradient of the line *RQ*.

c What do your results tell you about these lines?

d Find the gradient of the line *PQ*.

e Find the gradient of the line *SR*.

f What do your results tell you about the quadrilateral *ABCD*?

8 The quadrilateral *TUVW* is a kite.

Plot $T(1, 3)$, $U(3, 3)$ and $W(-4, -4)$ on a grid.

Find the coordinates of the fourth vertex, *V*.

Learn...

6.4 Lines through two given points and parallel lines

To find the equation of a line that goes through two given points, find the gradient and the intercept.

Example: *P* is the point $(-4, -2)$ and *Q* is the point $(4, 4)$.

Find the equation of the line *PQ*.

Solution:

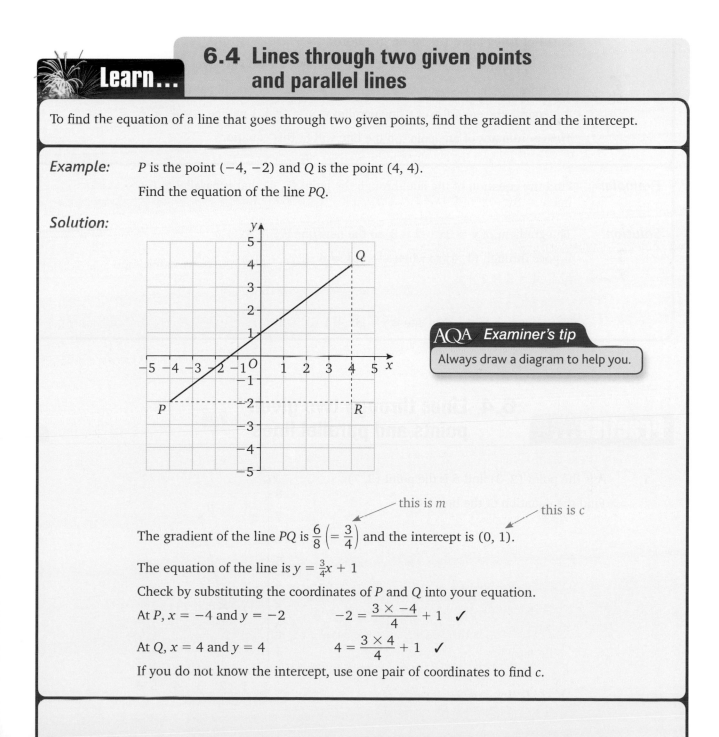

AQA Examiner's tip

Always draw a diagram to help you.

this is *m*

this is *c*

The gradient of the line *PQ* is $\frac{6}{8}\left(=\frac{3}{4}\right)$ and the intercept is $(0, 1)$.

The equation of the line is $y = \frac{3}{4}x + 1$

Check by substituting the coordinates of *P* and *Q* into your equation.

At *P*, $x = -4$ and $y = -2$ $-2 = \frac{3 \times -4}{4} + 1$ ✓

At *Q*, $x = 4$ and $y = 4$ $4 = \frac{3 \times 4}{4} + 1$ ✓

If you do not know the intercept, use one pair of coordinates to find *c*.

Example: P is the point (3, 7) and Q is the point (6, 1).

Find the equation of the line PQ.

Solution:

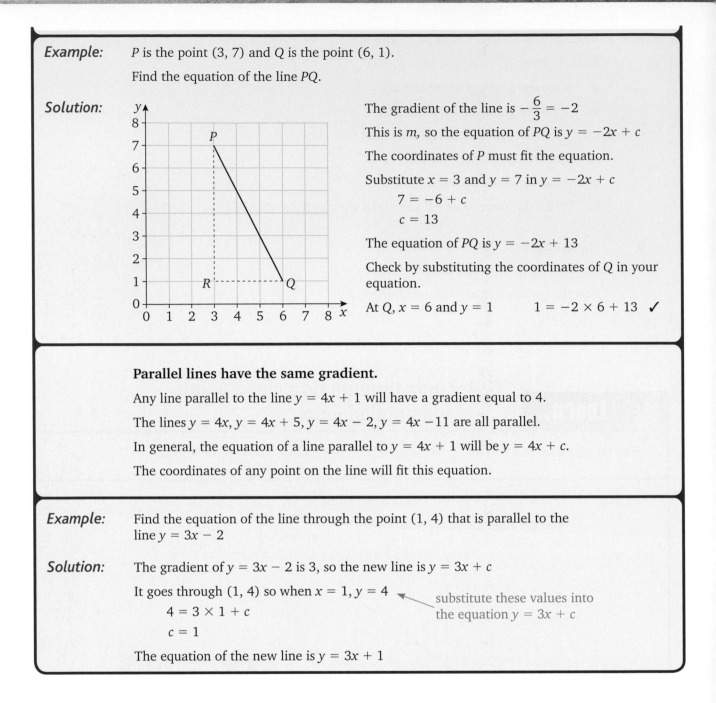

The gradient of the line is $-\dfrac{6}{3} = -2$

This is m, so the equation of PQ is $y = -2x + c$

The coordinates of P must fit the equation.

Substitute $x = 3$ and $y = 7$ in $y = -2x + c$

$$7 = -6 + c$$
$$c = 13$$

The equation of PQ is $y = -2x + 13$

Check by substituting the coordinates of Q in your equation.

At Q, $x = 6$ and $y = 1$ $1 = -2 \times 6 + 13$ ✓

Parallel lines have the same gradient.

Any line parallel to the line $y = 4x + 1$ will have a gradient equal to 4.

The lines $y = 4x$, $y = 4x + 5$, $y = 4x - 2$, $y = 4x - 11$ are all parallel.

In general, the equation of a line parallel to $y = 4x + 1$ will be $y = 4x + c$.

The coordinates of any point on the line will fit this equation.

Example: Find the equation of the line through the point (1, 4) that is parallel to the line $y = 3x - 2$

Solution: The gradient of $y = 3x - 2$ is 3, so the new line is $y = 3x + c$

It goes through (1, 4) so when $x = 1$, $y = 4$ substitute these values into the equation $y = 3x + c$

$$4 = 3 \times 1 + c$$
$$c = 1$$

The equation of the new line is $y = 3x + 1$

Practise...   **6.4 Lines through two given points and parallel lines**   k!   B

B

1 A is the point (2, 3) and B is the point (3, 7).

Find the equation of the line AB.

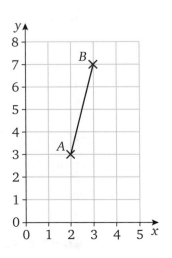

2   *C* is the point $(-2, -4)$ and *D* is the point $(0, 2)$.

Find the equation of the line *CD*.

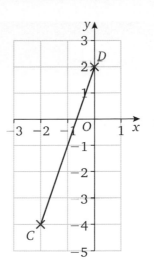

3   *E* is the point $(-1, 6)$ and *F* is the point $(5, 3)$.

Find the equation of the line *EF*.

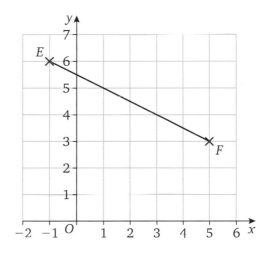

4   Find the equation of the line joining the points $(2, 7)$ and $(-2, 6)$.

5   Anthony says that the line $y = 2x$ is parallel to the line $y - 4 - 2x$

Explain why he is wrong.

6   Find the three pairs of parallel lines in these equations.

$y = 4x$	$y = 1 + 3x$	$x + y = 8$	$x = \dfrac{y}{4} + 2$
$y - 5x = 4$	$2x - y = 7$	$2y - 6x = 5$	$3x + y = 10$
$3y + x = 8$	$4x + y = 2$	$y = 3 - x$	$5y - x = 2$

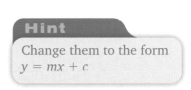

Hint

Change them to the form $y = mx + c$

7   Find the equation of the line through $(0, 2)$ that is parallel to $y = 3x - 4$

8   Find the equation of the line through $(1, 5)$ that is parallel to $y = 3 - 2x$

9   Find the equation of the line through $(-2, -3)$ that is parallel to $x + y - 4$

10   Find the equation of the line through $(4, -1)$ that is parallel to $3x + 2y = 10$

⚠ 11   The vertices of a triangle are $A(3, 6)$, $B(1, 2)$ and $C(7, 4)$.

M is the midpoint of the side *AB*.

N is the midpoint of the side *AC*.

a   Find the equation of the line *BC*.

b   Find the equation of the line *MN*.

c   Hence prove that *MN* is parallel to *BC*.

6 Assess

D

1   **a**   Draw the graph of $y = x - 3$ for values of x from -3 to 4.

    b   Write down the coordinates of the point where your graph crosses the y-axis.

2   **a**   Draw the graph of $2x + y = 7$ for values of x from 0 to 5.

    b   Write down the coordinates of the point where your graph crosses the line $y = 2$

3   **a**   Which of these points lie on the line $4x - 3y = 4$?

      $(1, 0)$ $(0, 1)$ $(3, 4)$ $(4, 4)$ $(7, 8)$ $(8, 7)$

      Show how you found your answers.

    b   Each of these points lies on two of the given lines.

      Match the points to their lines.

      Points: $A(-4, -3)$ $B(-1, 1)$ $C(-3, 6)$ $D(4, 3)$ $E(5, -2)$

      Lines: $y = 6$ $y + x = 3$ $3y = 4x + 7$ $4y - 3x = 0$ $y + 5x = 23$ $y + x = 0$

C

4   Write down the equation of the line that has:

    a   gradient 5 and intercept -6

    b   gradient -1 and intercept 4.

5   Rearrange each of these equations into the form $y = mx + c$

    a $y + 6x = 2$

    b $6x - 2y = 5$

6   Show that the lines $y = 9 - x$ and $x + y = 4$ are parallel.

7   The points $A(-3, -3)$ and $B(1, 5)$ are shown on the sketch.

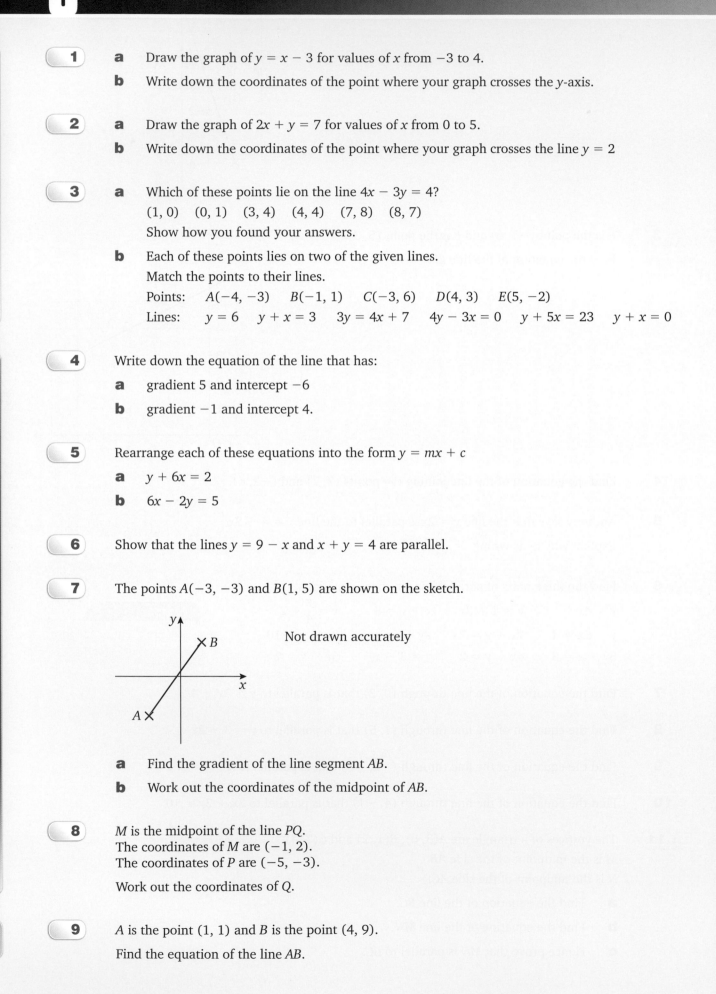

Not drawn accurately

    a   Find the gradient of the line segment AB.

    b   Work out the coordinates of the midpoint of AB.

8 M is the midpoint of the line PQ.

    The coordinates of M are $(-1, 2)$.

    The coordinates of P are $(-5, -3)$.

    Work out the coordinates of Q.

B

9 A is the point $(1, 1)$ and B is the point $(4, 9)$.

    Find the equation of the line AB.

10   Find the pair of parallel lines in this list.

$3x + 2y = 5$ $2y = 3x - 4$ $2x + 3y = 5$ $3x - 2y = 1$

11   Find the equation of the line through $(2, -3)$ that is parallel to $3y = 5 - 4x$

AQA Examination-style questions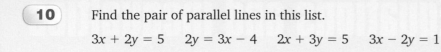

1   The grid shows the graphs of two straight lines A and B.

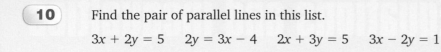

a   Write down the equation of line A.   *(2 marks)*

b   Write down the equation of line B.   *(1 mark)*

c   Write down a fact about the gradients of lines A and B.   *(1 mark)*

AQA 2007

7 Equations and inequalties

Objectives

Examiners would normally expect students who get these grades to be able to:

D

solve an equation such as
$3x + 2 = 6 - x$ or $4(2x - 1) = 20$

represent and interpret inequalities on a number line

C

solve an equation such as
$4x + 5 = 3(x + 4)$ or $\dfrac{x}{2} - \dfrac{x}{8} = 9$
or $\dfrac{2x - 7}{4} = 1$

solve an inequality such as $2x - 7 < 9$

find the integer solutions of an inequality such as $-8 < 2n \leqslant 5$

B

solve an equation such as
$\dfrac{2x - 1}{6} + \dfrac{x + 3}{3} = \dfrac{5}{2}$

solve an inequality such as
$3x + 2 \leqslant 4 - x$

represent linear inequalities in two variables, such as $x + y < 7$, as a region on a graph.

Did you know?

'Ink blots to space rockets'

$\bigcirc + 3 = 21$

What is the number under the blob?

You can guess the answer without knowing any algebra.

You can't design a space rocket by guesswork but this chapter will show you how to take the first steps in solving complicated equations.

Then you might end up designing the next space rocket.

Key terms

solve
unknown
brackets
denominator
inequality
integer
inverse operation
region

You should already know:

✔ how to collect like terms

✔ how to use substitution

✔ how to multiply out brackets by a single term, such as $3x(x + 2)$

✔ how to cancel fractions

✔ how to add and subtract fractions

✔ how to solve equations such as $2x + 3 = 11$

✔ how to draw graphs of linear equations.

7.1 Equations where the unknown (*x*) appears on both sides

Learn...

Follow these steps to **solve** the equation.

- Collect together on one side all the terms that contain the **unknown** letter (*x*).
- Collect together on the other side all the other terms.
- Remember signs belong with the term **after** them.

Example: Solve:

a $2x + 3 = 18 - x$

b $3y + 9 = 5y - 8$

Solution: a

$2x + 3 = 18 - x$

$2x + x + 3 = 18 - x + x$ Add x to both sides (this collects all the x terms together on the left-hand side).

$3x + 3 - 3 = 18 - 3$ Take 3 from both sides (this collects all the numbers on right-hand side).

$3x = 18 - 3$

$\dfrac{3x}{3} = \dfrac{15}{3}$ Divide both sides by 3.

$x = 5$

b

$3y + 9 = 5y - 8$

$3y - 3y + 9 = 5y - 3y - 8$ Take $3y$ from both sides (this collects all the y terms on the right-hand side). You could take $5y$ from both sides. You would get $-2y = -17$

$9 = 2y - 8$

$9 + 8 = 2y - 8 + 8$ Add 8 to both sides (this collects all the numbers on the left-hand side).

$17 = 2y$

$\dfrac{17}{2} = \dfrac{2y}{2}$ Divide both sides by 2.

$8.5 = y$

$y = 8.5$ Write the equation with y on the left.

7.1 Equations where the unknown (*x*) appears on both sides

Practise...   🎵 *k!*   D C B A A*

1   Solve these equations.

a $4x + 1 = 2x + 13$ e $6p + 2 = 9 + 4p$ i $7c - 1 = 3 - c$

b $2y - 3 = y + 4$ f $17 - 6q = 3 + q$ j $25 + 2d = 5d + 4$

c $5z - 2 = 8 + 3z$ g $2 - 3a = 7 + 2a$ k $6 - 7e = 3 - 6e$

d $9 - 3t = t + 3$ h $8b - 3 = 2b - 15$ l $5f + 10 = 2 + f$

2   Jared solves the equation $9x - 2 = 5 - 4x$
He writes down $5x - 2 = 5$

Is this correct?
Explain your answer.

D

AQA *Examiner's tip*

Set out each line of your working clearly so you can earn method marks even if your answer is wrong.

D

3   Ella solves the equation $5y + 6 = 2 - y$
She writes down $4y = 4$

Is this correct?
Explain your answer.

4   Dean solves the equation $3x - 11 = 4 + 2x$
He gets the answer $x = 7$

Can you find Dean's mistake?

5   Rick solves the equation $2y + 5 = 3 - 3y$
He gets the answer $y = -2$

Can you find Rick's mistake?

⚠ **6** $4z - 3 = \blacksquare - 2z$
The answer to this equation is $z = 5$

What is the number under the rectangle?

⚠ **7** $2a + \blacksquare = 5 - 7a$
The answer to this equation is $a = -1$

What is the number under the rectangle?

? **8**   If $b = 11$, find the value of $3b - 8$

Hence explain why $b = 11$ is not the solution of the equation $3b - 8 = 19 - 2b$

? **9**   If $c = -4$, find the value of $9 - 5c$

Hence explain why $c = -4$ is not the solution of the equation $6c + 13 = 9 - 5c$

Learn... 7.2 Equations with brackets

Your first step is usually to multiply out the **brackets**.

After this, you follow the rules for solving equations.

Example: Solve:

a $4(3x - 1) = 32$

b $7 - 3(y + 2) = 5 - 4y$

Solution: **a** $4(3x - 1) = 32$

$12x - 4 = 32$ Remember to multiply **both** terms in the bracket by 4.
$12x - 4 + 4 = 32 + 4$ Add 4 to both sides.
$12x = 36$ Divide both sides by 12.
$x = 3$

Alternative method:
$4(3x - 1) = 32$ Divide both sides by 4.
$3x - 1 = 8$
$3x - 1 + 1 = 8 + 1$ Add 1 to both sides.
$3x = 8 + 1$
$3x = 9$ Divide both sides by 3.
$x = 3$

This alternative method works because 4 is a factor of 32.
It cannot be used for all equations with brackets, as the next example shows.

b $7 - 3(y + 2) = 5 - 4y$

Multiply out the brackets first, then follow the rules for solving equations.

$7 - 3y - 6 = 5 - 4y$	Note: $-3 \times +2 = -6$
$1 - 3y = 5 - 4y$	The numbers on the left-hand side have been collected.
$1 - 3y - 1 = 5 - 4y - 1$	Subtract 1 from both sides.
$-3y = 4 - 4y$	
$-3y + 4y = 4 - 4y + 4y$	Add $4y$ to both sides.
$-3y + 4y = 4$	
$y = 4$	

AQA *Examiner's tip*

Don't try to do two steps at once – most students make mistakes if they rush their working.

Bump up your grade

You need to be able to solve equations which have brackets **and** the unknown occurring twice to get a Grade C.

Practise... 7.2 Equations with brackets D C B A A*

1 Solve these equations.

a $5(x + 3) = 55$

b $2(y - 4) = 16$

c $9 = 3(z - 7)$

d $7(b - 2) = 7$

e $13 = 2(c + 5)$

2 Solve these equations.

a $4(p + 2) - 2p + 9$

b $6(q - 3) = 17 - q$

c $2(5t - 1) = 13$

d $5a + 3 = 4(a - 2)$

e $3(2b - 3) = 1 + 7b$

f $8 + c = 5(c - 2)$

g $11d - 1 = 3(d + 1)$

h $2(1 - 2e) = 5 - 3e$

i $2 - 5f = 3(2 - f)$

j $6(2 + 3x) = 11x + 5$

k $3(y - 4) + 2(4y - 2) = 6$

3 Solve the equation $10 - 3(z + 2) = 7 - z$

4 Solve the equation $23 = 6 - 5(t - 4)$

5 Solve the equation $4(p - 3) - 3(p - 4) = 14$

6 Solve the equation $2(q - 9) - (7q - 3) + 25 = 0$

7 Natalie thinks of a number, adds 7 and then doubles the result. Her answer is 46.

Write this as an equation.
Solve the equation to find Natalie's number.

8 Rob thinks of a number, subtracts 8 and then multiplies the result by 5. His answer is 65.

Write this as an equation.
Solve the equation to find Rob's number.

Learn... 7.3 Equations with fractions

There are many methods of solving equations with fractions.
At some stage in solving an equation with a fraction, you have to clear the fraction by multiplying both sides by the **denominator.**

For example, if the equation contains $\frac{x}{3}$, you will need to multiply by 3.

If there is more than one fraction, say $\frac{3x}{5}$ and $\frac{x}{2}$, you will need to multiply by both denominators. In this case, this is $5 \times 2 = 10$

Harder equations have more than one term on the top of the fraction.
There are 'invisible brackets' around the terms on top of an algebraic fraction.

Example: Solve these equations.

     a $\frac{x}{3} - 2 = 5$

     b $\frac{5x}{6} - \frac{3x}{4} = 1$

     c $\frac{5x + 2}{4} = 3$

     d $\frac{2x - 1}{6} + \frac{x + 3}{3} = \frac{5}{2}$

Solution: **a** $\frac{x}{3} - 2 = 5$

Start by isolating the fraction.

$\frac{x}{3} - 2 + 2 = 5 + 2$ Add 2 to both sides so the fraction is on its own on the left-hand side.

$\frac{x}{3} = 7$

$x = 7 \times 3$ Multiply both sides by 3.

$x = 21$

     b $\frac{5x}{6} - \frac{3x}{4} = 1$

This equation has more than one fraction term.

The lowest common **denominator** is 12.

Multiply **each term** by 12 and then cancel. This should remove all the fractions.

$\overset{2}{\cancel{12}} \times \frac{5x}{\cancel{6}_1} - \overset{3}{\cancel{12}} \times \frac{3x}{\cancel{4}_1} = 12 \times 1$ Don't forget to multiply the right-hand side as well as the left-hand side.

$2 \times 5x - 3 \times 3x = 12 \times 1$

$10x - 9x = 12$

$x = 12$

     c $\frac{5x + 2}{4} = 3$ ⟵——— This is the same as $\frac{1}{4}(5x + 2) = 3$

This equation has two terms on the top of the fraction.

There are 'invisible brackets' around these terms.   You should put in the invisible brackets before you start your working.

$\overset{1}{\cancel{4}} \times \frac{(5x + 2)}{\cancel{4}_1} = 4 \times 3$ Multiply **both** sides by 4 and cancel.

$5x + 2 = 12$ Subtract 2 from both sides.

$5x = 12 - 2$

$5x = 10$ Divide both sides by 5.

$x = 2$

d $\dfrac{2x-1}{6}+\dfrac{x+3}{3}=\dfrac{5}{2}$

This equation shows you how to handle a complex equation with three fractions.

The lowest common denominator of 6, 3 and 2 is 6. (You could use larger common denominators like 18 or 24 but that would give you larger numbers to deal with.)

Put in the 'invisible brackets' to help you.

$${}^{1}\!\!\cancel{6}\times\dfrac{(2x-1)}{\cancel{6}_{1}}+{}^{2}\!\!\cancel{6}\times\dfrac{(x+3)}{\cancel{3}_{1}}={}^{3}\!\!\cancel{6}\times\dfrac{5}{\cancel{2}_{1}}$$ Multiply both sides of the equation by 6 and cancel.

$$(2x-1)+2(x+3)=3\times5$$ Multiply out the brackets.

$$2x-1+2x+6=15$$ Collect like terms.

$$4x+5=15$$ Subtract 5 from both sides.

$$4x=10$$ Divide both sides by 4.

$$x=2.5$$

Practise... 7.3 Equations with fractions 🔊   D C B A A*

1 Solve these equations.

a $\dfrac{x}{2}-5=4$

b $\dfrac{y}{5}+3=7$

c $5-1=\dfrac{z}{3}$

d $9-\dfrac{b}{2}=2$

e $\dfrac{c}{6}+5=2$

f $\dfrac{p}{3}+1=5-p$

g $\dfrac{q}{5}+3=6-q$

h $\dfrac{4x+1}{3}-11$

i $\dfrac{2y-7}{5}=3$

j $1=\dfrac{9-z}{3}$

k $\dfrac{1}{4}(p+3)=5$

l $\dfrac{1}{2}(3q+8)=13$

m $\dfrac{x}{5}+\dfrac{x}{3}=4$

n $\dfrac{y}{2}-\dfrac{y}{8}=3$

2 Ed and Gary solve the equation $\dfrac{4y-3}{5}-2y+3$

Ed gets the answer $y=-2$ and Gary gets $y=-3$

Check their answers to see which of them is correct.

3 Solve these equations.

a $\dfrac{x+1}{2}+\dfrac{x+2}{3}=2$

b $\dfrac{y+3}{6}+\dfrac{y-3}{2}=10$

c $\dfrac{z+5}{2}-\dfrac{z+3}{4}=4$

d $\dfrac{a-1}{5}-\dfrac{a+1}{6}=0$

e $\dfrac{3b+11}{4}-\dfrac{5b-3}{3}=1$

f $\dfrac{c}{7}-\dfrac{1-c}{14}=1$

> **AQA** *Examiner's tip*
>
> Take care with signs when the fractions are subtracted. Insert brackets to help you.
>
> $-(z+3)=-z-3$

4 Solve these equations.

a $\dfrac{1}{2}(5a-1)=a-5$

b $\dfrac{1}{8}(2b-5)=5-b$

c $c-7=\dfrac{1}{3}(11-c)$

d $\dfrac{3p}{2}=5-\dfrac{p}{6}$

e $\dfrac{q}{3}-\dfrac{1}{4}=\dfrac{q}{6}$

f $\dfrac{3t}{8}+\dfrac{1}{4}=\dfrac{2t}{5}$

g $\dfrac{d+10}{3}+\dfrac{d+1}{6}=\dfrac{3d+5}{2}$

h $\dfrac{e-2}{2}-\dfrac{e+2}{9}=\dfrac{2e+3}{18}$

i $\dfrac{p+4}{5}-\dfrac{2p+3}{6}=\dfrac{p}{15}$

j $\dfrac{3q-1}{3}-\dfrac{5q-3}{4}=\dfrac{7-q}{12}$

5 Explain why you cannot solve the equation $\dfrac{6p-5}{2}=4+3p$

Learn...   7.4 Inequalities and the number line

The four **inequality** symbols are shown in the table.

<	≤	>	≥
less than	less than or equal to	greater than	greater than or equal to

A number line shows the range of values for x.

An **open** circle shows that the range does not include that end of the line.
e.g. $x > 1$ or $y < 5$

A **closed** circle shows that the range includes that end of the line.
e.g. $x \leq 3$ or $y \geq 5$

This is the number line for $x > 1$

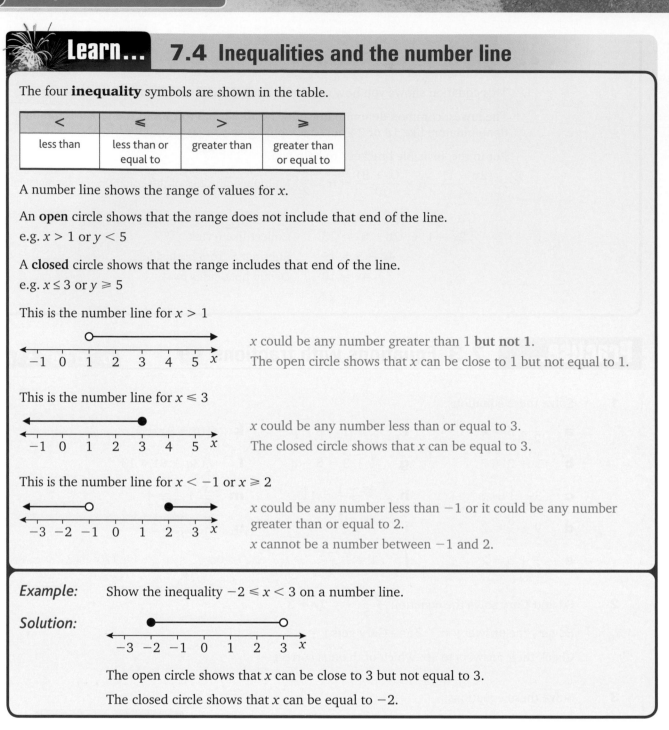

x could be any number greater than 1 **but not 1**.
The open circle shows that x can be close to 1 but not equal to 1.

This is the number line for $x \leq 3$

x could be any number less than or equal to 3.
The closed circle shows that x can be equal to 3.

This is the number line for $x < -1$ or $x \geq 2$

x could be any number less than -1 or it could be any number greater than or equal to 2.
x cannot be a number between -1 and 2.

Example: Show the inequality $-2 \leq x < 3$ on a number line.

Solution:

The open circle shows that x can be close to 3 but not equal to 3.

The closed circle shows that x can be equal to -2.

Practise...   7.4 Inequalities and the number line   k!   D C B A A*

D

1   Write down the inequalities shown by these number lines.

a

c

b

d

2   Show each of these inequalities on a number line.

a $x > 1$ **d** $x < 2$ **g** $-4 \leq x < 3$

b $x > -5$ **e** $x \leq -1$ **h** $x < 4$ or $x \geq 6$

c $x \geq 0$ **f** $-2 < x < 1$ **i** $x \leq -2$ or $x > 0$

3   Explain why it is incorrect to write $2 < x < -6$

4   Nic gets £10 a week in pocket money.
Nic asks Joe how much he gets each week.
Joe says 'I get more than £6 but less than you.'
Joe's pocket money is made up of pound coins and fifty pence pieces.

List the possible amounts Joe might get.

5   Natalie is five foot and six inches tall.
Olwen is five foot and two inches tall.
Pippa is taller than Olwen but not as tall as Natalie.

   a   Show Pippa's height on a number line.

   b   Explain why you cannot make a list of possible heights for Pippa.

Learn...   7.5 Solving inequalities

Some inequalities are very similar to equations.

The inequality $3x - 2 > 4$ is similar to the equation $3x - 2 = 4$

To solve this inequality, use **inverse operations** as you would with the equation.

$$3x - 2 > 4$$
$$3x - 2 + 2 > 4 + 2 \qquad \text{Add 2 to both sides.}$$
$$3x > 6 \qquad \text{Divide both sides by 3.}$$
$$x > 2$$

If you multiply or divide both sides of an inequality by a **negative number**, the inequality sign is **reversed**.

If $y > 5$, then $-y < -5$ Try this with a value for y, such as $y = 7$. 7 is greater than 5, but -7 is less than -5.

You may be asked to list **integer** values (whole numbers) that satisfy an inequality.

For example, the integers that satisfy $-3 \leqslant x < 5$ are $-3, -2, -1, 0, 1, 2, 3, 4$

Sometimes you have to combine these two skills, as in example **c** below.

Example: **a**   Solve the inequality $3x - 5 > 4$

        b   Solve the inequality $4 - 2x \leqslant 9 + 3x$

        c   List all the **integer** values of n such that $-5 < 2n \leqslant 6$

Solution: **a** $3x - 5 > 4$ Add 5 to both sides.
            $3x > 9$ Divide by 3.
            $x > 3$

        b $4 - 2x \leqslant 9 + 3x$ Subtract 4 from both sides.
            $-2x \leqslant 5 + 3x$ Subtract $3x$ from both sides.
            $-5x \leqslant 5$ Divide both sides by -5. (Remember to reverse the inequality sign.)
            $x \geqslant -1$

        c $-5 < 2n \leqslant 6$ Divide every term in the inequality by 2.
            $-2.5 < n \leqslant 3$

Integer values for n are: $-2, -1, 0, 1, 2, 3$

Practise... 7.5 Solving inequalities _k!_

1 Solve these inequalities.

    a $3x - 2 \geqslant 4$

    b $2y + 7 \leqslant 16$

    c $4z + 12 < 0$

    d $5 + 2p > 1$

    e $8 < 2 + 3q$

    f $5 > 13 - t$

2 Find the largest integer that satisfies the inequality $5 - 2x \geqslant 1$

3 Find the smallest integer that satisfies the inequality $7 < 3(2x + 9)$

4 List all the integer values of n such that:

    a $0 < 3n < 11$

    b $-4 < 2n \leqslant 6$

    c $-10 \leqslant 4n < 12$

    d $-5 \leqslant 5n \leqslant 8$

5 Solve these inequalities.

    a $7u - 5 > 3u - 1$

    b $8 - v < 2v + 11$

    c $5(w - 1) > 3(w + 2)$

    d $3x - 8 > 8x + 7$

    e $10 - 3y \geqslant 5 - y$

    f $7 - 2z \leqslant 4 + 3z$

⚠ 6 List all the pairs of positive integers, x and y, such that $3x + 4y \leqslant 15$

? 7 Jiffa is 14 years old.

She says to her Uncle Asif 'How old are you?'

He says 'In 9 years' time I shall be more than twice as old as I was when you were born.'

Write down an inequality and solve it to find the greatest age Asif could be.

Learn... 7.6 Inequalities and graphs _k!_

You can represent an inequality such as x > 1 as an area, or **region**, on a graph.

The boundary of this region will be the line $x = 1$

The convention is that 'strict inequalities', such as $x > -1$ or $y < 5$, are shown with a dashed line at the boundary.

'Included inequalities' such as $x \geqslant 1$ or $y \leqslant 5$ are shown with a solid line at the boundary.

Example: Show the region defined by each of these inequalities.

    a $x \geqslant 3$ **b** $y < -1$ **c** $x + y > 2$

Solution: **a** The inequality is $\geqslant$ so draw the boundary, $x = 3$, with a solid line.

Shade the region where $x \geqslant 3$

> **AQA Examiner's tip**
>
> Shade the region that is defined by the inequality.
> Write the inequality in this area.

b The inequality is $<$ so draw the boundary, $y = -1$, with a dashed line.

Shade the region where $y < -1$

c The inequality is $>$ so draw the boundary, $x + y = 2$, with a broken line.

Shade the region where $x + y > 2$

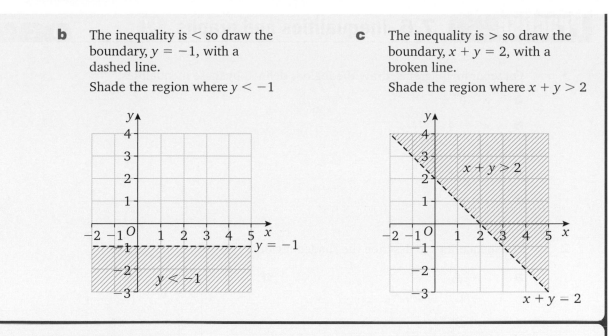

If you have a line that is not parallel to one of the axes, it is sometimes hard to decide which side of the line represents the inequality.

To help you decide:

* pick a point on one side of the line (use (0, 0) if the line does not go through the origin)
* check whether $x + y > 2$ is true for this point.

$0 + 0 > 2$ ✗ so this point is **not** on the side that represents the inequality.

If you represent a set of inequalities such as $x > 1$, $y \leqslant 2$ and $x + y < 5$ as regions on a graph, you can find number pairs that satisfy all the inequalities.

AQA **Examiner's tip**

If the line does not pass through the origin then test with (0, 0). This makes the working easier when substituting into the inequality.

If it does go through the origin, pick easy numbers like (1, 1).

Example: **a** Show the region defined by the inequalities $x + y \leqslant 5$, $x > 0$ and $y > 2$

b If x and y are integers, which points satisfy all three inequalities?

Solution: **a** Draw the three boundaries.

Shade above $y = 2$, to the right of $x = 0$ and below $x + y = 5$

To check your result, pick a point in the region such as (1, 3).

Checking that $x + y \leqslant 5$ $1 + 3 < 5$ ✓

Checking that $x > 0$ $1 > 0$ ✓

Checking that $y > 2$ $3 > 2$ ✓

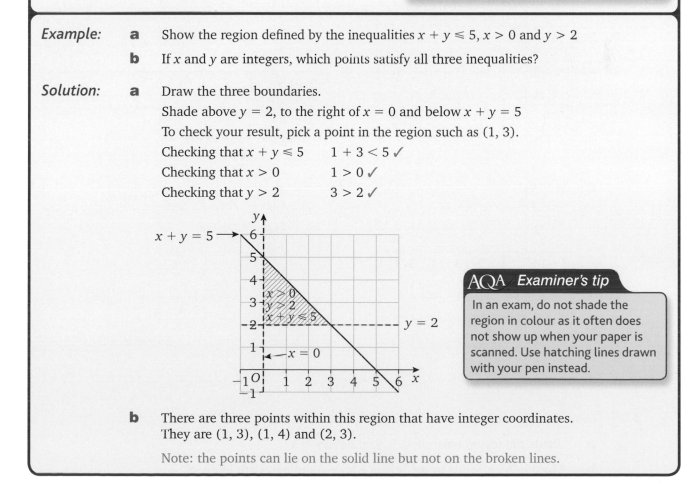

AQA **Examiner's tip**

In an exam, do not shade the region in colour as it often does not show up when your paper is scanned. Use hatching lines drawn with your pen instead.

b There are three points within this region that have integer coordinates. They are (1, 3), (1, 4) and (2, 3).

Note: the points can lie on the solid line but not on the broken lines.

Practise... 7.6 Inequalities and graphs k!

D C B A A*

B

1 On separate diagrams, draw the regions defined by these inequalities.

a $y < 0$

b $x > -4$

c $x \leq 2$

d $y \geq -1$

e $x + y > 4$

2 Use inequalities to describe the shaded regions.

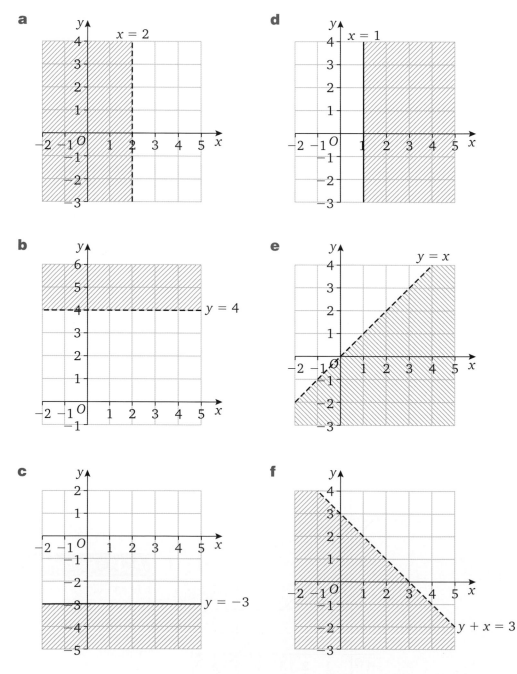

3 Draw x- and y-axes from 0 to 6.

a Shade the region where $x < 5$, $y > 2$ and $y \leq x$

b List the three points in the region whose coordinates are integers.

4 **a** Find the equations of the straight lines on these graphs.

b Use inequalities to describe the shaded regions.

i

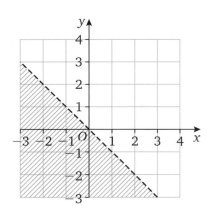

iii

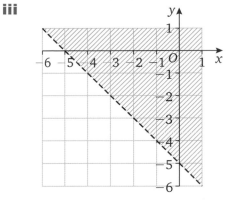

ii

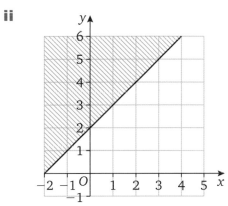

5 Draw x- and y-axes from 0 to 6.

a Shade the region where $y < 2x$, $y > \frac{1}{2}x$ and $x + y < 6$

b Dean says there are nine points in the region whose coordinates are integers. Is he correct? Explain your answer.

6 Describe with inequalities these regions bounded by blue lines.

a A

b B

c $E + F$

d D

e C

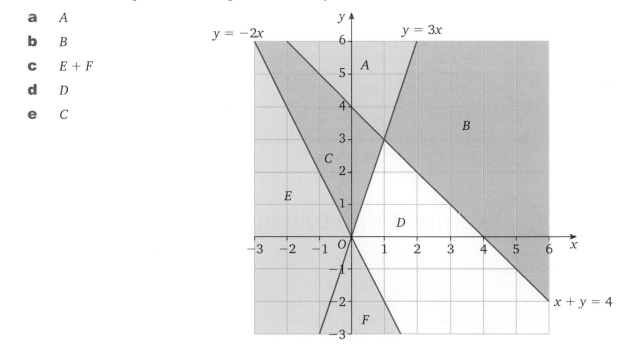

7 Assess

D

1 Solve these equations.

  a $p + 5 = 14 - 2p$ **c** $6m - 7 = 2m + 3$ **e** $5(u + 1) = 35$

  b $2q - 1 = 5 - q$ **d** $4 + 3n = n - 10$ **f** $49 = 7(3t - 2)$

2 Write down the inequalities shown by these number lines.

  a

  b

C

3 Solve these equations.

  a $3(v - 4) = 9 + 2v$ **c** $5(2x - 3) = 7 + 4(x - 1)$

  b $4(w - 2) + 2(3w + 1) = 44$ **d** $3(2t - 1) = 10 - 2(3t + 2)$

4 Solve these equations.

  a $\dfrac{y}{4} + 3 = 7$ **b** $4 - \dfrac{z}{3} = 6$ **c** $\dfrac{x}{5} + \dfrac{x}{10} = 6$

5 List all the integer solutions of the inequality $-8 < 3n \leqslant 9$

6 Solve these inequalities.

  a $6a - 7 \geqslant 5$ **b** $3b + 10 < 4$

7 Find the largest integer that satisfies the inequality $2x + 3 < 17$

B

8 Solve the inequality $3(y - 1) > 5y + 7$

9 Solve these equations.

  a $\dfrac{7x - 2}{5} + \dfrac{4 - 3x}{3} = \dfrac{1}{3}$ **b** $\dfrac{2 + 3y}{7} - \dfrac{y - 4}{3} = \dfrac{y}{2}$

10 Draw x- and y-axes from -3 to 5.

  a Shade the region where $y < 2x$, $x - 2y > 4$ and $x + 2y < 4$

  b List the five points in the region whose coordinates are integers.

11 Ramin went out with £7 in his pocket.
The £7 was made up of £1 coins and £2 coins.
Some coins fell through a hole in his pocket.
Now he has x £1 coins and y £2 coins.

  a Write down three inequalities that describe this.

  b Draw a graph of your inequalities and hence show that there are six possible different combinations of coins left.

AQA Examination-style questions

1 Bag A contains x counters.
Bag B contains 6 more counters than Bag A.
Bag C contains 4 times as many counters as Bag B.
The total number of counters in Bags A, B and C is 120.
Set up and solve an equation to work out the number of counters in Bag A.   *(6 marks)*

AQA 2005

8 Percentages

Objectives

Examiners would normally expect students who get these grades to be able to:

D

compare harder percentages, fractions and decimals

work out more difficult percentages of a given quantity

increase or decrease by a given percentage

express one quantity as a percentage of another

C

work out a percentage increase or decrease

B

understand how to use successive percentages

work out reverse percentage problems.

Key terms

percentage
VAT (Value Added Tax)
rate
amount
discount
deposit
credit
balance
interest
depreciation

Did you know?

I gave 110%!

Some sports personalities have claimed 'I gave 110%'

Is this possible?

When is it possible to have more than 100%?

What about these?

'I got more than 100% in the maths test!'

'The price went up by more than 100%'

'The company made a loss of more than 100%'

'I'm more than 100% certain that it happened.'

You should already know:

✔ about place values in decimals and how to put decimals in order of size

✔ how to simplify fractions

✔ how to change fractions to decimals and vice versa

✔ how to add, subtract, multiply and divide whole numbers, fractions and decimals.

Note that Unit 2 is a non-calculator unit so you will need to work without a calculator.

Learn... 8.1 Percentages, fractions and decimals

1% (1 per cent) means '1 part out of 100' or 'one hundredth'.

It is equivalent to the fraction $\frac{1}{100}$ and the decimal 0.01
In money it is equivalent to '1p in the £1'.

To write other percentages as fractions or decimals, divide by 100.

35 hundredths

For example, $35\% = \frac{35}{100} = \frac{7}{20}$ and $35\% = 35 \div 100 = 0.35$

Simplifying by dividing by 5   The figures move two places to the right.

To write a decimal or fraction as a percentage, you multiply by 100% (the inverse operation).

For example, $0.3 = 0.3 \times 100\% = 30\%$ and $\frac{2}{5} = \frac{2}{5_1} \times \frac{100^{20}}{1}\% = \frac{40}{1}\% = 40\%$

In some cases, like this one, you can also use equivalent fractions: $\frac{2}{5} = \frac{20}{50} = \frac{40}{100} = 40\%$

$\times 10$ $\times 2$

This is usually the easiest way to change a fraction to a percentage.

Hint

To remind yourself how to work with fractions and decimals, look at Chapter 3, pages 23–39.

Example: **a**   Which of these fractions is nearest in size to 30%?

$\frac{2}{5}$ $\frac{1}{3}$ $\frac{2}{7}$

b   Write down a fraction, in its simplest form, which is exactly equal to 30%.

Solution: **a**   Comparing decimals, fractions and percentages is easiest if they are all written as percentages.

$\frac{2}{5} = 40\%$ (see working above)

To change the other fractions to decimals, multiply them by 100:

$\frac{1}{3} \times \frac{100}{1}\% = \frac{100}{3}\% = 33\frac{1}{3}\%$ $\frac{2}{7} \times \frac{100}{1}\% = \frac{200}{7}\% = 28\frac{4}{7}\%$

Compare 40%, $33\frac{1}{3}\%$ and $28\frac{4}{7}\%$ with 30%

$28\frac{4}{7}\%$ is nearest, so $\frac{2}{7}$ is the fraction that is nearest to 30%

AQA Examiner's tip

Give the fraction from the question as your answer, not the percentage that you have worked out.

b   To change 30% to a fraction, divide it by 100:

$\div 10$

$30\% = \frac{30}{100} = \frac{3}{10}$

$\div 10$

Divide the top and bottom of the fraction until you get the smallest whole numbers you can. This is the simplest form.

There are many ways to find the percentage of a quantity.

Here are two ways to find 45% of £600:

$$45\% \text{ of } £600 = \frac{45}{\cancel{100}_1} \times \frac{\cancel{600}^6}{1} = \frac{270}{1} \qquad \text{or} \qquad 0.45 \times 600 = 45 \times 6 = 270 \quad \text{Using a 'decimal multiplier'.}$$

      45 hundredths of 600

Without a calculator, the best method is often to start by finding 1% or 10%

$1\% = \frac{1}{100}$ To find 1% of a quantity, divide it by 100.
                    In the example above, 1% of £600 = £6, so 45% is 45 × £6 = £270

$10\% = \frac{10}{100} = \frac{1}{10}$ To find 10% of a quantity, divide it by 10.

Example: Find:

         a   35% of £4.20   **b**   97% of £240

Solution: **a** $10\% \text{ of } £4.20 = \frac{£4.20}{10}$ $= £0.42$

                     $30\% \text{ of } £4.20 = 3 \times £0.42$ $= £1.26$ 30% is 3 × 10%

                     $5\% \text{ of } £4.20 = \frac{£0.42}{2}$ $= £0.21+$ 5% is half of 10%

                     $35\% \text{ of } £4.20 = 30\% + 5\%$ $= \textbf{£1.47}$

         b $1\% \text{ of } £240 = \frac{£240}{100}$ $= £2.40$

                                               Here is one way to check this:

                     $3\% \text{ of } £240 = 3 \times £2.40$ $= £7.20$ 3% is the same as 3p in every £.

                     $97\% \text{ of } £240 = £240 - £7.20 = \textbf{£232.80}$ So 3% of £240 = 240 × 3p = 720p

> AQA **Examiner's tip**
>
> Always check whether the answer looks reasonable.
> For example, 97% of £240 is nearly all of it, so £232.80 is reasonable.

Occasionally other ways may be quicker and easier.

For percentages with a simple, equivalent fraction, using these is quicker and easier.

For example:

$50\% = \frac{1}{2}$ **To find 50% of a quantity, divide it by 2.**

$25\% = \frac{1}{4}$ **To find 25% of a quantity, divide it by 4 (or halve it, then halve again).**

$75\% = 50\% + 25\%$ **To find 75% of a quantity, find 50% and 25%, then add.**
                         Halving, then halving again is the quickest way to do this.

8.1 Percentages, fractions and decimals

Practise...   (k!)   D   C   B   A   A*

1   Write these in order of size, smallest first.

     a $\frac{1}{4}$ 0.4   4% $\frac{4}{9}$

     b $\frac{16}{25}$ 0.67 $\frac{2}{3}$ 66% $\frac{13}{20}$ $62\frac{1}{2}\%$

2   **a**   Which of these is nearest in size to 0.4?   38% $\frac{3}{8}$ 43% $\frac{3}{7}$

     b   Which of these is nearest in size to $\frac{3}{4}$?   0.7   72% $\frac{7}{9}$ 0.79

D

D

3 Use three different ways to work out 25% of half a million pounds.

4 **a** Find:

      i   10% of 840 kg   **iv**   90% of 6 million   **vii**   6% of £3500

      ii   20% of 150 m   **v**   1% of 180 litres   **viii** 120% of £50

      iii 80% of 45 000   **vi**   4% of 750 km   **ix**   150% of £3000

   b Check each answer in part **a** using a different method.

      For example, if you found 10% of 840 g in part **a i** by dividing by 10 you

      could check using fractions: 10% of 840 $= \dfrac{10}{100} \times \dfrac{840}{1}$

      or using a multiplier: 10% of 840 $= 0.1 \times 840$

5 In a school, there are 630 boys and 660 girls.
90% of the boys and 95% of the girls have a mobile phone.
How many students altogether have mobile phones?

6 Paula earns £840 per week.
She spends 25% of this on rent and 40% on shopping.
How much does she have left?

> I divide by 10 to find 10%
> Then I divide by 2 to find
> 5%. Then I divide again by
> 2 to find 2½%. Adding the
> 10% and the 2½% gives
> the answer

7 Carl explains how he finds $12\frac{1}{2}$%

   a Use Carl's method to find $12\frac{1}{2}$% of £560.

   b Use a different way to find $12\frac{1}{2}$% of £560.

8 Gas and electricity companies charge 5% VAT on their bills
Find the VAT on each of these bills.

   a

Cost of electricity used
(without VAT) = **£96.40**

           Note: **VAT** is **Value Added Tax**.

   b

Gas you've used
(without VAT) = **£135.80**

9 A shop adds 17.5% VAT to all the goods it sells.
Find the VAT on each of these.

> **Hint**
> 17.5% = 10% + 5% + 2.5%

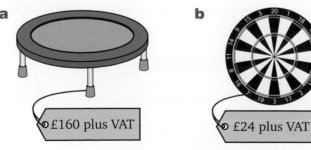

   a £160 plus VAT   **b** £24 plus VAT   **c** £16.80 plus VAT

C

10 There are 32 000 football supporters at a match.
65% of these are men, 25% are women and the rest are children.

   a How many more men than women are at the match?

   b What fraction of the football supporters at the match are children?

11   Karen says you can find 8% of £5200 by dividing 5200 by 8.
Sanjay says that you can find 8% of £5200 by multiplying 5200 by 0.8

Are either of these methods correct? Explain your answer.

! 12   Which is greater? $\frac{4}{5}$ of £2 million or 45% of £4 million

13   A science examination consists of a practical and a theory test.
70% of the candidates pass the practical. 45% pass the theory test.
These percentages include 25% of the candidates who pass both parts.

What fraction of the candidates fail both parts?

14   In 2009 a laptop cost £400 **excluding** VAT.
During 2009 the **rate** of VAT was reduced from 17.5% to 15%

How much less was the cost of the laptop **including** VAT after the VAT rate was reduced?

15   The table shows the tax rates in the country where Yusef lives.

Taxable income	Taxed at
Up to £40 000	20%
Amount over £40 000	40%

Yusef's taxable income is £45 000.

a   How much tax does Yusef pay?

b   How much extra tax will Yusef pay if he gets a 2% pay rise?

16   Rowan, Sue and Terry share a £60 000 inheritance.
Rowan gets 30% of what Sue gets and Terry gets 20% of what Sue gets.

a   Work out what each person gets.

b   Show how to check your answers to part **a**.

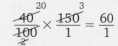

8.2 Increasing or decreasing an amount by a percentage

Learn...

Without a calculator, it is usually best to find the percentage increase or decrease first (using any of the methods in Learn 8.1). Then add the increase to the original **amount** or subtract the decrease from the original amount.

Sometimes there are more direct ways.

For example, suppose you want to reduce £150 by 60%

The final amount = 100% − 60% = 40% of £150

Here are three ways to find 40% of £150:

To reduce something by 60% you could:

find 60% of it then subtract
or just find 40% of it.

This way is quicker.

10% of £150 = £15
40% of £150 = £15 × 4 = £60

or $\dfrac{\overset{20}{\cancel{40}}}{\underset{2}{\cancel{100}}} \times \dfrac{\overset{3}{\cancel{150}}}{1} = \dfrac{60}{1}$

40 hundredths of £150

or   0.4 × 150 = 60

Using a multiplier 0.40 is the same as 0.4

Any method is acceptable. You could use a second method to check your answer.

Example: **a** Increase 800 by 15% **b** Decrease 500 by 7%

Solution: **a**

10% of 800	= 800 ÷ 10	= 80
5% of 800	= 80 ÷ 2	= 40 5% is half of 10%
15% of 800	= 10% + 5%	= 120
Increased amount	= 800 + 120	= **920**

b

1% of 500	= 500 ÷ 100	= 5
7% of 500	= 7 × 5	= 35
Decreased amount	= 500 − 35	= **465**

Practise...

8.2 Increasing or decreasing an amount by a percentage

D C B A A*

D

1
  a Increase £500 by 20%
  b Increase 750 kg by 40%
  c Decrease £650 by 30%
  d Decrease 360 km by 75%
  e Increase 80 000 by 5%
  f Increase £12.80 by 15%
  g Decrease 7000 by 45%
  h Decrease 480 by 95%

2 The normal price for an album is £15.
The shop reduces this by 20% in a sale.
What is the sale price?

3 A late offer gives 25% **discount** on a holiday that usually costs £720.

  a What does the holiday cost after the discount?

  b Check your answer using a different method.

4 The cost of a coach trip is £36.
What is the new price after a 5% increase?

5
  a Copy and complete these tables.

To increase by	10%	20%	90%
Multiply by			

To decrease by	10%	20%	90%
Multiply by			

  b Use the multipliers from your table to work out:

    i £400 increased by 10%
    ii 5000 increased by 20%
    iii 200 g increased by 90%

    iv £400 decreased by 10%
    v 5000 decreased by 20%
    vi 200 g decreased by 90%

  c Check your answers using a different method.

6 An evening cinema ticket costs £8. It costs $12\frac{1}{2}$% less in the afternoon.
What is the price in the afternoon?

7 Find the total cost of each of these.

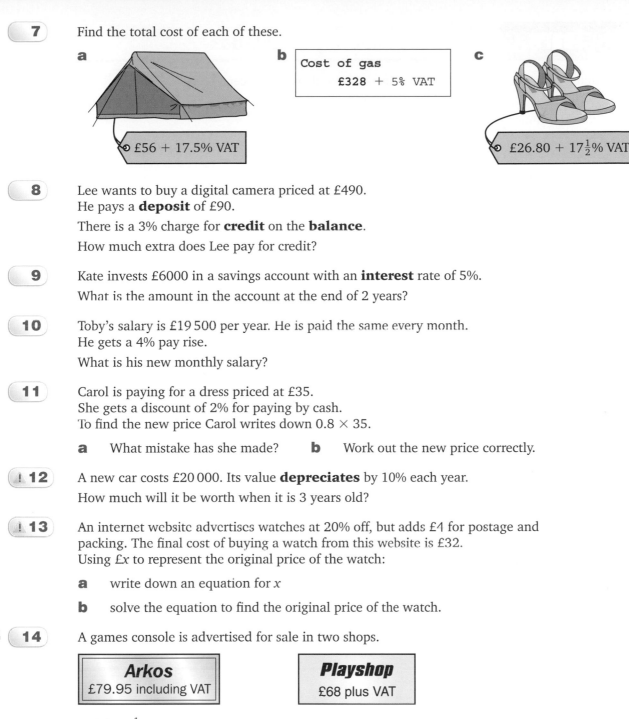

a

£56 + 17.5% VAT

b

| Cost of gas |
| £328 + 5% VAT |

c

£26.80 + 17½% VAT

8 Lee wants to buy a digital camera priced at £490.
He pays a **deposit** of £90.
There is a 3% charge for **credit** on the **balance**.
How much extra does Lee pay for credit?

9 Kate invests £6000 in a savings account with an **interest** rate of 5%.
What is the amount in the account at the end of 2 years?

10 Toby's salary is £19 500 per year. He is paid the same every month.
He gets a 4% pay rise.
What is his new monthly salary?

11 Carol is paying for a dress priced at £35.
She gets a discount of 2% for paying by cash.
To find the new price Carol writes down 0.8 × 35.

    a What mistake has she made?   **b** Work out the new price correctly.

12 A new car costs £20 000. Its value **depreciates** by 10% each year.
How much will it be worth when it is 3 years old?

13 An internet website advertises watches at 20% off, but adds £4 for postage and
packing. The final cost of buying a watch from this website is £32.
Using £x to represent the original price of the watch:

    a write down an equation for x

    b solve the equation to find the original price of the watch.

14 A games console is advertised for sale in two shops.

| **Arkos** |
| £79.95 including VAT |

| **Playshop** |
| £68 plus VAT |

VAT is 17½%

Which shop is cheaper and by how much?

15 A clothes shop aims to make at least 30% profit on everything it sells.
First the manager adds 30% to the cost price of an item.
Then he increases the result to a penny less than the next pound.
So, for example, if the 30% markup on an item gives £27.30,
the manager prices it at £27.99.

Find the manager's price for each item in the table.

Item	Cost price
Shirt	£12
Skirt	£25
Shorts	£7
Trousers	£36
Jacket	£47

16 A shop sells 200 g packets of peanuts. A poor peanut harvest means that the
shop now has to pay more for its supplies. The manager considers two options:

Option 1 Increase the price of a bag of peanuts by 20%

Option 2 Keep the price the same, but reduce the quantity by 20%

Which of these would you advise the manager to choose?
Give reasons for your choice and include calculations to support it.

Learn... 8.3 Successive percentages

You can use multipliers to combine the effect of more than one percentage.

For example, suppose you know that 60% of the adult population voted in an election and 40% of these voted for the winning party.

The percentage that voted for the winning party is **40% of 60%** of the adult population.

Multiplying the multipliers combines these percentages.

The percentage of the whole adult population that voted for the winning party: $0.6 \times 0.4 = 0.24$

Multiplier for 60% = 0.60   Multiplier for 40% = 0.40

This means only 24% of the population voted for the winning party; 76% didn't vote for them!

You can also use multipliers to combine percentage increases and decreases.

Example: A department store usually buys goods and sells them at a profit of 40%

In a sale it reduces its usual selling prices by 30%

a Does the department store still make a profit?

b What profit or loss does it make in the sale on a sofa which cost the store £750 to buy?

Solution: **a** The multiplier for the 40% markup is 1.40 = 1.4   The usual selling price is 140% of the cost price.

The multiplier for the 30% reduction is 0.70 = 0.7   The sale price is 70% of the usual selling price.

Multiplying these:

$1.4 \times 0.7 = 0.98$

This means the final sale price is 98% of the cost price.

The store makes a 2% loss on the goods it sells in the sale.

> AQA *Examiner's tip*
>
> Use multipliers to combine percentages.

b 1% of £750 = £750 ÷ 100 = £7.50   Using part **a** to answer part **b** is much quicker
2% of £750 = £7.50 × 2 = £15   than starting again.

Use the multiplier for 2% (0.02) to check: The loss on the sofa = 0.02 × 750 = £15.00

Practise... 8.3 Successive percentages 🄺   D C B A A*

B

1 In a school, 40% of the students come by public transport.
Of those who come by public transport, 5% use the train.

What percentage of all the school's students come by train?

2 In a town, 90% of the 20 000 adults who live there have a job.
Of these workers, 40% are female.

a How many adult females in this town have a job?

b How many adult males in this town have a job?

3 In a school, 80% of the students are going on a school trip.
Of these, 25% are going to London and the rest are going to a theme park.

a What percentage of all the students at the school are going:

i to London   **ii** to the theme park?

b The school has 1000 students. How many are going to London?

4 Jan saves 20% of what she earns.
60% of what she spends goes on clothes.

   a What percentage of Jan's earnings does she spend on clothes?

   b What percentage of her earnings does she spend on other things?

5 Phil buys a new car for £25 000.
The car's value depreciates by 20% in the first year after it is bought.
In the second year it depreciates by 15%

   a How much is the car worth after 2 years?

   b What is the overall percentage fall in its value?

6 Kelly earns £8.50 per hour. On promotion she gets a pay rise of 12%
After a year in her new job, Kelly expects to get another pay rise of 6%
Kelly says her new pay per hour will be 1.18 × £8.50.

   a Explain why this is not correct.

   b Write down a calculation that will give Kelly's new pay per hour.

7 A clothes shop reduces the price of its T-shirts by 30%
As a result it sells 50% more T-shirts than last week.

   a Work out the percentage increase in the shop's takings
   on T-shirts.

   b What disadvantages might this sale have?

8 At a college, 45% of the students are male.
Of these male students, 30% are on construction courses.
Of the female students, 10% are also on construction courses.

   What percentage of all the college's students are on construction courses?

9 In a school, 40% of the teachers are men and 10% of these teachers
wear spectacles.
Of the women teachers at the school, 15% also wear spectacles.

   Work out the percentage of all the teachers at the school who wear spectacles.

10 The table shows how the cost of manufacturing cricket bats is made up.

Cost	%
Labour	60
Materials	30
Overheads such as equipment, rent, power	10

The company buys some new equipment.
This increases overheads by 40% and materials by 10%, but reduces labour
costs by 50%

What is the overall effect on the cost of manufacturing the cricket bats?

11 A shop buys electrical goods and usually sells them at a profit of 50%
The manager wants to cut prices in a sale, but she does not want to make a loss.

What is the greatest percentage by which she can cut the usual prices without
making a loss?

12 Gemma and David share a lottery win in the ratio 1 : 3
Gemma says she is going to save 40% and spend the rest on a holiday.
David says he is going to save 60% and spend the rest on a car.

Overall, what percentage of the winnings will be saved?

Learn... 8.4 Writing one quantity as a percentage of another

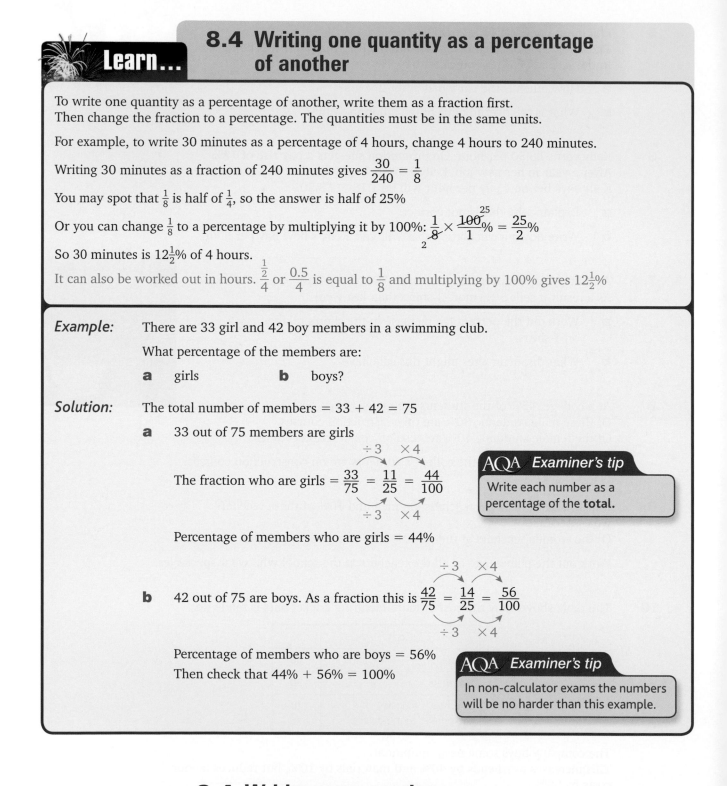

To write one quantity as a percentage of another, write them as a fraction first.
Then change the fraction to a percentage. The quantities must be in the same units.

For example, to write 30 minutes as a percentage of 4 hours, change 4 hours to 240 minutes.

Writing 30 minutes as a fraction of 240 minutes gives $\frac{30}{240} = \frac{1}{8}$

You may spot that $\frac{1}{8}$ is half of $\frac{1}{4}$, so the answer is half of 25%

Or you can change $\frac{1}{8}$ to a percentage by multiplying it by 100%: $\frac{1}{8} \times \frac{\overset{25}{100}}{1}\% = \frac{25}{2}\%$

So 30 minutes is $12\frac{1}{2}\%$ of 4 hours.

It can also be worked out in hours. $\frac{\frac{1}{2}}{4}$ or $\frac{0.5}{4}$ is equal to $\frac{1}{8}$ and multiplying by 100% gives $12\frac{1}{2}\%$

Example: There are 33 girl and 42 boy members in a swimming club.

What percentage of the members are:

a girls   **b** boys?

Solution: The total number of members = 33 + 42 = 75

a 33 out of 75 members are girls

The fraction who are girls $= \frac{33}{75} = \frac{11}{25} = \frac{44}{100}$

($\div 3$ $\times 4$)
($\div 3$ $\times 4$)

> **AQA** *Examiner's tip*
> Write each number as a percentage of the **total**.

Percentage of members who are girls = 44%

b 42 out of 75 are boys. As a fraction this is $\frac{42}{75} = \frac{14}{25} = \frac{56}{100}$

($\div 3$ $\times 4$)
($\div 3$ $\times 4$)

Percentage of members who are boys = 56%
Then check that 44% + 56% = 100%

> **AQA** *Examiner's tip*
> In non-calculator exams the numbers will be no harder than this example.

Practise... 8.4 Writing one quantity as a percentage of another

D C B A A*

1 Fiona gets £50 for her birthday. She spends £30 and saves the rest.

a What percentage does she spend?

b What percentage does she save?

2 A charity has raised £1280. Their target is £4000.
What percentage of the target do they still need to raise?

3 There were 12 rainy days in June.
What percentage of the month is this?

4 There are 33 girls and 27 boys in a youth club.
   a What percentage of the youth club members are:
      i girls **ii** boys?
   b Show how you can check your answers to part **a**.

5 Write the first quantity or number as a percentage of the second.
   a 60p, £1.50 **e** 240 cm, 4 m
   b 24 cm, 3 m **f** £1800, £30 000
   c 300 g, 2 kg **g** 14 000, 7 million
   d 200 ml, 2 litres **h** 8 hours, 1 day

   Hint
   1 m = 100 cm
   1 kg = 1000 g
   1 litre = 1000 ml

6 Mark gets an allowance of £25. He spends £4.25 on magazines.
What percentage of his allowance does he have left?

7 In a marathon, 25 women and 35 men start.
Only 18 of the women and 21 of the men complete it.
Work out:
   a the percentage of women who complete the marathon
   b the percentage of men who complete the marathon
   c the percentage of all those taking part who do not complete it.

8 Driving lessons cost £25 each with a discount of 20% if you buy 10 lessons.
So far Chris has saved up £140.
What percentage of the total cost of 10 lessons has Chris saved?

9 What percentage of the numbers between 1 and 25 (inclusive) are:
   a multiples of 6
   b factors of 12
   c prime numbers.

10 The VAT rate was reduced from 17.5% to 15% for one year.
Sally says that this reduced the VAT charged on her shopping by 2.5%
Tom says this is wrong. He thinks the VAT charged was reduced by over 14%
Who is correct? Explain your answer.

11 A mobile phone costs £15 per month plus 5 pence per minute for calls.
   a Write the monthly payment as a percentage of the total cost in a month when the time on calls is:
      i 100 minutes **iii** 300 minutes
      ii 200 minutes **iv** 400 minutes.
   b What happens to this percentage as the call time increases?

12 **a** What percentage of 2-digit numbers:
      i are multiples of 3 **ii** contain the digit 3?
   b What percentage of 3-digit numbers:
      i are multiples of 3 **ii** contain the digit 3?

D

C

B

Learn... 8.5 Finding a percentage increase or decrease

A percentage increase or decrease is always given as a percentage of the **original** amount.
This is also the case with percentage profit and loss.

To find an increase or decrease as a percentage:

Note: % change = $\dfrac{\text{change}}{\text{original amount}} \times 100\%$

- find the increase (or decrease) in the amount
- write the increase (or decrease) as a fraction of the **original** amount
- change the fraction to a percentage.

Example: Andy buys a bike for £300 and sells it a year later for £180.
What is his percentage loss?

Solution: The amount of money lost = £300 − £180 = £120

Writing this as a fraction of the **original**
amount gives $\dfrac{120}{300} = \dfrac{40}{100}$

Remember to divide by the original amount.

↑
original value

Andy lost 40%

Example: Each week Nina buys a magazine.
This week the price went up by 25 pence to £1.50.
What was the percentage increase in price?

Solution: The price last week was 150 − 25 = 125 pence.   You must have the same units.

To find the percentage increase $\dfrac{25}{125} = \dfrac{1}{5} = \dfrac{20}{100} = 20\%$

The price increased by 20%

Practise... 8.5 Finding a percentage increase or decrease

D C B A A*

C

1 The number of fish in a pond has gone down from 250 to 175.
What is the percentage decrease?

2 Shona invests £4800 in shares and sells them one year later
for £6000.

What is the percentage increase?

3 A day at a jet-ski centre usually costs £150.
If you take your own jet ski, it costs £120.

What is the discount for taking your own jet ski as a
percentage of the usual price?

4 Sam's pay rate goes up from £7.20 to £7.50 per hour.
Find the percentage increase.

> **Bump up your grade**
>
> For a Grade C you must be able to write an increase or decrease as a percentage.

5 A camera shop reduces the price of a digital camera from £60 to £40.
Tracy says the price is reduced by 50%

    a What mistake has she made?

    b What is the actual percentage reduction?

6 The table shows the prices of a football club's season tickets.

	Last year	This year
Adult	£280	£320
Under 16	£120	£135
Under 12	£90	£126

    a Work out which type of ticket has gone up by the greatest percentage.

    b Each year Wayne buys a season ticket for himself and his daughter who is
       now 13 years old.
       Work out the percentage increase in the total cost of the two tickets
       Wayne buys.

7 A sports shop sells tennis balls for 96 pence each
or £2.40 for a pack of three.
Marc buys a pack of three balls.

Work out how much he saves as a percentage of the
cost of buying the balls separately.

96p each or
£2.40 for
pack of 3

8 A property developer buys some land for £1 million.
He builds 25 houses on this land. It costs him £120 000 to build each house.
He sells the houses for £200 000 each.

Find the percentage profit.

9 Lisa says that it is not possible for something to increase by more than 100%

Do you agree? Explain your answer.

10 A supermarket sells crisps in a multi-pack of 12 packets for £2.16.
It also sells separate packets of crisps for 30 pence each.

    a What percentage do you save if you buy a multi-pack rather than separate
       packets of crisps.

    b Give two reasons why a shopper might decide to buy separate packets of
       crisps rather than a multi-pack.

11 A value x is increased by 20%
The value after this increase is $x + 40$.

What is the value of x?

12 What percentage extra do you get if you:

    a buy one, get one free

    b get three for the price of two

    c get an extra one free when you buy a pack of five?

Pack of 5.
Get 1 free!

Learn... 8.6 Reverse percentages

In a reverse percentage problem you start with the final amount and work back to the original amount. You can work this out using the **unitary** method. This method is based on finding the amount or cost of **one** unit (hence the name 'unitary'). Reverse percentage problems are solved by finding **1%**

Example: The price of a trampoline has been reduced by 40% in a sale.
The sale price is £90.

Work out:

a the price of the trampoline before the sale

b how much you save by buying the trampoline in the sale.

Solution: **a** The sale price = 100% − 40% = 60% of the original price

60% of the original price = £90

1% of the original price = $\dfrac{£90}{60}$ = £1.50 ← Find 1% of the original amount, then multiply by 100.

100% of the original price = 100 × £1.50 = £150

The original price was £150.

b If you buy the trampoline for £90 you will save £60.

Example: The number of downloads from a website has gone up this month by 20% to 48 000.

How many downloads were there last month?

Solution: 100% + 20%

120% of last month's figure = 48 000

1% of last month's figure = $\dfrac{48\,000}{120}$ = 400

100% of the last month's figure = 100 × 400 = 400 000

AQA *Examiner's tip*

Look out for questions like this when you are given the final amount and asked to find the **original** amount.

Practise... 8.6 Reverse percentages 🔊

D C B A A*

B

1 A surfboard is reduced by 20% in a sale. The sale price is £120.

Work out the price of the surfboard before the sale.

2 The cost of a rail journey has gone up by 10%. It now costs £55.

What was the price before the rise?

3 A garage reduces the price of a car by 30%
The reduced price is £10 500.

a What was the original price of the car?

b How much do you save by buying it now?

4 A headteacher says that the number of students who are absent from school today has gone up by 20% to 60 compared to yesterday.

How many children were absent yesterday?

5   In a 'back to school' sale a clothes shop reduces its prices of school uniforms by 30%

The table gives the sale prices.

Item	Sale price
Skirt	£14.00
Trousers	£8.40
Shirt	£4.20
Sweatshirt	£17.50

Work out what the prices were before the sale.

6   A holiday company gives 10% discount for early payments.
Jake makes an early payment of £738 for a holiday.

What was the cost before the early payment discount?

7   If 30% of a number is 63, what is the number?

8   Liam pays £2480 in tax. This is 20% of his taxable income.

What is Liam's taxable income?

9   Maria bought a scooter then sold it for £1650 at a loss of 25%

How much did she pay for it?

10   Gina buys a dress for £42. The price was reduced by 30% in a sale.
Gina wants to work out how much she has saved.
She writes down £42 ÷ 100 × 30 = £12.60

   a   Explain why Gina has got the wrong answer.

   b   Work out how much Gina saved.

11   A motorist pays £470 for a repair on her car.
This includes VAT at $17\frac{1}{2}\%$

What was the cost of the repair before VAT was added?

12   A company has 2970 female employees. 55% of their employees are male.

What is the number of male employees?

13   John is a car salesman. He earns a basic wage of £1800 per month plus 15% commission on any sales he makes.

What value of cars does John need to sell each year if he wishes to have an annual income of £45 000?

14   Natalie has £7056 in her bank account.
This is after two years in which 5% was added to the account at the end of each year.

How much did she have in the account two years ago?

8 Assess

D

1 A watch priced at £75 is reduced by 20% in a sale.
What is the sale price?

2 A plumber charges £460 plus VAT of $17\frac{1}{2}\%$
Work out the total bill.

3 In a school year, 81 out of 180 students are girls. What percentage is this?

4 Simon wants to buy a motorbike priced at £1500. The dealer offers him two options.

| Option 1 – 20% deposit plus 12 monthly payments of £105. | Option 2 – Single cash payment with a discount of 10%. |

a How much more does it cost if Simon chooses Option 1 rather than Option 2?

b Give one reason why Simon may still choose Option 1.

C

5 A bus fare goes up from 84 pence to £1.05.
What is the percentage increase?

6 A parents' association buys 50 Christmas trees for a total of £400 from a supplier
to sell at the school's Christmas sale.

a They sell 35 of the trees for £12 each.
Work out the percentage profit on these trees.

b At the end of the sale, they sell off the remaining trees for £5 each.
Work out the percentage loss on these trees.

c What was the overall profit or loss?

B

7 At a football match, 60% of the people are male and 80% of these support the home
team. Of the females at the match, 90% support the home team.
What percentage of all the people at the match supports the home team?

8 Dawn pays a deposit of £60 for an electric guitar. This is 40% of the full price.
She pays off the rest of the cost in six equal monthly payments.
How much is each monthly payment?

9 A clothes shop sells jackets for £75 and trousers for £52.
It makes 25% profit on the jackets and 30% profit on the trousers.
How much did the shop pay for each item?

A

10 A shop normally sells surfboards at a profit of 60%. The manager decides to reduce
prices in a sale, but still wishes to make 20% profit on the surfboards sold in the sale.
By what percentage of the normal selling price should the manager reduce prices in the sale?

AQA Examination-style questions 🔞

1 **a** In a sale the price of a television decreases from £750 to £660.
Work out the percentage decrease in price.   *(3 marks)*

   b In a sale the price of a camcorder decreases by 60%.
The sale price is £372.
Work out the price before the sale.   (3 marks)

2 The value of a vintage car rises from £36 000 to £63 000.
Work out the percentage increase in the price of the car.   (3 marks)

AQA 2008

Objectives

Examiners would normally expect students who get these grades to be able to:

D

use the terms square, positive square root, negative square root, cube and cube root

recall integer squares from 2×2 to 15×15 and the corresponding square roots

recall the cubes of 2, 3, 4, 5 and 10 and the corresponding cube roots

C

use index notation and index laws for positive powers

B

use index notation and index laws for negative powers

convert between ordinary and standard index form numbers

use standard index form for calculations involving multiplication and/or division

A

use index notation and index laws for fractional powers such as $16^{\frac{1}{2}}$ and $16^{0.5}$

A*

use index notation and index laws for fractional powers such as $8^{\frac{2}{3}}$ and $8^{-\frac{2}{3}}$

Key terms

indices
index
power
standard index form

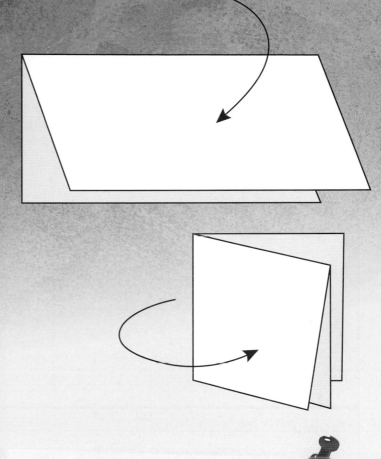

Did you know?

Folding paper

Did you know that it is impossible to fold a piece of paper more than 12 times?

If you fold the paper in half your paper is two sheets thick.

If you fold it in half again your paper is four sheets thick.

If you fold it in half again your paper is eight sheets thick.

How thick would your paper be after 12 folds?

Use the fact that paper is 0.1 millimetre or $\frac{1}{2540}$ inch thick.

You should already know:

✔ how to multiply numbers

✔ how to calculate squares and square roots

✔ how to calculate cubes and cube roots

✔ how to use algebra

✔ how to use reciprocals.

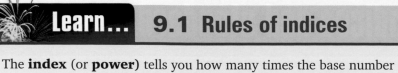

Learn... 9.1 Rules of indices

The **index** (or **power**) tells you how many times the base number is to be multiplied by itself. This means that 5^3 tells you that 5 (the base number) is to be multiplied by itself 3 times (the index or power).

5^3 — index (or power), base

So $5^3 = 5 \times 5 \times 5 = 125$

Rules of indices

$a^3 \times a^5 = (a \times a \times a) \times (a \times a \times a \times a \times a)$ $= a \times a \times a \times a \times a \times a \times a \times a$ $= a^8$	So $\quad a^3 \times a^5 = a^8$ In general $a^m \times a^n = a^{m+n}$
$a^7 \div a^3 = \dfrac{a^7}{a^3}$ $= \dfrac{a \times a \times a \times a \times a \times a \times a}{a \times a \times a}$ $= \dfrac{\cancel{a} \times \cancel{a} \times \cancel{a} \times a \times a \times a \times a}{\cancel{a} \times \cancel{a} \times \cancel{a}}$ $= a \times a \times a \times a$ $= a^4$	So $\quad a^7 \div a^3 = a^4$ In general $a^m \div a^n = a^{m-n}$
$(a^2)^3 = a^2 \times a^2 \times a^2$ $= (a \times a) \times (a \times a) \times (a \times a)$ $= a \times a \times a \times a \times a \times a$ $= a^6$	So $\quad (a^2)^3 = a^6$ In general $(a^m)^n = a^{m \times n}$

Example: Simplify the following.

		Number	*Algebra*	*Higher algebra*
	a	$6^3 \times 6^2$	$a^3 \times a^2$	$6a^3 \times 3a^2$
	b	$\dfrac{2^5}{2^2}$	$\dfrac{a^5}{a^2}$	$\dfrac{15a^5}{3a^2}$
	c	$(3^5)^2$	$(a^3)^2$	$(6a^2)^3$

Solution:

a
$$6^3 \times 6^2 \qquad a^3 \times a^2 \qquad 6a^3 \times 3a^2$$
$$= 6^{(3+2)} \qquad = a^{(3+2)} \qquad = 6 \times a^3 \times 3 \times a^2$$
$$= 6^5 \qquad = a^5 \qquad = 6 \times 3 \times a^3 \times a^2$$
$$= 18 \times a^{(3+2)}$$
$$= 18a^5$$

b
$$\frac{2^5}{2^2} \qquad \frac{a^5}{a^2} \qquad \frac{15a^5}{3a^2}$$
$$= 2^5 \div 2^2 \qquad = a^5 \div a^2 \qquad = \frac{15}{3} \times \frac{a^5}{a^2}$$
$$= 2^{(5-2)} \qquad = a^{(5-2)} \qquad = 5 \times a^{(5-2)}$$
$$= 2^3 \qquad = a^3 \qquad = 5a^3$$

c
$$(3^5)^2 \qquad (a^3)^2 \qquad (6a^2)^3$$
$$= 3^{3 \times 2} \qquad = a^{3 \times 2} \qquad = (6)^3 \times (a^2)^3$$
$$= 3^6 \qquad = a^6 \qquad = 216 \times a^{2 \times 3}$$
$$= 216 \times a^6$$
$$= 216a^6$$

Negative indices

$$a^2 \div a^5 = \frac{a \times a}{a \times a \times a \times a \times a}$$

$$= \frac{\cancel{a} \times \cancel{a}}{\cancel{a} \times \cancel{a} \times a \times a \times a}$$

$$= \frac{1}{a \times a \times a}$$

$$= \frac{1}{a^3}$$

$$a^2 \div a^5 = \frac{a^2}{a^5}$$

$$= a^{(2-5)}$$

$$= a^{-3}$$

So $\quad a^{-3} = \dfrac{1}{a^3}$

In general: $\quad a^{-n} = \dfrac{1}{a^n}$

Zero indices

$$a^3 \div a^3 = \frac{a \times a \times a}{a \times a \times a}$$

$$= \frac{\cancel{a}^1 \times \cancel{a}^1 \times \cancel{a}^1}{\cancel{a}^1 \times \cancel{a}^1 \times \cancel{a}^1}$$

$$= \frac{1}{1}$$

$$= 1$$

$$a^3 \div a^3 = \frac{a^3}{a^3}$$

$$= a^{(3-3)}$$

$$= a^0$$

So $\quad a^0 = 1$

In general: $\quad a^0 = 1$

Fractional indices

$$a^{\frac{1}{2}} \times a^{\frac{1}{2}} = a^{\frac{1}{2}+\frac{1}{2}} = a^1 = a \qquad \text{so } a^{\frac{1}{2}} = \sqrt{a} \text{ (since } \sqrt{a} \times \sqrt{a} = a)$$

$$a^{\frac{1}{3}} \times a^{\frac{1}{3}} \times a^{\frac{1}{3}} = a^{\frac{1}{3}+\frac{1}{3}+\frac{1}{3}} = a^1 = a \qquad \text{so } a^{\frac{1}{3}} = \sqrt[3]{a} \text{ (since } \sqrt[3]{a} \times \sqrt[3]{a} \times \sqrt[3]{a} = a)$$

In general: $\quad a^{\frac{1}{n}} = \sqrt[n]{a}$

Summary of rules of indices

$a^m \times a^n = a^{m+n}$	$a^m \div a^n = a^{m-n}$	$(a^m)^n = a^{m \times n}$
$a^{-m} = \dfrac{1}{a^m}$	$a^0 = 1$	$a^{\frac{1}{n}} = \sqrt[n]{a}$

Bump up your grade

You will need to use index notation and index laws for positive and negative powers for an award of Grade C.

Example: Work out:

a 3^{-2} **b** 999^0 **c** $100^{\frac{1}{2}}$ **d** $(-27)^{\frac{1}{3}}$ **e** $8^{\frac{2}{3}}$

Solution:

a $3^{-2} = \dfrac{1}{3^2}$ using negative indices

$\qquad = \dfrac{1}{9}$

b $999^0 = 1$ using zero indices

c $100^{\frac{1}{2}} = \sqrt{100}$ using fractional indices

$\qquad = 10$ -10 is also an acceptable answer

d $(-27)^{\frac{1}{3}} = \sqrt[3]{(-27)}$ using fractional indices

$\qquad = -3$

e $8^{\frac{2}{3}} = (8^2)^{\frac{1}{3}}$ or $(8^{\frac{1}{3}})^2$ using $(a^m)n = a^{m \times n}$

$\qquad (8^2)^{\frac{1}{3}} = (64)^{\frac{1}{3}} = 4$

$\qquad (8^{\frac{1}{3}})^2 = (2)^2 = 4$

AQA Examiner's tip

Remember that for square roots there are always two possible answers (one is positive and the other negative. You can write this using the $\pm$ symbol.

AQA Examiner's tip

It does not matter which way you answer this question although $(8^{\frac{1}{3}})^2$ is probably easier. Try to plan your work to make the mathematics easier.

Practise... 9.1 Rules of indices (k!)

D C B A A*

D

1 Work out:

a $3^2 + 4^2$

b $2^3 \times 3^2$

c $10^3 - \sqrt{100}$

d $\sqrt{225} - \sqrt[3]{125}$

e $\sqrt{5^2 + 12^2}$

f $\sqrt{3^2 \times 5^2}$

D
C

2 Find the value of each of the following.

a 7^2

b 4^2

c 11^2

d $(-3)^2$

e 2^3

f 10^4

g 1^5

h 2^5

i 3^4

j 4^3

k $(-10)^6$

l $(-2)^7$

3 Work out the value of each of the following.

a 9^2

b -2^5

c -3^4

d 5^1

e 4^6

f 12^0

g 1^2

h 1^{100}

i 3^{-1}

j 2^{-3}

k 4^{-6}

l 100^{-1}

m $2^{11} - 5^3$

n $2^6 + 6^2$

o $5^3 \times 10^{-4}$

p $10^8 - 10^6$

C

4 Simplify the following, leaving your answer in index form.

a $5^6 \times 5^2$

b $12^8 \times 12^3$

c $\dfrac{4^7}{4^3}$

d $7^{10} \div 7^5$

e $3^7 \div 3^{10}$

f $(9^2)^5$

g $\dfrac{4^2 \times 4^3}{4^6}$

C
B

5 Are the following statements true or false? Give a reason for your answer.

a $6^2 = 12$

b $1^3 = 1$

c $1^{-\frac{1}{2}} = -1$

d $16^{-\frac{1}{2}} = -4$

e $\dfrac{2^{10}}{4^5} = 1$

f $3^4 + 3^5 = 3^9$

g $10^{50} \times 10^{50} = 10^{100}$

h $(-216)^{\frac{1}{3}} = -6$

i $1\,000\,000^0 = 0$

B

6 Work out:

a $49^{\frac{1}{2}}$

b $121^{\frac{1}{2}}$

c $64^{\frac{1}{3}}$

d $8^{\frac{2}{3}}$

e $32^{\frac{2}{5}}$

f $4^{-\frac{1}{2}}$

g $1^{\frac{1}{3}}$

h $1^{-\frac{1}{3}}$

A

7 Put the following in order, starting with the smallest.

$64^{\frac{1}{3}}$ $\qquad$ $64^{\frac{1}{4}}$ $\qquad$ $(\frac{1}{64})^{\frac{1}{2}}$ $\qquad$ $64^{-\frac{1}{3}}$

8 Simplify the following.

> **Hint**
>
> Write $2x^2 \times 3x^5$ as $2 \times x^2 \times 3 \times x^5$
> $= 2 \times 3 \times x^2 \times x^5$
> $= 6 \times x^2 \times x^5$

a $2x^2 \times 3x^5$

b $\dfrac{3a^6}{6a^2}$

c $5c^2 \times 2c^7$

d $(4b^2)^3$

e $\dfrac{c^6 \times c^9}{c^5}$

f $\dfrac{5c^2 \times 2c^7}{c^6}$

A*

9 Work out:

a $8^{\frac{2}{3}}$ **b** $-8^{\frac{2}{3}}$ **c** $(-8)^{\frac{2}{3}}$ **d** $32^{\frac{2}{5}}$ **e** $(-125)^{\frac{2}{3}}$

10 Simplify $\dfrac{15a^7b^6c^3}{3a^4b^9c^{-2}}$

11 4^{3^2} can be ordered as $(4^3)^2$ or $4^{(3^2)}$

Marc says they are the same.

Is Marc correct?

Give a reason for your answer.

12 The number 64 can be written as 8^2 in index form.

Write down five other ways that it can be written in index form.

13 **a** Find the product of $7xy^2$ and $3x^4y^3$.

> **Hint**
> Write $7xy^2$ as $7 \times x \times y^2$

b Write down five other expressions which give the same product as your answer in part **a**.

14 Amy notices that $\sqrt{4} \times \sqrt{9} = \sqrt{4 \times 9}$

Does this always work?

Give some examples.

What happens if you divide the two numbers?

Learn... 9.2 Standard index form 🄺

Standard index form is a shorthand way of writing very large and very small numbers.

Standard index form numbers are always written as follows.

n is a positive or negative integer

$$A \times 10^n$$

A is a number between 1 and 10 ($1 \leqslant A < 10$)

Converting from standard index form

To convert from standard index form to ordinary form use the following information.

$10^1 = 10$

$10^2 = 10 \times 10 = 100$

$10^3 = 10 \times 10 \times 10 = 1000$

$10^4 = 10 \times 10 \times 10 \times 10 = 10\,000$

$10^5 = 10 \times 10 \times 10 \times 10 \times 10 = 100\,000$

$10^6 = 10 \times 10 \times 10 \times 10 \times 10 \times 10 = 1\,000\,000$ (1 million)

$10^{-1} = \dfrac{1}{10^1} = \dfrac{1}{10} = 0.1$

$10^{-2} = \dfrac{1}{10^2} = \dfrac{1}{100} = 0.01$

$10^{-3} = \dfrac{1}{10^3} = \dfrac{1}{1000} = 0.001$

$10^{-4} = \dfrac{1}{10^4} = \dfrac{1}{10\,000} = 0.0001$

$10^{-5} = \dfrac{1}{10^5} = \dfrac{1}{100\,000} = 0.00001$

$10^{-6} = \dfrac{1}{10^6} = \dfrac{1}{1\,000\,000} = 0.000001$

AQA *Examiner's tip*

Remember that multiplying by 10^{-1} is the same as dividing by 10, multiplying by 10^{-2} is the same as dividing by 10^2, etc.

Example: Write in ordinary form:

a **i** 5×10^6 **b** **i** 4×10^{-3}

ii 6.225×10^5 **ii** 7.295×10^{-6}

Solution: **a** **i** $5 \times 10^6 = 5 \times 1\,000\,000 = 5\,000\,000$

ii $6.225 \times 10^5 = 6.225 \times 100\,000 = 622\,500$

b **i** $4 \times 10^{-3} = 4 \times 0.001 = 0.004$

ii $7.295 \times 10^{-6} = 7.295 \times 0.000001 = 0.000007295$

You can work these out by counting how many places the decimal point has to move.

5.0000000 (move the decimal point 6 places to the right) gives $5\,000\,000.0$

0004. (move the point 3 places to the left) gives 0.004

Converting to standard index form

To convert to standard index form write your number in the form $A \times 10^n$

where A is a number between 1 and 10

and n is a positive or negative integer.

Example: Convert these ordinary form numbers into standard index form.

a $701\,000$

b 0.00000000153

Solution: **a** $701\,000$

$A = 7.01$, so $701\,000 = 7.01 \times 100\,000 = 7.01 \times 10^5$

b 0.00000000153

$A = 1.53$, so $0.00000000153 = 1.53 \times 0.000000001 = 1.53 \times 10^{-9}$

Adding, subtracting, multiplying and dividing standard index form numbers

Use the rules of indices to multiply and divide standard index form numbers.

$a^m \times a^n = a^{m+n}$

$a^m \div a^n = a^{m-n}$

$(a^m)^n = a^{m \times n}$

$a^{-m} = \dfrac{1}{a^m}$

$a^0 = 1$

Example: Work out the following, leaving your answer in standard index form.

a $6 \times 10^8 \times 8 \times 10^{-3}$

b $\dfrac{6 \times 10^8}{8 \times 10^{-3}}$

c $5 \times 10^3 + 7 \times 10^4$

d $7.3 \times 10^5 - 2.4 \times 10^5$

Solution:

a $6 \times 10^8 \times 8 \times 10^{-3} = 6 \times 8 \times 10^8 \times 10^{-3}$ rearranging the order

$$= 48 \times 10^8 \times 10^{-3}$$

$$= 48 \times 10^{8-3} \qquad \text{using the rules of indices for } 10^8 \times 10^{-3}$$

$$= 48 \times 10^5 \qquad \text{this is not yet in standard index form}$$

$$= 4.8 \times 10^1 \times 10^5 \qquad \text{writing 48 as } 4.8 \times 10^1$$

$$= 4.8 \times 10^{1+5} \qquad \text{using the rules of indices for } 10^1 \times 10^5$$

$$= 4.8 \times 10^6$$

b $\dfrac{6 \times 10^8}{8 \times 10^{-3}} = \dfrac{6}{8} \times \dfrac{10^8}{10^{-3}}$

$$= 0.75 \times 10^{8--3} \qquad \text{using the rules of indices for } 10^8 \div 10^{-3}$$

$$= 0.75 \times 10^{11} \qquad \text{remembering that } 8 - -3 = 11$$

$$= 7.5 \times 10^{-1} \times 10^{11} \qquad \text{writing 0.75 in standard index form as } 7.5 \times 10^{-1}$$

$$= 7.5 \times 10^{-1+11} \qquad \text{using the rules of indices for } 10^{-1} \times 10^{11}$$

$$= 7.5 \times 10^{10}$$

c $5 \times 10^3 + 7 \times 10^4 = 5000 + 70\,000$ writing numbers in ordinary form

$$= 75\,000 \qquad \text{adding}$$

$$= 7.5 \times 10^4 \qquad \text{converting back to standard index form}$$

d $7.3 \times 10^5 - 2.4 \times 10^5$

$$= (7.3 - 2.4) \times 10^5 \qquad \text{since the powers of 10 are the same}$$

$$= 4.9 \times 10^5$$

AQA *Examiner's tip*

Watch out for shortcuts when adding and subtracting numbers that have the same power of 10.

Practise... 9.2 Standard index form (k!) D C B A A*

1 Write the following ordinary form numbers in standard index form.

a	4200	**c**	700 100	**e**	15	**g**	0.013
b	590 000 000	**d**	8 600 000 000	**f**	0.0008	**h**	0.000000178

2 Write the following numbers in ordinary form.

a	4×10^5	**c**	7.005×10^3	**e**	9×10^{-1}	**g**	9.99×10^{-10}
b	6.0×10^2	**d**	3.401×10^1	**f**	4.75×10^{-4}		

3 The mass of an electron is approximately 0.00000000000000000000000000000910938 kilograms.

Write this number as a standard index form number.

4 Write the number 60^3 in standard index form.

B

B
A

5 Work out the following.

a $(4 \times 10^4) \times (2 \times 10^7)$

g $(5 \times 10^{-4})^2$

b $(3.3 \times 10^6) \times (3 \times 10^4)$

h $\dfrac{4 \times 10^4}{2 \times 10^3}$

c $(4.5 \times 10^5) \times (2 \times 10^{11})$

i $\dfrac{3.9 \times 10^5}{1.3 \times 10^8}$

d $(5 \times 10^5) \times (3 \times 10^9)$

j $\dfrac{2.2 \times 10^1}{5.5 \times 10^{-6}}$

e $(2.5 \times 10^8) \times (5 \times 10^{-3})$

k $(2.2 \times 10^6) \div (4.4 \times 10^4)$

f $(1.5 \times 10^7)^2$

6 Given that $p = 4 \times 10^2$ and $q = 2 \times 10^{-1}$, work out:

a $p \times q$ b $p \div q$ c $p + q$ d $p - q$ e p^2

A

7 The distance to the edge of the observable universe is approximately 4.6×10^{26} metres.

Express this distance in kilometres, giving your answer in standard index form.

8 The speed of light is approximately 3.0×10^8 m/s.

How far will light travel in one week?

Give your answer in standard index form.

⚠ 9 The mass of the Sun is approximately 2×10^{30} kg
and the mass of the Earth is approximately 6×10^{24} kg.

How many times heavier is the Sun than the Earth?

⚙ 10 The following table shows the diameters of the planets
of the solar system.

Planet	Diameter (km)
Mercury	4.9×10^3
Venus	1.2×10^4
Earth	1.3×10^4
Mars	6.8×10^3
Jupiter	1.4×10^5
Saturn	1.2×10^5
Uranus	5.2×10^4
Neptune	4.9×10^4

Place the planets in order of size, starting with the
smallest first.

❓ 11 Ali says that $(4 \times 10^4) + (2 \times 10^4) = (6 \times 10^4)$

Brian says that $(4 \times 10^4) + (2 \times 10^4) = (6 \times 10^8)$

Who is correct?

Give a reason for your answer.

9 Assess

1 **a** Sam says all numbers have two square roots.
Gareth says some numbers have no square roots.

Who is right? Give a reason for your answer.

b Livia joins in the conversation and says that all numbers have two cube roots.

Is she right? Give a reason for your answer.

2 Work out the following, leaving your answers as single powers.

a	$4^6 \times 4^2$	**e**	$6^4 \times 6^2 \times 6^3$	**i** $5^8 \div 5^7$
b	$11^5 \times 11^3$	**f**	$10^4 \div 10^2$	**j** $2^3 \div 2^3$
c	$(5^3)^2$	**g**	$21^7 \div 21^5$	
d	$7^5 \times 7$	**h**	$16^{10} \div 16^9$	

3 Find the value of:

a $3^2 \times 4^2$ **b** $5^4 \div 5^2$ **c** $6^5 \times 6^3 \div 6^4$ **d** $\dfrac{(10^8 \times 10^7)}{10^7 \times 10^6}$

4 Which is greater:

a 3^5 or 5^3 **b** 11^2 or 2^{11} **c** 2^4 or 4^2?

5 Which of the following statements is true?

The sum of the squares of two odd numbers is always odd.
The sum of the squares of two odd numbers is always even.
The sum of the squares of two odd numbers could be odd or even.

Give a reason for your answer.

6 The diameter of the dwarf planet Pluto is 2.27×10^3 km.

The diameter of Neptune is 4.86×10^4 km.

Express the diameter of Pluto to the diameter of Neptune as a ratio in the form $1:n$
Give your answer to a suitable degree of accuracy.

7 Find the values of the following, leaving your answers as fractions where appropriate.

a	5^{-1}	**c** $12^3 \div 12^4$	**e** $2^6 \div 2^8$	**g** $(\frac{1}{2})^{-3}$
b	23^0	**d** 3^{-2}	**f** $(\frac{1}{4})^0$	

8 Work out:

a	$81^{\frac{1}{2}}$	**c** $27^{-\frac{1}{3}}$	**e** $-64^{\frac{2}{3}}$	**g** $32^{\frac{3}{5}}$	**i** $(-125)^{-\frac{2}{3}}$
b	$225^{\frac{1}{2}}$	**d** $1^{\frac{2}{3}}$	**f** $(-64)^{\frac{2}{3}}$	**h** $9^{-\frac{1}{2}}$	

AQA Examination-style questions 🔑

1 $x^a \times x^b = x^7$
$(x^a)^b = x^{10}$
Work out the values of a and b.

(3 marks)

AQA 2008

10 Real-life graphs

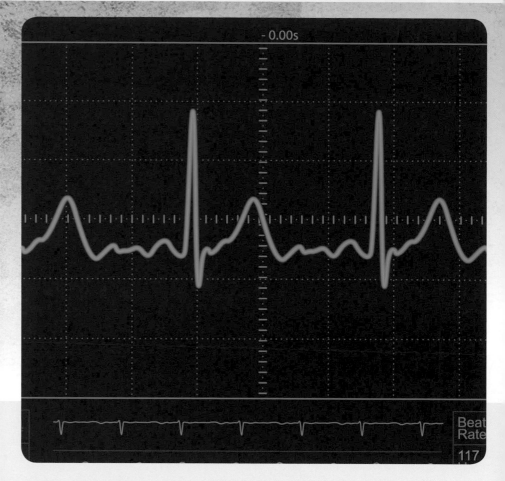

- 0.00s

Beat Rate

117

Objectives

Examiners would normally expect students who get these grades to be able to:

D

interpret real-life graphs

find simple average speed from distance–time graphs

recognise from a distance–time graph when the fastest average speed takes place

C

find the average speed in km/h from a distance–time graph with time in minutes

B

discuss and interpret graphs modelling real situations.

Did you know?

…how important graphs can be?

Graphs that record information such as heart rate, heart beats and blood pressure are very important. Real-life graphs such as these are used in hospitals and can save lives.

You should already know:

✔ how to plot points

✔ how to draw, scale and label axes

✔ how to plot and interpret a line graph

✔ how to plot and use conversion graphs

✔ how to solve simple problems involving proportion

✔ common units for measuring distance, speed and time

✔ how to interpret horizontal lines on a distance–time graph

✔ how to find distances from distance–time graphs.

Key terms

speed
gradient

Learn... 10.1 Distance–time graphs

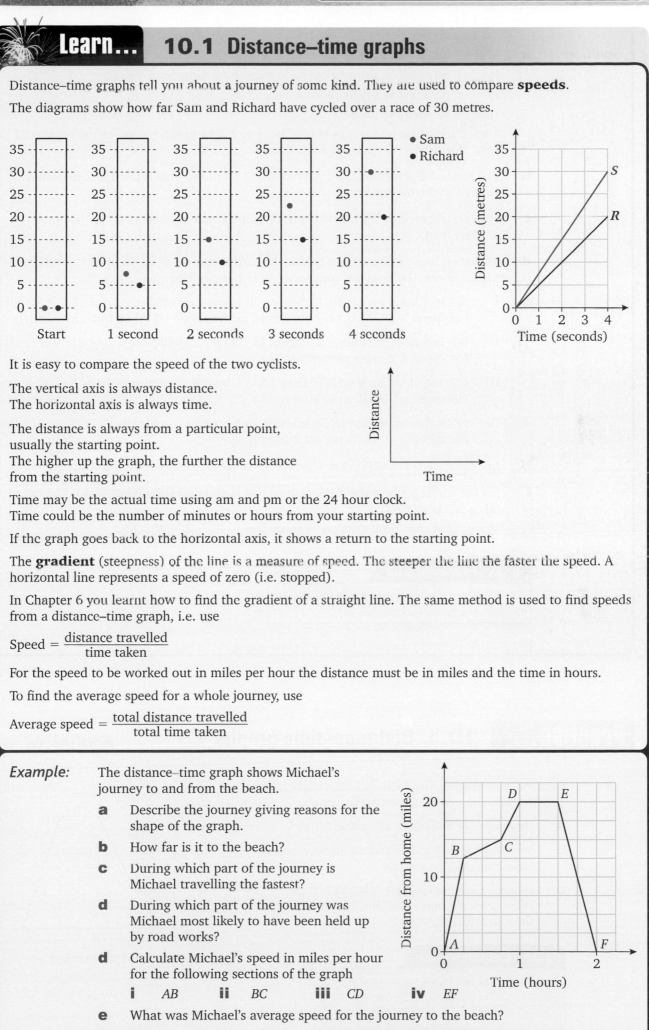

Distance–time graphs tell you about a journey of some kind. They are used to compare **speeds**.

The diagrams show how far Sam and Richard have cycled over a race of 30 metres.

It is easy to compare the speed of the two cyclists.

The vertical axis is always distance.
The horizontal axis is always time.

The distance is always from a particular point, usually the starting point.
The higher up the graph, the further the distance from the starting point.

Time may be the actual time using am and pm or the 24 hour clock.
Time could be the number of minutes or hours from your starting point.

If the graph goes back to the horizontal axis, it shows a return to the starting point.

The **gradient** (steepness) of the line is a measure of speed. The steeper the line the faster the speed. A horizontal line represents a speed of zero (i.e. stopped).

In Chapter 6 you learnt how to find the gradient of a straight line. The same method is used to find speeds from a distance–time graph, i.e. use

$$\text{Speed} = \frac{\text{distance travelled}}{\text{time taken}}$$

For the speed to be worked out in miles per hour the distance must be in miles and the time in hours.

To find the average speed for a whole journey, use

$$\text{Average speed} = \frac{\text{total distance travelled}}{\text{total time taken}}$$

Example: The distance–time graph shows Michael's journey to and from the beach.

a Describe the journey giving reasons for the shape of the graph.

b How far is it to the beach?

c During which part of the journey is Michael travelling the fastest?

d During which part of the journey was Michael most likely to have been held up by road works?

d Calculate Michael's speed in miles per hour for the following sections of the graph

i AB   **ii** BC   **iii** CD   **iv** EF

e What was Michael's average speed for the journey to the beach?

f What was Michael's average speed over the two hours?

Solution:

a Michael left home at *A* and travelled at a constant speed for $\frac{1}{4}$ hour to *B*.

He then travelled at a slower constant speed for $\frac{1}{2}$ hour from *B* to *C*.

He then travelled at a faster constant speed for $\frac{1}{4}$ hour from *C* to *D*.

He then stopped for $\frac{1}{2}$ hour.

Then it took $\frac{1}{2}$ hour to return home from *E* to *F*. The graph returns to the horizontal axis. This shows the return journey home.

b The furthest distance Michael goes from *A* is 20 miles. This is the distance from *A* (home) to *D* (the beach).

c Michael is travelling fastest between *AB* as the gradient (steepness) of the line is greatest then.

d Michael is likely to have been held up by road works between *BC* as he is travelling much slower. The gradient (steepness) of the line is least then.

e **i**   *AB*: In $\frac{1}{4}$ hour, he travels 12.5 miles. In 1 hour he would travel $4 \times 12.5 = 50$ miles
His speed is 50 miles per hour (mph) (as he would travel 50 miles in 1 hour).

ii   *BC*: In $\frac{1}{2}$ hour, he travels 2.5 miles. In 1 hour he would travel $2 \times 2.5 = 5$ miles
His speed is 5 miles per hour (mph).

iii   *CD*: In $\frac{1}{4}$ hour, he travels 5 miles. So in 1 hour he would travel $4 \times 5 = 20$ miles
His speed is 20 miles per hour (mph).

iv   *EF*: In $\frac{1}{2}$ hour, he travels 20 miles. So in 1 hour he would travel $2 \times 20 = 40$ miles
His speed is 40 miles per hour (mph).

e In 1 hour, he travels 20 miles. His average speed is 20 miles per hour (mph)

f For the whole journey the distance travelled is 40 miles (there **and** back). The time taken is 2 hours.

Average speed = total distance ÷ total time = $40 \div 2 = 20$ mph.

> **AQA** *Examiner's tip*
>
> Remember to divide by the time **in hours** when you want to find the average speed in miles per hour, or km per hour.

Practise... 10.1 Distance–time graphs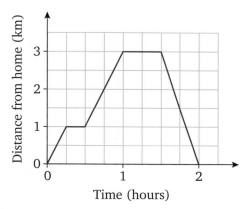

D C B A A*

1 Sam walks to town to buy a CD and then walks home. The distance–time graph shows his journey.

a How far does Sam walk altogether?

b Sam stops to talk to a friend on his way into town. How long does he stop for?

c When is Sam walking at his fastest? What is his average speed for this part of the journey?

> **AQA** *Examiner's tip*
>
> The horizontal axis has 4 squares for each hour. This tells you each square is $\frac{1}{4}$ hour. Remember $\frac{1}{4}$ hour = 0.25 hours.

2   Helen completed a short mountain-bike trail.
The distance–time graph shows her ride.

a   What was the total distance Helen travelled?

b   Helen enjoyed the ride as there was a really fast section.

   i   Between which letters on the graph is this indicated?

   ii   How long was this section? Give your answer in km.

   iii   How long did it take Helen to ride this section?

c   There was one very steep uphill section.

   i   Between which two letters on the graph is this indicated?

   ii   How long was this section?

   iii   How long did it take Helen to get up the hill?

d   Calculate the average speed in km/h for each of the eight sections of the ride.

e   Calculate Helen's average speed for the whole ride.

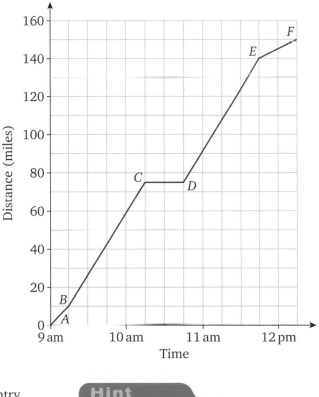

3   A coach travels from Kendal to Birmingham. The journey is shown in the distance–time graph.

a   The coach stops at some services.

   i   What time does it stop at the services?

   ii   How long does the coach stop for?

   iii   How far are the services from Kendal?

b   At what stage on the graph does the coach join the motorway?

c   How far is the coach from Birmingham when it leaves the motorway?

d   Work out the average speed in mph for each of the five stages in the journey.

e   Find the average speed of the coach between Kendal and Birmingham.

4   Giovanni goes for a ride on his bike in the country.

He starts from the car park and rides for 30 minutes at a steady 12 mph.

He then goes up a hill at 8 mph for 15 minutes.

At the top he stops to admire the view for 15 minutes.

He then rides down back to the car park, which takes him 30 minutes.

Work out Giovanni's average speed in mph for the whole journey.

Hint

You may use a distance–time graph to help answer Question 4.

AQA   *Examiner's tip*

When asked to find the average speed in km/h when time is given in minutes remember to divide by the time taken in **hours**.

5 The graph shows the journeys of four students to school in the morning.

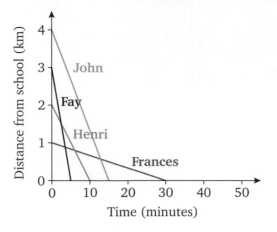

The four students used different ways to get to school.
One student walked, one cycled, one caught the bus and one used the train.

a How did each student travel to school?
Give reasons for your answers.

b Calculate the speed of each student in km/h.

6 Hamish goes for a ride on his bike. His journey is shown in the distance–time graph.

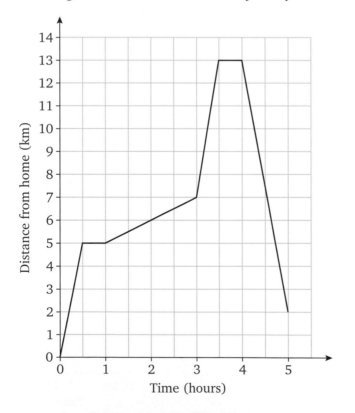

a When did Hamish fall off his bike?

b When was Hamish going fastest?

c Describe his journey in words.

d What was his average speed for the whole journey?

e What could be changed in the graph for his average speed to have been 5 km/h?

f How would the graph be different if Hamish had been unable to cycle after he fell off?

Learn... 10.2 Other real-life graphs

Graphs are useful for tracking changes in a variable such as value, population size, height of a ball or temperature over time.

Examples of graphs

A. Graph showing temperature of a cup of coffee from the time it is made.

C. Graph showing population growth for a population.

B. Graph showing height of a ball from the time it is thrown.

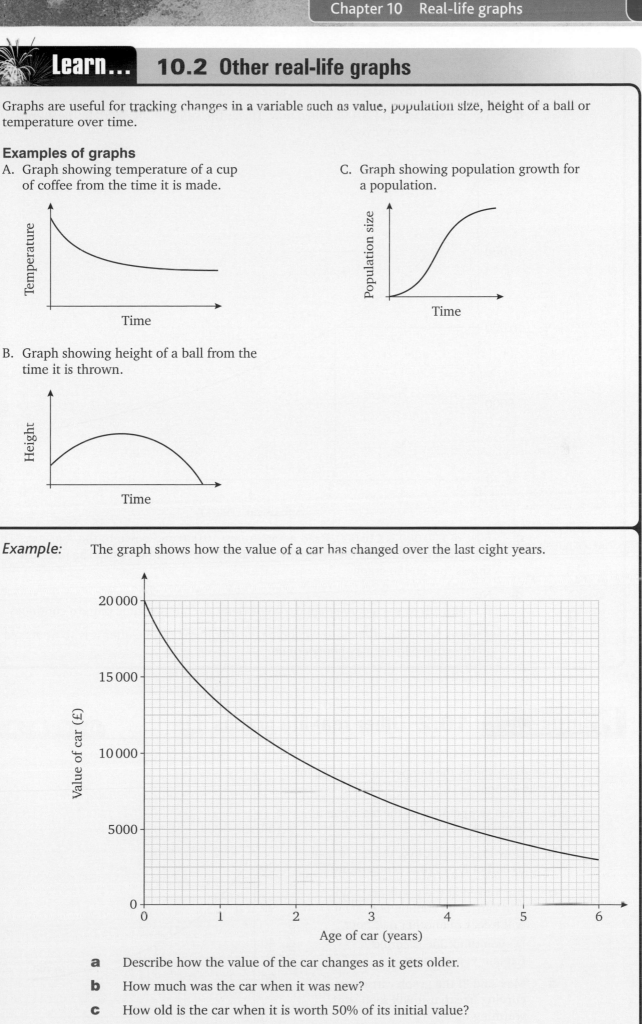

Example: The graph shows how the value of a car has changed over the last eight years.

   a Describe how the value of the car changes as it gets older.

   b How much was the car when it was new?

   c How old is the car when it is worth 50% of its initial value?

   d Is it appropriate to use the graph to find the value of the car when it is 10 years old? Explain your answer.

Solution: **a**   The car starts decreasing in value very quickly at the start. As it gets older its value continues to decrease, but it loses value less quickly.

       b   The car was worth £20 000 when new. This is the value at the 'start' of the graph, when the age was 0 years.

       c   50% of £20 000 is £10 000. Read across from £10 000 and down to the 'Age' axis. The car is almost two years old when it is worth 50% of its initial value. The blue arrow shows this on the graph.

       d   No.
            It is difficult to use a curve to make predictions, even if the same pattern continues.

            There is no information as to what happens to the car's value after it is six years old so the same pattern may not continue.

Practise...   10.2 Other real-life graphs   🕊️   D C B A A*

D

1   The graph shows the temperature of a cup of tea as it cools.

    a   What temperature is the tea when it is made?

    b   How long does it take the tea to cool to half of its original temperature?

    c   Joe looked at the graph and said 'If it carries on cooling like this it will freeze in another half hour'.

        Do you think Joe is correct? Explain your answer.

    d   Max said 'If the graph carries on curving like that it will soon start warming up again'.

        Do you think Max is correct? Explain your answer.

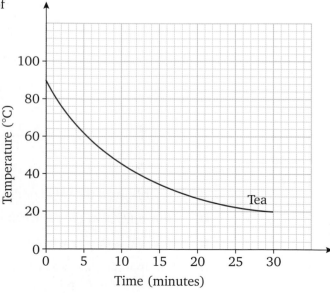

2

The following graph shows how power (kW) and torque (Nm) vary with the speed of the engine (rpm) for a particular car engine.

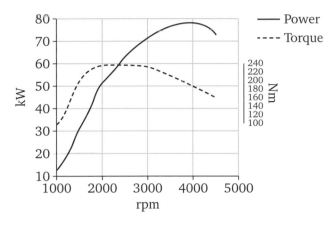

a   John said that the torque was at its highest at 4000 rpm.
What mistake has John made?

b   Describe any pattern in the graph showing torque.

c   Is it appropriate to continue the graph to predict values for 7000 rpm?
Give a reason for your answer.

3

The diagrams below show eight empty bottles. Each bottle is to be filled with water at a constant rate. There are eight graphs, one for each picture. The graph shows how the depth of water, *d*, in each bottle varies with time, *t*.

Match each bottle with its graph.

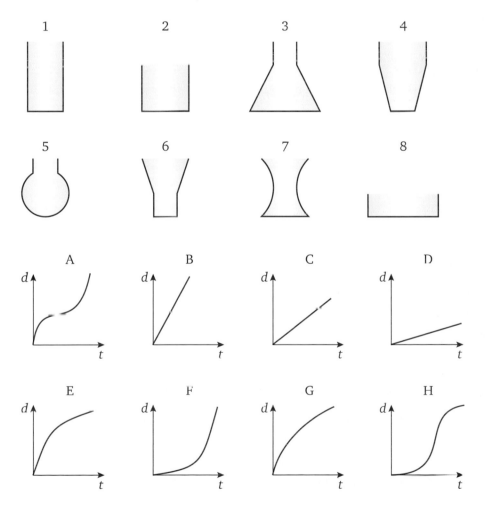

B

4   The following graph shows the depth of water at the end of a pier over a weekend.

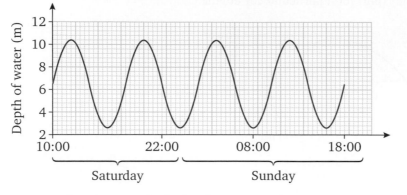

a   At what time are the high tides on Saturday?

b   What is the maximum depth of water at the end of the pier?

c   What is the minimum depth of water at the end of the pier?

d   What is the length of time between consecutive high tides?

e   Cara is on holiday and wants to fish from the end of the pier. She thinks the best time to fish is when the tide has been fully out and is on its way in.
She has to leave at 17:00 on Saturday to go for tea. She has to leave at 12:00 on Sunday for lunch.

How much time will she be able to spend fishing on:

i   Saturday   **ii**   Sunday morning?

f   Wendy sails her boat from the end of the pier.
She needs at least 5 metres of water to launch and land her boat safely.
She launches her boat at 11 o'clock on Saturday morning.

i   How long does she have before she will not be able to land her boat?

ii   If she is late arriving, what is the next earliest time that she will be able to land her boat?

5   The following graph shows the daylight hours throughout the year at Longtown in hours.

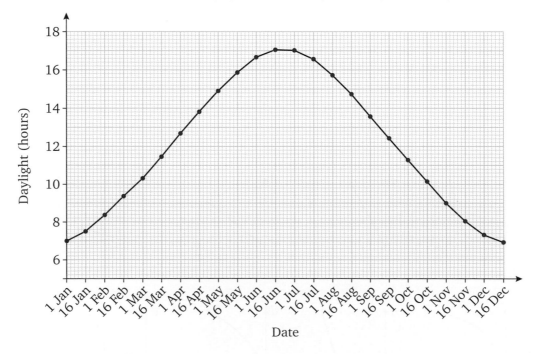

Date

Use the graph to find:

a   the daylight hours for the longest day

b   the daylight hours for the shortest day

c   the number of hours daylight on George's birthday, 16 April.

6   The following graph shows the thinking distances (blue) and stopping distances (red) for different speeds. (Source: Highway Code.)

The thinking distance is the distance travelled by a car between the driver deciding to brake and actually starting to brake.

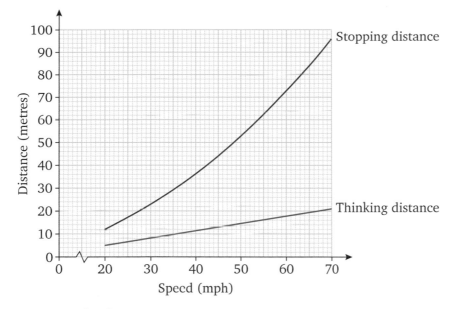

a   Describe the patterns in:

   i   the thinking distance

   ii   the stopping distances.

b   Use the graph to find:

   i   the thinking distance for a car travelling at 40 mph

   ii   the thinking distance for a car travelling at 55 mph

   iii   the **stopping** distance for a car travelling at 30 mph

   iv   the **stopping** distance for a car travelling at 40 mph.

c   The braking distance is the difference between the thinking distance and the stopping distance.

Fred said 'the braking distance for travelling at 60 mph is two times the braking distance for travelling at 30 mph'. Is Fred correct? Explain your answer.

7

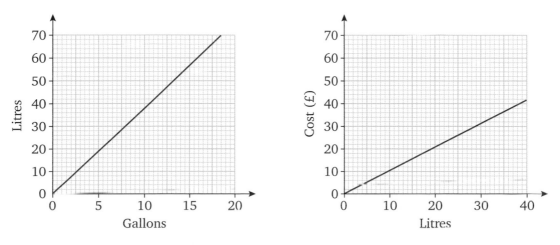

Andrew is filling his car with fuel.
The tank will hold 15.5 gallons when full.
The car's trip computer said the car had 3 litres left in the tank when he stopped at the filling station.

How much will it cost Andrew to fill his car's fuel tank?

10 Assess

D
C

1   Colin takes his dog Ben for a walk over Cartmel Fell.
The distance–time graph shows his distance from home.

a   What time did Colin and Ben set off?

b   Colin had his lunch the first time they stopped.

    i   What time was this?

    ii   How long did they stop for lunch?

c   What was their average speed in km per hour before lunch?

d   On the way back they stopped several times for Colin to admire the view.
At what times did Colin make these stops?

e   How far did they walk?

f   What was their average speed in km/h for the whole walk?

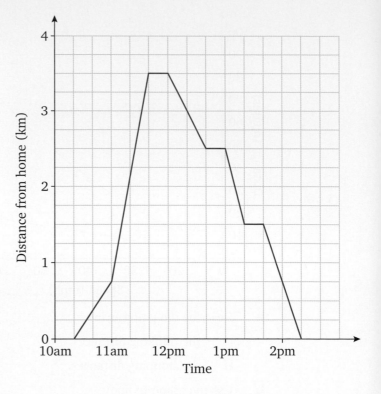

2   Sophie and Beckie are running to keep fit.

a   Beckie and Sophie go for a training run one night. Describe their runs.

b   What does the graph show about Sophie between *A* and *B*?
Give a possible reason for this.

c   Work out Sophie's average speed in miles per hour for the whole run.

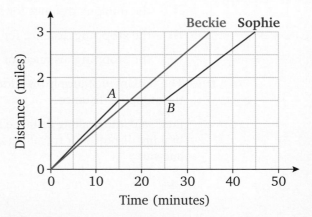

C

3   The graph shows the journey of a car as it accelerates and then slows down.

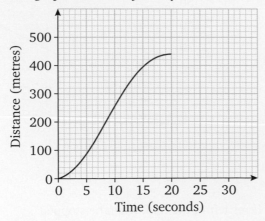

Calculate the average speed of the car for this journey.
State your units clearly.

4   Paul lives 10 miles from the nearest railway station. It takes him 30 minutes to drive to the station in his car. He travels at a constant speed.

a   He sets off at 15:10 to meet his son at the station. Copy the axes and draw a distance–time graph to show his journey.

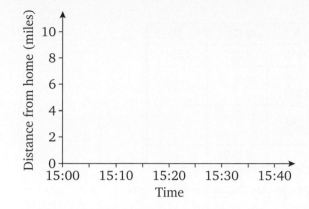

b   Paul's son Sam arrives at the station at 15:00 and starts to walk home. He walks at a steady 4 mph.
Add a graph of his walk to your distance–time graph.

c   Assuming Paul and Sam take the same route:

i   what time do they meet?

ii   how far has Sam walked when they meet?

5   The graph shows the path of a cricket ball through the air when thrown.

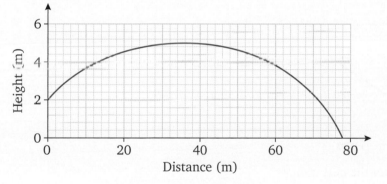

a   What was the total distance thrown?

b   What was the maximum height reached by the ball?

c   What horizontal distance had been travelled when the ball was at its highest?

d   Give a possible reason why the height of the ball started at 2 metres.

AQA Examination-style questions

1   This is part of a train timetable.

Train		A	B	C	D
Eastville	*depart*	0915	0948	1021	1054
Fraize	*arrive*	0927	1000		1109
	depart	0930	1003	↓	
Gamstone	*arrive*	1025	1058	↓	
	depart	1028			
Hunby	*arrive*	1055		1140	

a   Which train, A, B, C or D, is shown in this distance–time graph?

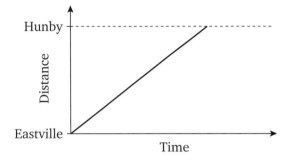

                                               (1 mark)

b   Which train is shown this distance–time graph?

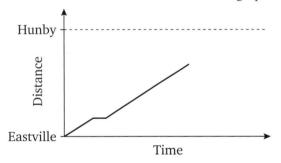

                                               (1 mark)

c   Here is the timetable for the next train.

Train		E
Eastville	*depart*	1135
Fraize	*arrive*	1147
	depart	1150
Gamstone	*arrive*	↓
	depart	
Hunby	*arrive*	1310

Copy the axes below. Sketch the distance–time graph for train E.

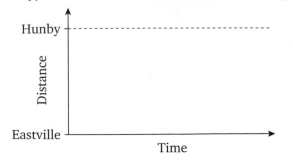

                                               (2 marks)

AQA 2006

2   Viki has a mobile phone contract.
       It has a basic monthly charge and some free minutes.
       The graph shows how the total monthly charge is calculated for her mobile phone
       contract for up to 500 minutes of calls.

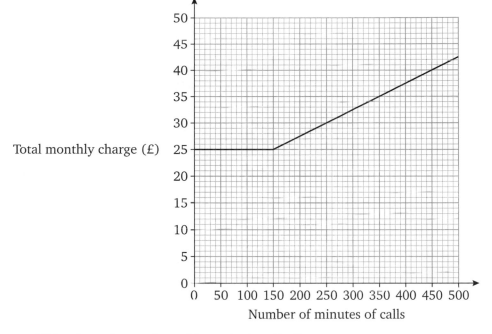

Total monthly charge (£)

Number of minutes of calls

a   Write down the number of free minutes of calls.   (1 mark)

b   Work out the charge per minute for the other calls.   (3 marks)

AQA 2009

Formulae

Objectives

Examiners would normally expect students who get these grades to be able to:

D

substitute numbers into formulae such as

$$C = \frac{(A + 1)D}{9}$$

derive complex expressions and formulae

distinguish between an expression, an equation, an identity and a formula

C

rearrange linear formulae such as $p = 3q + 5$

B

rearrange formulae involving brackets, indices, fractions and square roots

A

rearrange formulae where the variable appears twice.

I used the formula: cooking time = 20 per pound weight + 20 to work out how long the chicken needed. Perhaps the time should have been in minutes not hours!

Did you know?

Formulae can be very useful

Formulae are used in everyday life, for example in cooking instructions. Be careful to check that the units you are working with make sense!

You should already know:

✔ order of operations (BIDMAS)

✔ the four rules applied to negative numbers

✔ the four rules applied to fractions

✔ how to calculate the squares, cubes and other powers of numbers

✔ how to write simple formulae using letters and symbols

✔ how to simplify expressions

✔ how to expand brackets such as $4(x + 2)$

✔ how to factorise expressions

✔ how to solve linear equations.

Key terms

formula
expression
substitute
equation
identity
term
subject

Learn... 11.1 Substitution and writing formulae 🄺

When you write **formulae** you need to remember the following.

If a stands for a number then $2 \times a$ can be written as $2a$. Write the number in front of the letter.

The **expression** $3x + 5$ means multiply x by 3 then add 5.

The expression $5(y - 2)$ means subtract 2 from y then multiply the answer by 5.

To **substitute** numbers into a formula, always write down the formula first. Then replace the letters with the values you are given, and write this down. Then start the working out.

AQA *Examiner's tip*

You can use brackets to help you do calculations in the correct order.

Remember BIDMAS applies to algebra as well as arithmetic.

AQA *Examiner's tip*

Be careful when you choose your own letters in problems. Some letters are easily confused with numbers.

Z and 2 can get confused.

I and 1 can get confused.

b and 6 can get confused.

q and 9 can get confused.

S and 5 can get confused.

Example: Georgia is using the formula $s = ut + \frac{1}{2}at^2$ in science. She needs to find s when

    a $u = 2, t = 3, a = 0.5$ **b** $u = 5, a = -1, t = 6$

Solution: **a** $s = ut + \frac{1}{2}at^2$ Write the formula down first.

         $s = 2 \times 3 + \frac{1}{2} \times 0.5 \times 3^2$ Replace the letters by their values.

         $s = 6 + 2.25$

         $s = 8.25$

    b $s = ut + \frac{1}{2}at^2$

         $s = 5 \times 6 + \frac{1}{2} \times (-1) \times 6^2$ Using brackets can help with signs.

         $s = 30 - 18$

         $s = 12$

AQA *Examiner's tip*

Remember to show all stages of your working; you gain method marks for this in an examination.

Example: A rectangle is 5 cm longer than it is wide. The width is c.
Show that the area of the rectangle can be found using the formula $A = c^2 + 5c$

Solution: For a rectangle, area is length multiplied by width.

The width is c.

The length is $c + 5$.

Area = length $\times$ width

Area = $(c + 5) \times c$

Area = $c^2 + 5c$

Example: The instructions for cooking a lamb joint are as follows.

Allow 60 minutes for each kg plus an extra 30 minutes.

    a   Write a formula for this rule. Use w for the weight in kg and t for the time needed in minutes.

    b   How much time is needed to cook a lamb joint weighing 750 g?

    c   Rachel is cooking a lamb joint. It has already been in the oven for 90 minutes. She correctly works out that it needs a further 45 minutes. How much does the lamb joint weigh?

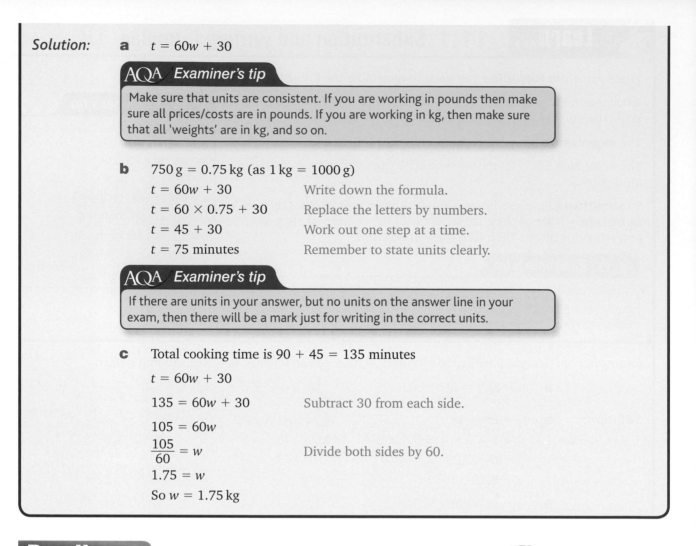

Solution:

a $t = 60w + 30$

> **AQA** *Examiner's tip*
>
> Make sure that units are consistent. If you are working in pounds then make sure all prices/costs are in pounds. If you are working in kg, then make sure that all 'weights' are in kg, and so on.

b $750\,g = 0.75\,kg$ (as $1\,kg = 1000\,g$)

$t = 60w + 30$	Write down the formula.
$t = 60 \times 0.75 + 30$	Replace the letters by numbers.
$t = 45 + 30$	Work out one step at a time.
$t = 75$ minutes	Remember to state units clearly.

> **AQA** *Examiner's tip*
>
> If there are units in your answer, but no units on the answer line in your exam, then there will be a mark just for writing in the correct units.

c   Total cooking time is $90 + 45 = 135$ minutes

$t = 60w + 30$	
$135 = 60w + 30$	Subtract 30 from each side.
$105 = 60w$	
$\dfrac{105}{60} = w$	Divide both sides by 60.
$1.75 = w$	
So $w = 1.75\,kg$	

Practise... 11.1 Substitution and writing formulae 🔑 D C B A A*

D

1   A particular type of coach has 56 seats.

   a   How many seats are there on 2 coaches?

   b   How many seats are there on 3 coaches?

   c   Write down a formula showing how to work out the number of seats from the number of coaches. Use S for the number of seats and C for the number of coaches.

2   Write down a formula for the total cost of:

   a x lollies at 70p each and y lollies at 80p each

   b c cakes at 90p each and b biscuits at 20p each.
Use T for the total cost.
Why is it not a good idea to use C for the total cost in part **b**?

3   A cookery book gives this rule to roast a chicken.

> **Total time = 40 minutes per kilogram plus 20 minutes**

Write a formula for the time needed to roast a chicken using this rule.
Use w for the weight in kg and t for the time in minutes.

4   Kate has £2 to spend. She buys x biros at y pence each.

   a   Write down an expression for the total amount she spends.

   b   Write down a formula for the amount of change she receives. Use C to stand for her change in pence.

D

5   Phil bought x cups of tea and y cups of coffee from his local cafe for himself and his friends. The tea cost 80p per cup, and the coffee cost 90p per cup.

Which one of the following could be a formula for the total cost in pence, C?

$C = 90x + 80y$

$C = 80x + 90y$

$C = 80x90y$

Explain your answer, and state why the other formulae are not correct.

6   PizzaQuick works out its delivery charge with the following formula.

Delivery charge (£) = number of pizzas × 0.75 + 1.50

a   Work out the delivery charge for three pizzas.

b   Richard pays a delivery charge of £6. How many pizzas did he order?

c   Mary is charged £8 for delivery. Explain how you know that Mary was not charged correctly?

7   Mrs Bujjit is working out the wages at the factory. She uses the following formula.

Wages equal hours worked multiplied by rate per hour.

a   Write this formula in algebra.

b   How much does Ellen earn if she is paid £7 an hour and she works for 30 hours?

c   How much does Francis earn if he works for 25 hours and is paid £8 an hour?

d   How many hours did Ruth work if her hourly rate is £12.50 and she earned £475?

8   In geography, Fiona is converting degrees Fahrenheit into degrees Celsius.

She uses the formula: $C = \dfrac{5(F - 32)}{9}$

Find C if:

a $F = 77$ **b** $F = 32$ **c** $F = -31$ **d** $F = -13$

9   The rule for finding out how far away thunderstorms are is:

'Count the number of seconds between the lightning and the thunder. Divide the answer by 5. The answer gives the distance in miles.'

a   Write a formula for this rule.
Use s to stand for the number of seconds and d to stand for the distance in miles.

b   In a thunderstorm, Jan counts 12 seconds between lightning and thunder. How far away is the thunderstorm?

c   Jamie counts for 8 seconds. A thunderstorm is 3.5 miles away. How many more seconds does he have to wait before he hears the thunder?

10   Rachel is doing an experiment in science. She uses the following formula.

Average speed $= \dfrac{\text{Total distance travelled}}{\text{Total time taken}}$

She uses this formula to work out that if an object has an average speed of 20 m/s and travels for 10 seconds then it must have travelled 2 m.

What mistake has Rachel made?

C

11 Sean and Dee organise a quiz evening.

A quiz team is made up of four people.

Each team is charged £8 to enter the quiz.

Sean and Dee spend £20 on prizes and £25 on food and drink.

There are x teams at the quiz evening.

On average, each team member spends £3 on refreshments.

Write down an expression in x for the profit they make.

12 Use the formula $v = ut - \frac{1}{2}at^2$ to find v when:

a $u = 2, t = 3, a = 4$

b $u = 12, t = 2, a = -6$

c $u = 1, t = 3, a = -2$

! 13 Tom is calculating the interest on some savings.

He uses I to stand for interest in the formula $I = \dfrac{PTR}{100}$

a If the principal (P) = £300, the time (T) = 2 years and the rate (R) = 0.5%, calculate the interest.

b How long would he have to save if he wanted £45 interest?

! 14 Natland Taxis use the formula $C = 3m + 4.5$ to work out the cost of journeys for customers.

C is the total charge in pounds and m is the number of miles for the journey.

Every journey has a minimum charge and a charge for each mile.

a What is Natland Taxis' minimum charge?

b What is the cost per mile?

15 Sedgwick Tool Hire charge £18 to hire a cement mixer for 1 day.
They charge £9 for every extra day.

Harry says the formula for the total charge is $C = 18d + 9$
He uses d for the number of days and C for the total charge.

a Explain why Harry's formula is not correct.

b Write down what Harry's formula should be.

c Use the internet to find some costs for tool hire.
Write down some formulae for the cost of tool hire.

Learn...   11.2 Changing the subject of a formula   (k!)

You need to be able to identify whether an algebraic statement is a **formula**, an **equation**, an **expression** or an **identity**.

A **formula** tells you how to work something out. It can be written using words or symbols and will always have an equals sign. There will be at least two letters involved.

For example: **Area of a rectangle is equal to length multiplied by width** is a formula in words.

$A = L \times W$ is the same formula in symbols, where A stands for area, L for length and W for width.
From this formula, you can work out the area of any rectangle if you know its length and width. L and W can have any value.
You can tell this is a formula, it tells you what to do with L and W to work out, A. There is an equals sign, and there are more than 2 two letters being used.

An **equation** is two expressions separated by an equals sign. You are often asked to solve an equation, in which case there will be only one letter, but it may appear more than once.

For example, $x + 3 = 7$ is an equation, x is equal to 4. This is the only possible value of x as any other number added to 3 does not equal 7.

You can tell this is an equation, there is an expression on each side of the equals sign. There is only one letter involved. It can be solved to find a value of x.

Formulae and equations can sometimes look very similar.

An **expression** is just a collection of **terms**. An expression does not have an equals sign.

For example: $3x + 2y - 5$ is an expression.

You can tell this is an expression as it is just a collection of terms. There is no equals sign.

An **identity** is a statement that is true whatever the value of the symbols.
For example: $3x + 4x \equiv 7x$ is always true ($\equiv$ is the identity symbol).

Changing the subject of a formula

The **subject** of a formula is the letter on the left-hand side of the equals sign.

P is the subject of the formula $P = 3L + 2$

You can change the subject of this formula to make L the subject.
You will then have a formula telling you what to do to P to work out L.
You use the same strategies that you learned when you solved equations.

> **Hint**
> Remember that what you do to one side of an equation, you must also do to the other side.

Example: **a**   Make L the subject of the formula $P = 3L + 2$

b   Make r the subject of the formula $M = nr^2$

c   Make x the subject of each of the following formulae.

     i $c(5 - x) = e$ **ii** $f = \sqrt{\dfrac{h + i}{x}}$ **iii** $\dfrac{a + bx}{cx} = d$

Solution: **a**

$P = 3L + 2$	Write the formula down first.
$P - 2 = 3L + 2 - 2$	Subtract 2 from both sides.
$P - 2 = 3L$	
$\dfrac{P - 2}{3} = \dfrac{3L}{3}$	Divide both sides by 3.
$\dfrac{P - 2}{3} = L$	
$L = \dfrac{P - 2}{3}$	Put L on the left hand side as the subject of the formula.

b

$M = nr^2$	Write the formula down first.
$\dfrac{M}{n} = r^2$	Divide both sides by n.
$\pm\sqrt{\dfrac{M}{n}} = r$	Take the square root of both sides (remember the square root of a number can be + or −).
$r = \pm\sqrt{\dfrac{M}{n}}$	Rewrite the formula with r as the subject.

c   **i**

$c(5 - x) = e$	Write the formula down first.
$5c - cx = e$	Multiply out the brackets.
$5c = e + cx$	Add cx to both sides (to get a positive term involving x).
$5c - e = cx$	Subtract e from both sides.
$\dfrac{5c - e}{c} = x$	Divide both sides by c.
$x = \dfrac{5c - e}{c}$	Rewrite with x as the subject.

ii

$$f = \sqrt{\frac{h + i}{x}}$$ Write the formula down first.

$$f^2 = \frac{h + i}{x}$$ Square both sides.

$$f^2 x = h + i$$ Multiply both sides by x.

$$x = \frac{h + i}{f^2}$$ Divide both sides by f^2.

iii

$$\frac{a + bx}{cx} = d$$ Write the formula down first.

This formula is different to the others, as the 'new' subject, x, appears twice.

$$a + bx = dcx$$ Multiply both sides by cx.

$$a = dcx - bx$$ Subtract bx from both sides. (This gathers all the terms in x on one side of the equal sign.)

$$a = x(dc - b)$$ Factorise (you only take the x out as common factor here. It is important to get the x on its own.)

$$\frac{a}{(dc - b)} = x$$ Divide both sides by the contents of the bracket (leaving just x on its own).

$$x = \frac{a}{(dc - b)}$$ Rewrite to make x the subject.

Bump up your grade

To get a Grade C you need to learn how to rearrange formulae.

11.2 Changing the subject of a formula

Practise...

D C B A A*

D

1 In this chapter you will have met these words:

expression, formula, equation, identity.

Choose the correct word to describe each of the following.

a $p = a + b + c + d$ **e** $5 = 1 - 2q$

b $2x + 5y - 4z$ **f** $9k - 3$

c $7m + 3m \equiv 10m$ **g** $c = 25h - 9$

d $3h = 6$ **h** $3z + 5 = 26$

C

2 Rearrange the formula $M = n + 42$ to make n the subject.

3 Rearrange each of these formulae to make y the subject.

a $5 + y = c$ **b** $64 + 2y = f$ **c** $d = 24 + 3y$ **d** $j = 4y - 3k$

4 Rearrange each of these formulae to make x the subject.

a $gx + t^2 = s^2$ **c** $kx - 19 = n$

b $m = 7x - 49$ **d** $y - x = 50$

5 Which of the following is a correct rearrangement of $m = 4x - 3$?

A $x = \frac{m - 3}{4}$ **C** $x = \frac{m - 4}{3}$ **E** $x = \frac{3 - m}{4}$

B $x = \frac{m + 3}{4}$ **D** $x = m + \frac{3}{4}$ **F** $x = \frac{m + 4}{3}$

6 Sam rearranges the formula $y = \dfrac{3}{x}$ to make x the subject.

She gets the answer $x = \dfrac{y}{3}$

Is she correct? Give a reason for your answer.

7 The formula for finding the speed of an object is $s = \dfrac{d}{t}$ where s stands for speed, d for distance and t for time.

   a Rearrange the formula to make d the subject.

   b Rearrange the formula to make t the subject. (It may be easier to use your answer to part **a** as your starting point.)

8 Rearrange each of these formulae to make x the subject.

   a $x^2 - b = 9$

   b $ax^2 = y$

   c $gx^2 - c = d$

9 Anne is using the formula $V = \pi r^2 h$ to find r.

She rearranges the formula and gets $r = \dfrac{\sqrt{V}}{\pi h}$

Is she correct?

Give a reason for your answer.

10 Rearrange these formulae to make x the subject.

   a $f(x + g) = h$ **c** $r + s - t\sqrt{x}$

   b $l = m(n - x)$ **d** $a = 3x + bx$

! 11 The formula to find the length of the diagonal, d, of a rectangle l units long and w units wide is $d = \sqrt{l^2 + w^2}$

   a Make l the subject of the formula.

   b Find the length of l when $d = 30\,cm$ and $w = 18\,cm$.

! 12 Rearrange the formula $y = \dfrac{x + a}{x - a}$ to make x the subject.

! 13 Brian and Amy are rearranging the formula $T = 2\pi\sqrt{\dfrac{l}{g}}$ to make l the subject.

Brian gets $l = \dfrac{T^2 g}{2\pi}$ for his answer and Amy gets $l = \dfrac{T^2 g}{4\pi}$

Is either of them correct? Give a reason for your answer.

! 14 Make the letter in square brackets the subject of the formula.

   a $x(a - b) = h(a - x)$ $[x]$

   b $E = \frac{1}{2}m(v^2 - u^2)$ $[u]$

15 **a** Find a formula for the sum (S) of three consecutive whole numbers $n, n + 1,$ and $n + 2$.

   b Rearrange the formula to make n the subject.

   c Find the three consecutive whole numbers whose sum is 369.

? 16 Choose a 2 × 2 square from the grid.
Draw the square and add opposite corners.

For example:

1	2	3	4	5	6
7	8	9	10	11	12
13	14	15	16	17	18
19	20	21	22	23	24
25	26	27	28	29	30
31	32	33	34	35	36

| 14 | 15 | $14 + 21 = 35$
|----|----|
| 20 | 21 | $15 + 20 = 35$

Try some more 2 × 2 squares from this grid.

This square
n	
$n+6$	
is from this grid.

Fill in the missing numbers. Write down a formula for the diagonal sum, d, in terms of n.

What happens for 3 × 3 squares?

4 × 4 squares?

Try this for a larger grid such as this one.

1	2	3	4	5	6	7
8	9	10	11	12	13
15	16	17

Extend this to a grid g units wide.

11 Assess

D
C

1 The formula for a sequence is $t_n = 5n - 3$, where t_n is the nth term.

a Use this formula to find the 7th term in the sequence.

b Which term in the sequence is equal to 92?

2 A cup of coffee costs £1.80 and a cup of tea costs £1.20 at Strickland's snack bar.

a Write a formula for the total cost, T, of x coffees and y teas.

b Janet buys 3 coffees and 4 teas. Use your formula to find the total cost of these drinks.

3 Jessica is x years old.
Paul is 2 years older than Jessica.

a Write down an expression for Paul's age.

b Nick is three times as old as Paul.

Write down an expression for Nick's age.

4 Wooden joists are used in houses to support ceilings and floors.

The safety rule for joists 2 inches wide is:

'find depth in inches by dividing the span in feet by two, then add two to the result'

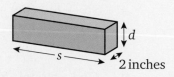

Lynn is a builder.

a Write down a formula that Lynn could use showing depth in terms of span.

b Find d when s is 16 feet.

c If d is 8 inches what is the largest span this rule allows?

5 George is using the formula $K = \dfrac{5(F - 32)}{9} + 273$

   a Find K if $F = 41$

   b Find F if $K = 303$

   c Make F the subject of the formula.

6 Rearrange the formula $m = 4(3c + d) - 1$ to make c the subject.

7 Make y the subject of the straight-line equation $3x + 4y = 12$

8 Make c the subject of the formula $E = mc^2$

9 Make x the subject of the following formulae.

   a $y - x^2 = 9$

   b $y = \sqrt{x}$

   c $3y = 2x^2 + 3$

   d $5y - 2x = mx + 4$

10 A shop uses the following formula to work out the total cost when customers pay by instalments.

$d = 0.1C$

$C = d + 36m$

C is the total cost in pounds.
d is the deposit in pounds.
m is the monthly payment in pounds.

The total cost of a chair is £800.

Work out the monthly payments.

AQA Examination-style questions 🔑

1 A shopkeeper uses this formula to calculate the total cost when customers pay by monthly instalments.

$$C = d + 24 \times m$$

C is the total cost in pounds.
d is the deposit in pounds.
m is the monthly instalment in pounds.

   a The deposit for a wardrobe is £16.
      The monthly payments are £10.
      What is the total cost? *(2 marks)*

   b How many years does it take to finish paying for goods using this formula? *(1 mark)*

   c The total cost of a sofa is £600.
      The deposit is £120.
      Work out the value of the monthly instalment. *(3 marks)*

AQA 2009

2   A teacher sets an extended task.
Any task that is handed in late has the original mark reduced using this formula.

$$R = \frac{(N + 9) \times M}{40}$$

R is the reduction.
N is the number of days late.
M is the original mark.

a   Adam hands in his task one day late.
His original mark is 32.
Work out his new mark.   *(3 marks)*

b   Belinda hands in her task 5 days late.
Her mark is reduced by 7 marks.
Work out her original mark.   *(3 marks)*

AQA 2008

Objectives

Examiners would normally expect students who get these grades to be able to:

C

solve a problem using step by step deductions

B

factorise an expression such as $x^2 - 5x + 14$ or $x^2 - 9$

solve an equation such as $x^2 - 5x + 14 = 0$

A

factorise an expression such as $3x^2 + 7x + 2$ or $3x^2 - 27$

simplify an expression such as $\dfrac{x^2 + 3x + 2}{x^2 - 1}$ by factorising

solve an equation such as $3x^2 + 7x + 2 = 0$ by factorising

derive a proof using reasoning and logic

A*

solve an equation such as $\dfrac{3}{x - 2} + \dfrac{4}{x - 1} = 2$

solve an equation such as $x^2 - 8x + 11 = 0$ by completing the square.

Key terms

quadratic expression   coefficient

factorise   consecutive

expand

Did you know?

Quadratic equations

The history of algebra began in ancient Egypt and Babylon. People there learned to solve linear ($ax = b$) and quadratic ($ax^2 + bx = c$) equations, as well as equations such as $x^2 + y^2 = z^2$. The use of quadratic equations can be traced back to 2000 BCE when they were solved by methods like the ones used today.

You should already know:

✔ how to collect like terms

✔ how to multiply brackets by a single term

✔ how to multiply two brackets together

✔ how to solve a linear equation

✔ how to simplify algebraic fractions.

Learn... 12.1 Factorising quadratic expressions (k!)

A quadratic expression is always in the form $ax^2 + bx + c$

Factorising is the inverse operation to **expanding**.

Example: If the answer is $x^2 + 5x + 6$, what was in the brackets?

Solution:

×	x	?
x	x^2	
?		$+6$

To get x^2, the brackets must start with x and x.

To get $+6$, the second terms must multiply to $+6$, so could be:

+ 1 and + 6
or + 2 and + 3
or − 1 and − 6
or − 2 and − 3

Possible factors: $(x + 1)(x + 6)$
$(x + 2)(x + 3)$
$(x − 1)(x − 6)$
$(x − 2)(x − 3)$

Each pair of brackets multiplies to x^2 . . . . $+ 6$ but only one multiplies to $x^2 + 5x + 6$

Check them by multiplying out.

Notice that the brackets with negative numbers will not produce a middle term of $+ 5x$

The factors are $(x + 2)(x + 3)$.

Example: If the answer is $y^2 + 3y − 10$, what was in the brackets?

Solution:

×	y	?
y	y^2	
?		-10

To get y^2, the brackets must start with y and y

To get $−10$, the second terms must multiply to $−10$, so could be:

+ 1 and − 10
or + 2 and − 5
or − 1 and + 10
or − 2 and + 5

Possible factors: $(y + 1)(y − 10)$
$(y + 2)(y − 5)$
$(y − 1)(y + 10)$
$(y − 2)(y + 5)$

> AQA **Examiner's tip**
>
> If you can multiply out brackets correctly, then you can factorise correctly too.
>
> Always check your answer by multiplying out to see if you arrive back at the quadratic.

Each pair of brackets multiplies to y^2 . . . . $− 10$ but only one multiplies to $y^2 + 3y − 10$

Check them by multiplying out.

The factors are $(y − 2)(y + 5)$.

The difference of two squares

These are quadratic expressions like $a^2 - 9$, $b^2 - 25$, $x^2 - y^2$

They have no bx term.

Example: Factorise $a^2 - 9$

Solution: $a^2 - 9 = a^2 - 3^2$

To get a^2, the brackets must start with a and a.

To get -9, the second terms must multiply to -9.

so could be:

$+ 1$ and $- 9$

or $- 1$ and $+ 9$

or $+ 3$ and $- 3$

If the term in a has vanished, it must have been made up from $+ 3a$ and $- 3a$.

The factors are $(a + 3)(a - 3)$.

Practise... 12.1 Factorising quadratic expressions *k!* D C B A A*

B

Factorise:

1 $a^2 + 9a + 20$

2 $b^2 + 10b + 24$

3 $c^2 - 9c + 18$

4 $d^2 - 7d + 12$

5 $e^2 + 8e - 20$

6 $f^2 + 4f - 21$

7 $m^2 - 2m - 15$

8 $n^2 - n - 20$

9 $p^2 + 6p + 9$

10 $q^2 - 4q + 4$

11 $r^2 - 4$

12 $v^2 - 49$

13 $w^2 - 5w - 24$

14 $x^2 + 10x - 24$

15 $y^2 + y - 30$

16 $t^2 - 4t - 32$

17 $h^2 + 7h - 18$

18 $k^2 - 13k + 22$

19 $x^2 + 23x + 42$

20 $y^2 + 2y - 63$

⚠ 21 Factorise:

a $x^2 - 5xy + 4y^2$ b $p^2 + pq - 12q^2$ c $a^2 - b^2$ d $4c^2 - 25d^2$

? 22 Use your knowledge of the difference of two squares to work out:

a $31^2 - 30^2$ b $57^2 - 43^2$

? 23 The factors of $x^2 + kx + 12$ are $(x + a)(x + b)$ where a and b are positive integers.

Show that there are three possible values of k.

? 24 The factors of $y^2 + nx - 15$ are $(y + c)(y + d)$ where c and d are integers.

Show that there are four possible values of n.

Learn... 12.2 Factorising harder quadratic expressions

In this section, the **coefficient** of x^2 is not equal to 1, so the brackets will not both start with x. There may be many possible pairs of brackets.

Example: Factorise $2x^2 + 15x + 7$

Solution:

×	2x	?
x	$2x^2$	
?		+7

To get $2x^2$, the brackets must start with $2x$ and x.

To get $+7$, the second terms must multiply to $+7$, so could be:

    $+1$ and $+7$.

or -1 and -7

However, -1 and -7 will not give $+15x$ as the middle term.

Possible factors: $(2x + 1)(x + 7)$

                  $(2x + 7)(x + 1)$

Each pair of brackets multiplies to $2x^2 + \ldots\ldots + 7$ but only one multiplies to $2x^2 + 15x + 7$

Check them by multiplying out.

The factors are $(2x + 1)(x + 7)$.

Example: Factorise: $6y^2 - 5y - 4$

Solution:

×	2y	?
3y		
?		−4

or

×	y	?
6y		
?		−4

To get $6y^2$, the brackets could start with $2y$ and $3y$, or with y and $6y$.

To get -4, the second terms must multiply to -4, so could be:

    $+2$ and -2

or $+1$ and -4

or -1 and $+4$

Possible factors: $(2y + 2)(3y - 2)$ $(y + 2)(6y - 2)$

                  $(2y - 2)(3y + 2)$ $(y - 2)(6y + 2)$

                  $(2y + 1)(3y - 4)$ $(y + 1)(6y - 4)$

                  $(2y - 1)(3y + 4)$ $(y - 1)(6y + 4)$

                  $(2y + 4)(3y - 1)$ $(y + 4)(6y - 1)$

                  $(2y - 4)(3y + 1)$ $(y - 4)(6y + 1)$

Each pair of brackets multiplies to $6y^2 + \ldots\ldots - 4$ but only one multiplies to $6y^2 - 5y - 4$

Check them by multiplying out.

The factors are $(2y + 1)(3y - 4)$.

Example: Factorise completely $6z^2 - 26z - 20$

Solution: This quadratic has the factor 2.

$6z^2 - 26z - 20 = 2(3z^2 - 13z - 10)$

The factors of $3z^2 - 13z - 10$ are $(3z + 2)(z - 5)$.

The factors of $6z^2 - 26z - 20$ are $2(3z + 2)(z - 5)$.

AQA *Examiner's tip*

You will be told to 'factorise completely' when there are three factors. Don't forget to write all three factors in your answer.

12.2 Factorising harder quadratic expressions

Practise...

D C B A A*

Factorise:

1 $2a^2 + 7a + 3$

2 $3b^2 + 5b + 2$

3 $2c^2 - 5c + 3$

4 $5d^2 - 2d + 7$

5 $7e^2 - 2e - 5$

6 $3f^2 + f - 2$

7 $2x^2 - 7x - 4$

8 $3y^2 + 7y - 6$

9 $5m^2 - 11m - 12$

10 $3n^2 - 28n + 9$

11 $5p^2 + 13p + 6$

12 $2q^2 + 15q + 18$

13 $4t^2 - 12t + 9$

14 $9u^2 + 30u + 25$

15 $4v^2 + 8v + 3$

16 $4w^2 - 21w + 5$

17 $4x^2 - 9$

18 $9y^2 - 25$

A

Factorise completely:

19 $2x^2 + 10x + 8$

20 $3y^2 - 9y + 6$

21 $5z^2 - 45$

22 $3b^2 - 27$

Factorise:

! 23 $2x^2 + 7xy - 15y^2$

! 24 $4p^2 + pq - 5q^2$

25 One of the factors of $3x^2 + kx + 8$ is $(x + 2)$.

Find the value of k.

26 One of the factors of $5y^2 - y - n$ is $(5y + 1)$.

Find the value of n.

Learn... 12.3 Simplifying algebraic fractions

To simplify algebraic fractions, you should factorise the numerator and/or the denominator. Then divide the numerator and denominator by common factors.

Example: Simplify $\dfrac{x^2 + 3x + 2}{x^2 - 1}$

Solution:

Factorise the numerator $x^2 + 3x + 2 = (x + 1)(x + 2)$

Factorise the denominator $x^2 - 1 = (x - 1)(x + 1)$

Rewrite the fraction as $\dfrac{(x + 1)(x + 2)}{(x - 1)(x + 1)}$

Divide top and bottom by the common factor $\dfrac{\cancel{(x + 1)}(x + 2)}{(x - 1)\cancel{(x + 1)}} = \dfrac{x + 2}{x - 1}$

AQA Examiner's tip

If there is no common factor in a question like this you are likely to have made an error.

Practise... 12.3 Simplifying algebraic fractions 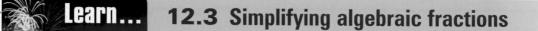 D C B A A*

Simplify:

1 $\dfrac{c^2 + 2c + 1}{4c + 4}$

2 $\dfrac{y^2 - 4}{3y - 6}$

3 $\dfrac{w^2 - 4w + 4}{5w - 10}$

4 $\dfrac{t^2 + 11t + 18}{t^2 + 9t + 14}$

5 $\dfrac{x^2 + 3x - 4}{x^2 + 7x + 12}$

6 $\dfrac{y^2 - 2y - 3}{y^2 - 6y + 9}$

7 $\dfrac{x^2 + 3x - 4}{x^2 - 1}$

8 $\dfrac{3z^2 + 5z - 2}{9z^2 - 1}$

9 $\dfrac{2x^2 + x - 6}{x^2 - 4}$

10 $\dfrac{5a^2 + 7a + 2}{5a^2 - 13a - 6}$

11 $\dfrac{4m^2 - 9}{2m^2 - 3m - 9}$

Simplify:

⚠ 12 $\dfrac{x^3 + x^2 - 2x}{x - 1}$

⚠ 13 $\dfrac{a^2 + 9a + 20}{3a - 15} \times \dfrac{a^2 - a - 20}{a^2 + 8a + 16}$

⚠ 14 $\dfrac{c^2 - 2c - 3}{c^2 - 5c + 6} \times \dfrac{2c - 6}{c^2 - 1}$

Learn... 12.4 Solving quadratic equations by factorising

If $p \times q = 0$, then either p or q (or both of them) must be 0.

$7 \times 0 = 0$

$0 \times 4 = 0$

$0 \times 0 = 0$

This is the basis for solving quadratic equations by factorising.

If $(x - 2) \times (x + 5) = 0$ then either $(x - 2) = 0$ or $(x + 5) = 0$ and x can be either 2 or −5.

Example: Solve the equation $x^2 - 5x - 14 = 0$

Solution: Factorising gives $(x - 7)(x + 2) = 0$

Either $(x - 7) = 0$ or $(x + 2) = 0$
         $x = 7$ $x = -2$

The solutions are $x = 7$ or -2

Example: Solve the equation $x^2 - 3x = 0$

Solution: Factorising gives $x(x - 3) = 0$ Here the 'first bracket' is just x.

Either $x = 0$ or $(x - 3) = 0$
                       $x = 3$

The solutions are $x = 0$ or 3

Example: Solve the equation $2x^2 - 9x - 5 = 0$

Solution: Factorising gives $(2x + 1)(x - 5) = 0$

Either $(2x + 1) = 0$ or $(x - 5) = 0$
         $x = -\frac{1}{2}$ $x = 5$

The solutions are $x = -\frac{1}{2}$ or 5

Hint

If $(2x + 1) = 0$ then $2x = -1$
so $x = -\frac{1}{2}$

Practise...

12.4 Solving quadratic equations by factorising

k!   D C B A A*

Solve these equations.

1 $(m - 3)(m + 2) = 0$

2 $(n + 1)(2n - 5) = 0$

3 $x^2 - 5x + 4 = 0$

4 $y^2 - 2y - 15 = 0$

5 $b^2 + 5b - 84 = 0$

6 $c^2 - c - 12 = 0$

7 $p^2 + 5p = 14$

8 $q^2 + 27 = 12q$

9 $t^2 = 100$

10 $a^2 + 7a = 0$

B

AQA   *Examiner's tip*

Rearrange a quadratic equation in the form .... $= 0$ before you factorise.

11 $2b^2 - 8b = 0$

12 $2x^2 - 9x - 5 = 0$

13 $3y^2 + 8y - 3 = 0$

14 $5z^2 + 12z + 4 = 0$

15 $5t^2 - 3t - 14 = 0$

16 $2p^2 + 13p = 7$

A

A

17   The quadratic equation $x^2 + 2x - p = 0$ has a solution $x = -5$

Work out the value of p.

18   The quadratic equation $y^2 + qy - 12 = 0$ has a solution $y = 3$

Work out the value of q.

⚠ **19**   The length of the rectangle PQRS is x cm and its width is $(x - 5)$ cm.

A triangle *PTU*, where $PT = 6$ cm and $PU = 4$ cm, is removed from one corner of the rectangle as shown.

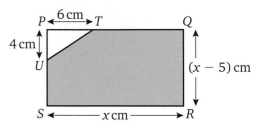

   a   Show that the shaded area is $(x^2 - 5x - 12)$ cm.

   b   The shaded area is 164 cm².

       Form a quadratic equation and solve it to find the length of the rectangle.

20   **a**   The quadratic equation $x^2 - 14x + 49 = 0$ has only one solution. Why?

       b   Write down another quadratic equation that has only one solution.

21   Anna thinks of a number, squares it and then adds twice the original number. The result is 99.

Write down a quadratic equation and solve it to find the two possible numbers that Anna started with.

22   A rectangular garden is y metres long.
The width of the garden is 5 metres less than the length.
The area of the garden is 234 square metres.

Form a quadratic equation in y and solve it to find the length of the garden.

 **Learn...**

12.5 Solving fractional equations that lead to quadratics

To solve an equation containing fractions, you often need to simplify the fractions by adding or subtracting them first. if the denominators are expressions in x, when you multiply by the denominators you will produce a quadratic equation.

Example: Solve the equation $\dfrac{3}{x - 2} + \dfrac{4}{x - 1} = 2$

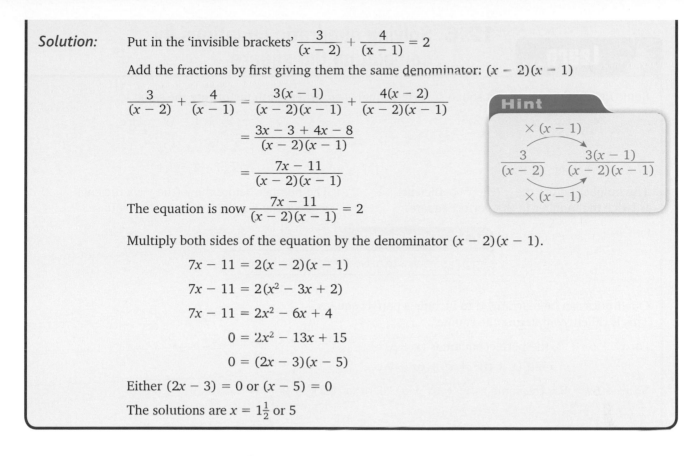

Solution: Put in the 'invisible brackets' $\dfrac{3}{(x-2)} + \dfrac{4}{(x-1)} = 2$

Add the fractions by first giving them the same denominator: $(x-2)(x-1)$

$$\dfrac{3}{(x-2)} + \dfrac{4}{(x-1)} = \dfrac{3(x-1)}{(x-2)(x-1)} + \dfrac{4(x-2)}{(x-2)(x-1)}$$

$$= \dfrac{3x - 3 + 4x - 8}{(x-2)(x-1)}$$

$$= \dfrac{7x - 11}{(x-2)(x-1)}$$

Hint

$$\times (x-1)$$

$$\dfrac{3}{(x-2)} \qquad \dfrac{3(x-1)}{(x-2)(x-1)}$$

$$\times (x-1)$$

The equation is now $\dfrac{7x - 11}{(x-2)(x-1)} = 2$

Multiply both sides of the equation by the denominator $(x-2)(x-1)$.

$$7x - 11 = 2(x-2)(x-1)$$

$$7x - 11 = 2(x^2 - 3x + 2)$$

$$7x - 11 = 2x^2 - 6x + 4$$

$$0 = 2x^2 - 13x + 15$$

$$0 = (2x - 3)(x - 5)$$

Either $(2x - 3) = 0$ or $(x - 5) = 0$

The solutions are $x = 1\frac{1}{2}$ or 5

12.5 Solving fractional equations that lead to quadratics

Practise...   **k!**   D C B A A*

Solve:

1 $x - \dfrac{8}{x+2}$

2 $\dfrac{2}{a^2} - \dfrac{3}{a} = 9$

3 $2x = x + \dfrac{35}{2-x}$

4 $\dfrac{10}{x+3} - \dfrac{2}{x} = 1$

5 $\dfrac{x}{x-1} - \dfrac{4}{x} = 1$

6 $\dfrac{4}{x+3} - \dfrac{3}{x+4} = 1$

7 $\dfrac{7}{x+2} - \dfrac{1}{x-1} = \dfrac{3}{4}$

8 $\dfrac{1}{y} + \dfrac{1}{y+1} = \dfrac{7}{12}$

9 $\dfrac{2}{x+2} + \dfrac{3}{2x-1} = 1$

10   A girl walks a distance of 20 kilometres and then cycles back.
She takes 3 hours 45 minutes less for the return journey and her average speed
is 12 km/h greater than on the first part of her journey.

a   Show that $\dfrac{4}{x} - \dfrac{4}{x+12} = \dfrac{3}{4}$ where x km/h is her average walking speed.

b   Solve this equation to find her average walking speed.

A

Learn... 12.6 Solving quadratic equations by completing the square

Some quadratics are perfect squares. Perfect squares are where both factors are the same.

$$x^2 + 6x + 9 = (x + 3)^2$$

half of $+6 = +3$

The number before the x (the x coefficient) is twice the number in the perfect square.

$$y^2 - 2y + 1 = (y - 1)^2$$

half of $-2 = -1$

The number before the y (the y coefficient) is twice the number in the perfect square.

> **AQA** *Examiner's tip*
>
> Your first step is to halve the coefficient of x.

Quadratics can be rearranged to include a perfect square. This is called 'completing the square'.

For $x^2 + 6x + 7$, the perfect square is $(x + 3)^2$

and $(x + 3)^2 = x^2 + 6x + 9$

So $x^2 + 6x + 7$ is the same as $x^2 + 6x + 9 - 2$ or $(x + 3)^2 - 2$

$+7 = +9 - 2$

For $y^2 - 2y - 5$, the perfect square is $(y - 1)^2$

and $(y - 1)^2 = y^2 - 2y + 1$

So $y^2 - 2y - 5$ is the same as $y^2 - 2y + 1 - 6$ or $(y - 1)^2 - 6$

$-5 = +1 - 6$

You can use this method to solve any quadratic equation, giving the answer in surd form.

Example: Solve the equation $x^2 + 6x + 7 = 0$ by completing the square.

Solution: Complete the square as shown above $(x + 3)^2 - 2 = 0$

Add 2 to both sides $(x + 3)^2 = 2$

Take the square root of both sides $x + 3 = \pm\sqrt{2}$

Write the answer in the form '$x = ...$' $x = -3 \pm\sqrt{2}$

> **AQA** *Examiner's tip*
>
> If the number on the right of the equation is negative, the equation cannot be solved, so check you have not made a mistake.

Example: Solve the equation $y^2 - 2y - 5 = 0$ by completing the square.

Solution: Complete the square as shown above $(y - 1)^2 - 6 = 0$

Add 6 to both sides $(y - 1)^2 = 6$

Take the square root of both sides $y - 1 = \pm\sqrt{6}$

Write the answer in the form '$y = ...$' $y = 1 \pm\sqrt{6}$

12.6 Solving quadratic equations by completing the square

Practise...

D C B A A*

1 $x^2 + 4x + 1 \equiv (x + 2)^2 - a$

Work out the value of a.

2 $y^2 - 14y + 8 \equiv (y - 7)^2 + b$

Work out the value of b.

Solve these equations by completing the square.

Give your answers in surd form.

> **Hint**
>
> Start by looking for a common factor.

3 $x^2 + 2x - 1 = 0$

4 $y^2 - 6y + 1 = 0$

5 $z^2 + 8z - 2 = 0$

6 $t^2 - 4t - 8 = 0$

7 $p^2 + 12p + 30 = 0$

8 $q^2 + 4q + 2 = 0$

9 $u^2 + 3 = 8u$

10 $v^2 + 22 = 20v$

11 $2a^2 - 4a - 8 = 0$

12 $3c^2 - 18c + 3 = 0$

13   You are given the identity $x^2 + mx + 25 \equiv (x + n)^2$

Work out the values of m and n.

14   You are given the identity $x^2 - px + 121 \equiv (x + q)^2$

Work out the values of p and q.

15   You are given the identity $4x^2 + 12x + 3 \equiv (2x + a)^2 + b$

Work out the values of a and b.

16   Explain why you cannot solve the equation $y^2 + 3y + 5 = 0$

Learn...   **12.7 Algebraic proof**

A proof is a series of logical mathematical steps that confirms the truth of a mathematical statement.

You must use correct notation and symbols in your proof. Algebra can be used to solve many mathematical proofs.

Proof questions might require you to offer some explanation.

Example: Show that if n is a positive even number then $n^2 - n$ is even.

Solution: $n^2 = n \times n$ and even $\times$ even = even.

Also even $-$ even = even.

Alternative solution

$n^2 - n = n(n - 1)$

n is even, and so $n - 1$ is odd.

Even $\times$ odd = even.

Example: Prove that $2(9x - 14) - 3(x - 1) \equiv 5(3x - 5)$

Solution: Work from the left hand side (LHS) of the identity only.

Multiply out, simplify and factorise the expression on the left to reach the expression on the right.

$$\text{LHS} \quad 2(9x - 14) - 3(x - 1) = 18x - 28 - 3x + 3$$
$$= 15x - 25$$
$$= 5(3x - 5)$$
$$= \text{RHS}$$

AQA Examiner's tip

Remember the symbol $\equiv$ means 'identical to'.

AQA Examiner's tip

Never work with both sides of the identity together.

AQA Examiner's tip

If your solution is incorrect, check your signs when multiplying.

Example: If $5(2x + 1) - 3(x - 3) \equiv a(x + b)$

Work out the values of a and b.

Solution:
$$\text{LHS} \quad 5(2x + 1) - 3(x - 3) = 10x + 5 - 3x + 9$$
$$= 7x + 14$$
$$= 7(x + 2)$$

From RHS $a = 7$ and $b = 2$

Example: If $(2x + 9)^2 \equiv 4(x - 1)^2 + a(4x + b)$

Work out the values of a and b.

Solution:
$$\text{LHS } (2x + 9)^2 = (2x + 9)(2x + 9)$$
$$= 4x^2 + 36x + 81$$
$$\text{RHS } 4(x - 1)^2 + a(4x + b) = 4(x^2 - 2x + 1) + 4ax + ab$$
$$= 4x^2 - 8x + 4 + 4ax + ab$$

Compare the coefficients of x on each side
$$36 = -8 + 4a$$
$$4a = 44$$
$$a = 11$$

Compare the number terms on each side.
$$81 = 4 + 11b$$
$$b = 7$$

Example: Prove that the difference between two **consecutive** square numbers is always an odd number.

Solution: Let the first number be x and the square of this number is x^2.

The next consecutive number is $x + 1$ and the square of this number is $(x + 1)^2$.

You need to prove that the difference between x^2 and $(x + 1)^2$ is an odd number.

The difference can be written as $(x + 1)^2 - x^2$
$$= (x^2 + 2x + 1) - x^2$$
$$= 2x + 1$$

Since the number $2x$ is always an even number then the number $2x + 1$ must be an odd number.

So the difference between two consecutive square numbers is always an odd number.

AQA Examiner's tip

It is a good idea to take the smaller number from the larger number when finding the difference, so you don't get a negative answer.

Practise...   12.7 Algebraic proof 🄺

D C B A A*

1   Prove that $5(2x + 5) + 11(x - 2) \equiv 3(7x + 1)$

2   Prove that $11(x - 1) + 4(x + 14) \equiv 15(x + 3)$

3   If $4(x - 3) + a(3x + 11) \equiv 10(x + b)$

     Work out the values of a and b.

4   Prove that the sum of two consecutive odd numbers is always an even number.

5   Prove that the sum of three consecutive numbers is equal to three times the middle number.

6   Tasha says that $(a + b)^2 = a^2 + b^2$

     Show that Tasha is incorrect.

7   Part of a number grid is shown.

     The shaded shape is called B_{11} because it has 11 in the top left-hand corner.

     a   This is B_n.

       Copy and fill in the empty boxes on B_n.

     b   Farakh notices that $11 \times 20 = 220$

       and that $19 \times 12 = 228$

       Show, using algebra, that the difference of the products of the diagonals is always 8.

1	2	3	4	5	6	7	8
9	10	11	12	13	14	15	16
17	18	19	20	21	22	23	24
25	26	27	28	29	30	31	32
33	34	35	36	37	38	39	40
41	42	43	44	45	46	47	48
49	50	51	52	53	54	55	56
57	58	59	60	61	62	63	64

8   Prove that the product of three consecutive even numbers is a multiple of 8.

9   Prove that if you add the squares of three consecutive numbers and then subtract two, the answer is a multiple of 3.

10   Prove that $\dfrac{n + 1}{n} - \dfrac{n}{n + 1} = \dfrac{2n + 1}{n(n + 1)}$

11   The nth triangle number is given by the formula $\frac{1}{2}n(n + 1)$.

     a   Write down the first three triangle numbers.

     b   Prove that the sum of any two consecutive triangle numbers is always a square number.

12   Take a 3-digit number such that the three digits are different.

     Reverse the number.

     Subtract the smaller number from the bigger one.

     If the difference is a 2-digit number add a zero before it.

     Reverse the new 3-digit number and add the reversed number to the difference.

     Explain why the answer is always 1089.

12 Assess

D

1 Prove that $5(x - 4) + 2(4x - 3) \equiv 13(x - 2)$.

B

2 Prove that the product of two odd numbers is always an odd number.

3 If $\dfrac{4x - 2}{3} - \dfrac{x - a}{4} \equiv \dfrac{13(x + 1)}{12}$

Work out the value of a.

4 Factorise:

a $a^2 + 3a + 2$ e $m^2 - 9$ i $r^2 - 2r - 35$ m $5z^2 - 27z + 10$

b $c^2 - 4c + 3$ f $n^2 - 5n - 24$ j $t^2 + t - 2$ n $2w^2 + 5w - 3$

c $f^2 - f - 12$ g $p^2 + 12p + 11$ k $3x^2 - 7x + 2$ o $6u^2 + 11u + 3$

d $h^2 + 8h - 20$ h $q^2 + 21q + 20$ l $5y^2 + 14y - 3$ p $4v^2 - 13v + 10$

5 Factorise completely:

a $18x^2 - 2$ b $3y^2 - 24y + 21$ c $2t^2 - 18t - 20$ d $8x^2 + 20x - 12$

A

6 Simplify:

a $\dfrac{x^2 + 5x + 4}{x^2 + x - 12}$ c $\dfrac{z^2 + 5z - 24}{z^2 - 5z + 6}$

b $\dfrac{y^2 - 2y - 35}{y^2 - 25}$ d $\dfrac{25 - x^2}{x^2 + 7x + 10}$

7 Solve these equations.

a $(a - 2)(a + 6) = 0$ f $f^2 = 3f + 40$

b $b^2 + 8b + 7 = 0$ g $k^2 = 1$

c $c^2 - 9c + 8 = 0$ h $m^2 - 14m - 32 = 0$

d $d^2 + d = 6$ i $2n^2 - 7n + 5 = 0$

e $e^2 - 5e = 0$ j $3p^2 - p - 14 = 0$

8 One solution of the equation $x^2 - 5x + p = 0$ is $x = 3$
Work out the value of p.

9 One solution of the equation $y^2 - qy - 25 = 0$ is $y = -1$
Work out the value of q.

A*

10 If $\dfrac{x^2 - 9}{x^2 + 4x - a} \equiv \dfrac{x + 3}{x + 7}$

Work out the value of a.

11 The nth term of a sequence is given by the formula $\frac{1}{2}n(n - 1)$

a Write down the first three terms of the sequence.

b Prove that the sum of any two consecutive terms of the sequence is always a square number.

A*

12 Solve these equations by completing the square.
Give your answers in surd form.

a $x^2 + 10x + 4 = 0$ **c** $z^2 - 16z + 12 = 0$

b $y^2 - 4y + 1 = 0$ **d** $5c^2 + 30c - 40 = 0$

13 You are given the identity $x^2 - ax + 49 \equiv (x - b)^2$
Work out the values of a and b.

14 Solve $\dfrac{x}{x + 1} + \dfrac{2}{1 - x} = 1$

15 Solve $\dfrac{3}{2x + 1} - \dfrac{1}{x - 5} = \dfrac{4}{3}$

16 The area of this rectangle is $56\,\text{cm}^2$.

Form a quadratic equation in y and solve it to find the length of the rectangle.

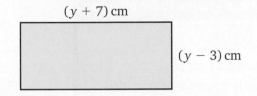

$(y + 7)\,\text{cm}$

$(y - 3)\,\text{cm}$

17 The dimensions of this cuboid are all in cm.

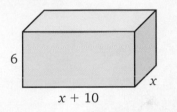

6

x

$x + 10$

The volume of the cuboid is $450\,\text{cm}^3$.

Form a quadratic equation in x and solve it to find the width of the cuboid.

AQA Examination-style questions

1 **a** Find the values of a and b such that:
$$x^2 + 10x + 40 = (x + a)^2 + b$$
(2 marks)

b Hence, or otherwise, write down the minimum value of $x^2 + 10x + 40$
(1 mark)

AQA 2005

2 **a** n is a positive integer.

i Explain why $n(n + 1)$ must be an even number.
(1 mark)

ii Explain why $2n + 1$ must be an odd number.
(1 mark)

b Expand and simplify $(2n + 1)^2$.
(2 marks)

c Prove that the square of any odd number is always 1 more than a multiple of 8.
(3 marks)

AQA 2004

Objectives

Examiners would normally expect students who get these grades to be able to:

B

solve a pair of simultaneous equations such as $x + 3y = 9$ and $3x - 2y = 5$

A

solve a pair of simultaneous equations such as $y = 4x + 5$ and $y = x^2$

Key terms

simultaneous equations
eliminate
substitution

DEUTSCHE BUNDESPOST

60

EUROPA

GOTTFRIED WILHELM LEIBNIZ · 1646 – 17[?]
1980

Did you know?

A real problem-solver

The idea of solving simultaneous equations is credited to Gottfried Leibniz, who was born in 1646. He was a German philosopher and mathematician who also invented the binary system, which formed the basis for computer technology nearly 300 years after his birth! He is such an important figure in German history that his picture appeared on a German postage stamp.

You should already know:

✔ how to solve a linear equation

✔ how to multiply out brackets

✔ how to rearrange an equation to make y or x the subject

✔ how to solve a quadratic equation by factorisation or by completing the square.

Learn... 13.1 Solving simultaneous equations by elimination

To solve **simultaneous equations**, make sure the coefficients of one of the variables in both equations match.

Then add or subtract terms in the equations to **eliminate** that variable. For example:

$$3x + 2y = 7$$
$$7x - 2y = 13$$

These equations are ready to be added. The y coefficients match as $+ 2y$ added to $- 2y$ equals zero.

Adding these equations gives $10x = 20$, which can be solved.

$$3x + 4y = 11$$
$$5x + 4y = 9$$

These equations are ready to be subtracted. The coefficients match as $+ 4y$ subtracted from $+ 4y$ equals zero.

Subtracting these equations gives $2x = -2$, which can be solved.

Example: Solve the simultaneous equations:

$$2x + y = 11$$
$$x - y = 1$$

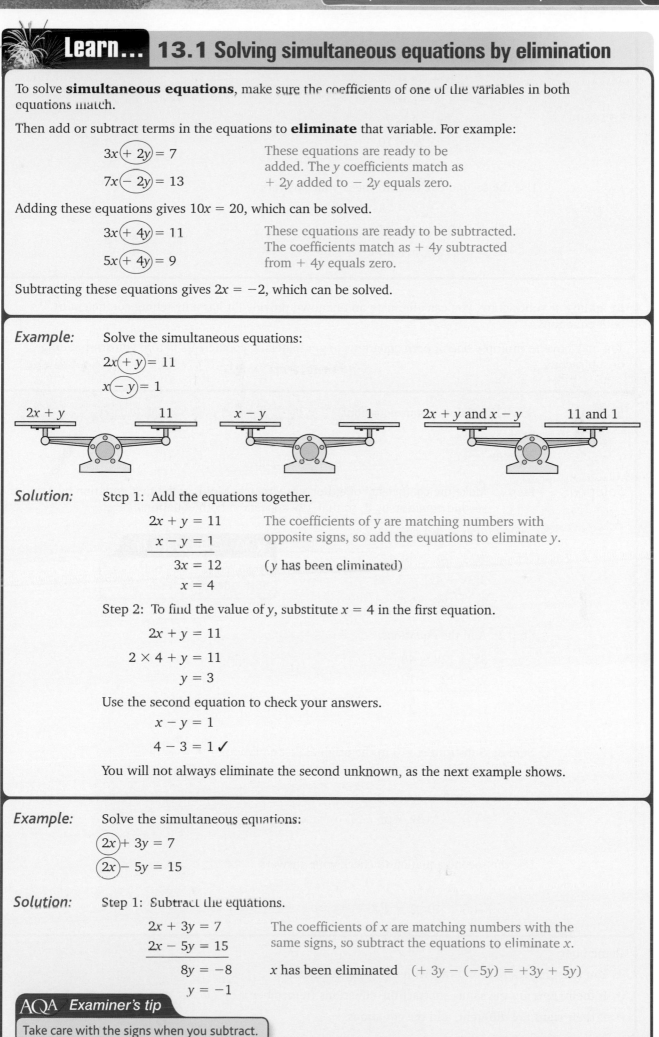

| $2x + y$ | 11 | $x - y$ | 1 | $2x + y$ and $x - y$ | 11 and 1 |

Solution: Step 1: Add the equations together.

$$2x + y = 11$$
$$\underline{x - y = 1}$$
$$3x = 12$$

The coefficients of y are matching numbers with opposite signs, so add the equations to eliminate y.

(y has been eliminated)

$$x = 4$$

Step 2: To find the value of y, substitute $x = 4$ in the first equation.

$$2x + y = 11$$
$$2 \times 4 + y = 11$$
$$y = 3$$

Use the second equation to check your answers.

$$x - y = 1$$
$$4 - 3 = 1 ✓$$

You will not always eliminate the second unknown, as the next example shows.

Example: Solve the simultaneous equations:

$$2x + 3y = 7$$
$$2x - 5y = 15$$

Solution: Step 1: Subtract the equations.

$$2x + 3y = 7$$
$$\underline{2x - 5y = 15}$$
$$8y = -8$$

The coefficients of x are matching numbers with the same signs, so subtract the equations to eliminate x.

x has been eliminated $(+ 3y - (-5y) = +3y + 5y)$

$$y = -1$$

AQA   *Examiner's tip*

Take care with the signs when you subtract.

Step 2: To find the value of x, substitute $y = -1$ in the first equation.

$$2x + 3y = 7$$
$$2x + 3 \times -1 = 7$$
$$2x - 3 = 7$$
$$2x = 10$$
$$x = 5$$

Use the second equation to check your answers.

$$2x - 5y = 15$$
$$2 \times 5 - 5 \times -1 = 15$$
$$10 + 5 = 15 \checkmark$$

By adding or subtracting, you can eliminate an unknown provided it has a matching coefficient in both equations.

You may have to multiply one or both equations to get matching coefficients before you start adding or subtracting.

Example: Solve the simultaneous equations:

$$2x + 3y = 12$$
$$3x - 4y = 1$$

Solution: Step 1: Make the coefficients of either x or y match. Multiply the first equation by 4 and the second equation by 3, so that $12y$ appears in both equations.

$$4(2x + 3y) = 4 \times 12$$
$$8x \boxed{+ 12y} = 48$$
$$3(3x + 4y) = 3 \times 1$$
$$9x \boxed{- 12y} = 3$$

> **AQA** *Examiner's tip*
>
> Don't forget to multiply **both sides** of each equation.

Step 2: Add the equations.

$$8x + 12y = 48$$
$$\underline{9x - 12y = 13}$$
$$17x = 51$$
$$x = 3$$

Step 3: Substitute $x = 3$ in the original first equation.

$$2x + 3y = 12$$
$$2 \times 3 + 3y = 12$$
$$3y = 6$$
$$y = 2$$

Use the second equation to check your answers.

$$3x - 4y = 1$$
$$3 \times 3 - 4 \times 2 = 1 \checkmark$$

Remember:

- You must have a pair of terms with matching coefficients.
- If their <u>s</u>igns are the <u>s</u>ame, <u>s</u>ubtract the equations (remember it by s s s).
- If their signs are different, add the equations.

Practise...

13.1 Solving simultaneous equations by elimination (k!)

D C B A A*

B

1 Solve these simultaneous equations by elimination.

a $4x + y = 1$
$3x - y = 13$

e $5p + 2q = 3$
$7p + 2q = 11$

i $3x + 2y = 10$
$3x - y = 8$

b $2a + 3b = 13$
$5a - 3b = 22$

f $4r - 3t = 12$
$2r - 3t = 9$

j $e + 3f = 21$
$e - f = 1$

c $5c + d = 15$
$4c + d = 11$

g $3x + 5y = 2$
$3x + 2y = 8$

k $2x - y = 16$
$2x + 3y = 8$

d $7m + 4n = 6$
$m - 4n = 10$

h $4c + 5d = 6$
$3c - 5d = 8$

l $2x - 3y = 0$
$2x + 5y = 4$

2 Write down a pair of simultaneous equations with the solution $x = 6, y = 1$

3 Write down a pair of simultaneous equations with the solution $x = 2, y = -5$

4 Solve these simultaneous equations by elimination.

a $5a + 4b = 7$
$3a + 2b = 5$

d $4m + 3n = 1$
$3m - 2n = 5$

g $2e + 3f = 2$
$e + 6f = 4$

b $2p + q = 10$
$5p + 3q = 27$

e $9r + 4t = 7$
$2r - 5t = 31$

h $3x - 4y = 5$
$2x + y = -4$

c $2c + 3d = 5$
$3c - 2d = 14$

f $7x - 12y = 39$
$5x - 4y = 5$

⚠ 5 Solve these simultaneous equations.

$55x + 45y = 75$

$45x + 55y = 25$

> **Hint**
> Add the equations and divide by the coefficient of x.
> Subtract the equations and divide by the coefficient of x.
> Now you have two, much simpler, equations to solve.

⚠ 6 Solve this set of three simultaneous equations to find x, y and z.

$x + y + z = 15$

$x + y - z = 9$

$x - y + z = 1$

> **Hint**
> Try adding pairs of equations.

⚙ 7

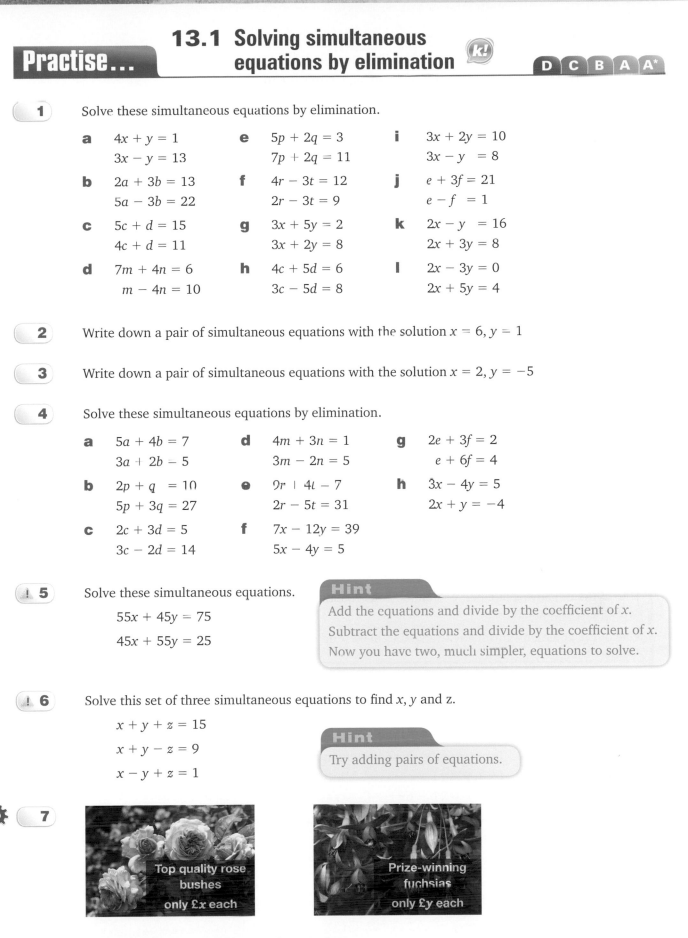

Top quality rose bushes

only £x each

Prize-winning fuchsias

only £y each

Anita buys five rose bushes and three fuchsias.
Her bill is £48.

Sonia buys two rose bushes and three fuchsias.
Her bill is £25.50.

Write down a pair of simultaneous equations and solve them to find x and y.

8 Dan sells decorative storage boxes in two sizes.
The cost of four small boxes and three large boxes is £63.
The cost of five small boxes and two large boxes is £56.
Find the cost of one small box.

9 Jack is x years old.
Jill is y years old.
The sum of their ages is 60 years.
Jack is 6 years older than Jill.
Write down a pair of simultaneous equations and solve them to find x and y.

10 Hasif has 17 coins in his pocket.
Some are 5p coins and the rest are 10p coins.
The total value of the coins is £1.40.
How many 5p coins does he have?

11 Paul is thinking of a fraction $\dfrac{x}{y}$

If he adds 4 to the numerator and the denominator, his fraction equals $\dfrac{3}{5}$

If he subtracts 6 from the numerator and the denominator, his fraction equals $\dfrac{1}{3}$

What is Paul's fraction?

12 The ages of Jasmin and Sara are in the ratio $2 : 3$
In 4 years' time, their ages will be in the ration $3 : 4$
How old are Jasmin and Sara now?

Learn... 13.2 Solving simultaneous equations by substitution

One of the unknowns in a pair of simultaneous equations can also be eliminated by **substitution** from one equation to the other.

One of the equations must be rearranged to make x or y the subject.

Example: Solve the simultaneous equations:
$$4x + 5y = 16$$
$$6x + y = 11$$

Solution: Step 1: Rearrange the second equation to make y the subject.
$$6x + y = 11$$
$$y = 11 - 6x$$

The equation which has y rather than $5y$ is easier to rearrange and substitute.

Step 2: Substitute this expression for y into the first equation.
$$4x + 5(11 - 6x) = 16$$
$$4x + 55 - 30x = 16$$
$$-26x = -39$$
$$26x = 39$$
$$x = 1.5$$

Step 3: Substitute this value for x into the formula.
$$y = 11 - 6x$$
$$y = 11 - 6 \times 1.5$$
$$= 2$$

AQA **Examiner's tip**

It is easy to forget Step 3 and lose marks.

The substitution method is especially useful when there is one linear equation and one quadratic equation. Then the substitution leads to a quadratic in one unknown.

Example: Solve the simultaneous equations:

$y = 3x - 2$ linear equation

$y = x^2$ quadratic equation

Solution: Step 1: Make sure the linear equation expresses y in terms of x.

$y = 3x - 2$

Step 2: Substitute this expression in the quadratic equation.

$y = x^2$

$3x - 2 = x^2$

Step 3: Rearrange the new equation to the quadratic form.

$x^2 - 3x + 2 = 0$

Step 4: Solve the equation.

$(x - 2)(x - 1) = 0$

Either $x - 2 = 0$, when $x = 2$

or $x - 1 = 0$, when $x = 1$

Step 5: Substitute each value of x in the linear equation to find the corresponding value of y.

$y = 3x - 2$

$y = 6 - 2 = 4$ First pair of values is $(2, 4)$

$y = 3 - 2 = 1$ Second pair of values is $(1, 1)$

Step 6: Check your answers also satisfy $y = x^2$.

$x = 1, y = 1^2 = 1$

$x = 2, y = 2^2 = 4$

> **AQA** *Examiner's tip*
>
> Show your answers as pairs of values:
>
> $x = 2$ belongs with $y = 4$
>
> $x = 1$ belongs with $y = 1$

Example: Solve the simultaneous equations $x + y = 5$

$y = 3x^2 + 4x - 7$

Solution: Step 1: Use the linear equation to express y in terms of x

$y = 5 - x$

Step 2: Substitute this expression in the quadratic equation

$5 - x = 3x^2 + 4x - 7$

Step 3: Simplify the new equation and rearrange to the quadratic form

$0 = 3x^2 + 5x - 12$

Step 4: Solve the equation

$0 = (3x - 4)(x + 3)$

Either $3x - 4 = 0$, when $x = \frac{4}{3}$

or $x + 3 = 0$, when $x = -3$

Step 5: Substitute each value of x in the linear equation to find the corresponding value of y

$\frac{4}{3} + y = 5$

$y = \frac{11}{3}$ First pair of values is $(\frac{4}{3}, \frac{11}{3})$

$-3 + y = 5$

$y = 8$ Second pair of values is $(-3, 8)$

Practise...

13.2 Solving simultaneous equations by substitution

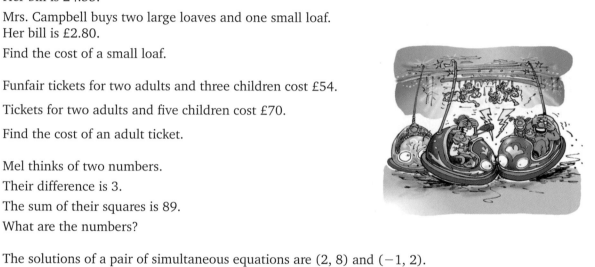

D C B A A*

B

1 Solve these simultaneous linear equations by substitution.

a $a = b - 1$
    $a + 2b = 8$

c $m - 5n = 13$
    $2m + n = 4$

e $3p - q = 12$
    $5p - 7q = 20$

b $c = 3d - 2$
    $c + 5d = 14$

d $2x + y = 9$
    $3x + 2y = 9$

f $3v - 2w = 19$
    $2v + w = 29$

A

2 Solve these simultaneous equations by substitution.

a $y = 7x + 2$
    $y = 4x^2$

c $y = 2x + 11$
    $y = 2x^2 - 7x + 6$

e $2x - y = 1$
    $y = 2x^2 - 8x + 11$

g $y + 3x = 7$
    $y = 4x^2 - 5x + 1$

b $b + 14a = 5$
    $b = 3a^2$

d $d = 1 - c$
    $d = 2c^2 - 3c - 3$

f $x - y = 1$
    $y = 5x^2 + 7x - 9$

h $x + 2y = 2$
    $y = x^2 - 6x + 7$

3 Mrs. Jackson buys three large loaves and two small loaves. Her bill is £4.55.

Mrs. Campbell buys two large loaves and one small loaf. Her bill is £2.80.

Find the cost of a small loaf.

4 Funfair tickets for two adults and three children cost £54.

Tickets for two adults and five children cost £70.

Find the cost of an adult ticket.

5 Mel thinks of two numbers.

Their difference is 3.

The sum of their squares is 89.

What are the numbers?

6 The solutions of a pair of simultaneous equations are (2, 8) and (−1, 2).

The first equation is $y = 3x^2 - x - 2$

The second equation is linear.

Find the second equation.

> **Hint**
> You are looking for the equation of a line.

13 Assess

B

1 Solve these simultaneous equations.

a $3a - b = 11$
    $2a + b = 9$

d $3m + 2n = 28$
    $m - n = 1$

g $y = 7x$
    $2y = 5x - 9$

b $7c + d = 10$
    $3c + d = -2$

e $p + 3q = 13$
    $2p + q = 11$

h $y = 6 - 2x$
    $4x + 3y = 10$

c $3e - 2f = 9$
    $e + 2f = 15$

f $2r - 3t = 10$
    $3r + 5t = 15$

A

2 Solve these simultaneous equations.

a $y = x^2$
    $y = 6x - 8$

b $y = 2x^2$
    $5x + y = 3$

c $y + 3x = 7$
    $y = 4x^2 - 5x + 1$

d $3x - 2y = 1$
    $y = 2x^2 + 5x - 8$

A

3 Samir makes a rectangular run for his pet rabbit.

He has 5 metres of fencing to make the run.

He wants the run to have an area of 1.5 square metres.

Write down two simultaneous equations in x and y, the length and width of the run.

What are the dimensions of Samir's rabbit run?

4 Joe thinks of two negative numbers.

The sum of their squares is 125.

Their difference is 9.

What are the numbers?

5 The solutions of a pair of simultaneous equations are $(3, 8)$ and $(-2, 13)$.

The first equation is $y = 2x^2 - 3x - 1$

The second equation is linear.

Find the second equation.

AQA Examination-style questions

1 In a 'magic' triangle each side has the same total.

In this magic triangle each side has a total of 24.

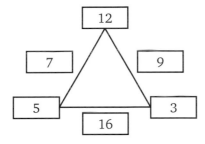

Here is another 'magic' triangle in which the sum of the three expressions on each of the three sides is the same.

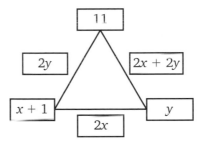

Complete the 'magic' triangle.

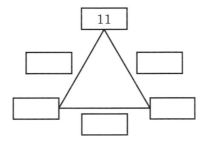

(7 marks)

AQA 2008

Consolidation

So far you have covered the following topics:

Prime factors

Sequences

Fractions and decimals

Surds

Working with symbols

Graphs of linear functions

Equations and inequalities

Percentages

Indices and standard index form

Real-life graphs

Formulae

Quadratic equations and algebraic proof

Simultaneous equations

All these topics will be tested in this chapter and you will find a mixture of problem solving and functional questions. You won't always be told which bit of maths to use or what type a question is, so you will have to decide on the best method, just like in your exam.

Example: Tom, Lee and Sam are trying to win some marbles in a game.

Tom wins $\frac{2}{5}$ of the marbles.

Lee and Sam win the remaining marbles in the ratio $7 : 5$

What percentage of the marbles does Lee win?

(4 marks)

Solution:

> ### Hint
>
> This is a multi-step problem. This means you have to plan your method.
>
> You are likely to gain more marks for your attempt if you work systematically, one step at a time, showing the method for each step.

You don't know how many marbles that Tom, Lee and Sam are trying to win but, because the answer required is a percentage, a good method is to assume that the number is 100.

It actually doesn't matter which number you choose but 100 makes the arithmetic in the problem much simpler.

Start by working out the number of marbles Lee and Sam win.

$\frac{2}{5}$ of $100 = 100 \div 5 \times 2 = 40$ marbles

$100 - 40 = 60$ marbles

or

$\frac{3}{5}$ of $100 = 100 \div 5 \times 3 = 60$ marbles

Next share the number of marbles won by Lee and Sam in the ratio $7 : 5$

For every 7 marbles that Lee gets Sam gets 5.

$7 + 5 = 12$

So for every 12 marbles Lee gets 7.

$60 \div 12 = 5$

There are 5 lots of 12 marbles in 60 marbles.

$5 \times 7 = 35$

So *Lee gets 35 marbles.*

Finally give the answer as a percentage.

35 as a percentage of 100 is 35%

So *Lee gets 35% of the marbles.*

> ### Mark scheme
> - 1 mark for working out that Lee and Sam have won 60 marbles.
> - 2 marks for working out that Lee gets 35 marbles.
> - 1 mark for the final answer.

Alternative solution:

First work out the fraction of marbles won by Lee and Sam.

$1 - \frac{2}{5} = \frac{3}{5}$

Then work out what fraction of these marbles that Lee wins.

$7 + 5 = 12$

Lee gets $\frac{7}{12}$ of the $\frac{3}{5}$ of the marbles.

Next calculate $\frac{7}{12}$ of $\frac{3}{5}$

$\frac{7}{12} \times \frac{3}{5} = \frac{21}{60}$

Finally change this fraction to a percentage.

$\frac{21}{60} = \frac{7}{20} = \frac{35}{100} = 35\%$

So *Lee gets 35% of the marbles.*

Example: **a**   Show that $\sqrt{80} + \sqrt{125} = 9\sqrt{5}$ *(2 marks)*

b   Given that $(\sqrt{80} + \sqrt{125})^{-1} = \frac{\sqrt{p}}{q}$

Where p and q are integers, find the values of p and q.   *(3 marks)*

Solution: For the first part of this question you have to change the form of the surds. Then you need to simplify.

a $\sqrt{80} + \sqrt{125} = \sqrt{(16 \times 5)} + \sqrt{(25 \times 5)}$

$\sqrt{(16 \times 5)} + \sqrt{(25 \times 5)} = 4\sqrt{5} + 5\sqrt{5} = 9\sqrt{5}$

> AQA *Examiner's tip*
>
> Always make sure that you write your answer in the space provided.

> ### Mark scheme
> - 1 mark is given for either $4\sqrt{5}$ or $5\sqrt{5}$
> - 1 mark is given for showing the addition $4\sqrt{5} + 5\sqrt{5}$

For part **b** you will need to use your answer to part **a**.

b   Rationalise your answer to part a.

$$(\sqrt{80} + \sqrt{125})^{-1} = (9\sqrt{5})^{-1} = \frac{1}{9\sqrt{5}}$$

$$\frac{1}{9\sqrt{5}} = \frac{1}{9\sqrt{5}} \times \frac{\sqrt{5}}{\sqrt{5}} = \frac{\sqrt{5}}{9 \times \sqrt{5} \times \sqrt{5}} = \frac{\sqrt{5}}{9 \times 5} = \frac{\sqrt{5}}{45}$$

$$p = 5, q = 45$$

> **Hint**
>
> To rationalise your answer here, multiply the top and bottom by $\sqrt{5}$

Mark scheme

- 1 mark is given for $\dfrac{1}{9\sqrt{5}}$ this is a method mark.
- 1 mark is given for $\dfrac{\sqrt{5}}{9 \times \sqrt{5} \times \sqrt{5}}$ this is another method mark.
- 1 mark is given for $p = 5$, and $q = 45$

Considation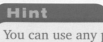

1   There are three piles of magazines.
Two of the piles are 30 cm high.
The other pile is 13.2 cm high.
Each magazine is 0.6 cm thick.
How many magazines are there in total?

2   Bill buys x packets of mints.
Each packet of mints cost 45 pence.
He pays with a £5 note.

a   Write an expression, in terms of x, for the change that Bill should receive. Give your expression in pence.

b   Bill receives £3.65 change. Write down and solve an equation to work out the number of packets of mints that Bill buys.

     You **must** show your working.

3   The Ancient Egyptians used unit fractions like this: $\overline{|||} = \frac{1}{3}$

A unit fraction has a numerator of 1.

The Ancient Egyptians made other fractions by adding unit fractions together.

For example, $\frac{2}{3}$ can be made by adding $\frac{1}{2}$ and $\frac{1}{6}$

$$\frac{1}{2} + \frac{1}{6} = \frac{3}{6} + \frac{1}{6} = \frac{4}{6} = \frac{2}{3}$$

> **Hint**
>
> You can use any pair of these fractions or all three.

a   What other fractions can you make using $\frac{1}{2}$, $\frac{1}{3}$, and $\frac{1}{4}$?

b   An Ancient Egyptian farmer shares 5 loaves between 8 people working in his fields.

     i   What fraction of a loaf does each worker get? Give your answer as two unit fractions added together.

     ii   Describe how the farmer cuts the loaves to make sure each worker receives exactly the same amount.

c   Repeat part **b** for 3 loaves shared between 4 workers.

4 Ben has a collection of 210 DVDs.

Each of his DVDs is 14 mm wide.

He stores his DVDs in a special unit that has five shelves.

Each shelf is 700 mm long.

How many more DVDs can Ben store before the unit is full?

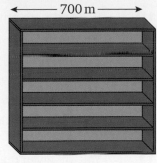
700 m

D

5 Each of these quantities has been rounded to the nearest whole number.

Write down the minimum possible size of each quantity.

a   34 cm   **b**   60 kg   **c**   15 litres   **d**   £55

6

Three friends have some sweets.

They eat three-fifths of the sweets in the morning.

In the afternoon, the remaining sweets are shared equally between the three friends.

What fraction of the original number of sweets does each friend receive in the afternoon?

7 Last year Gordon ran his local marathon in a time of 3 hours and 10 minutes. Before this year's race he says:

'My target is to have a time that is at least 1% faster than last year.'

He runs this year's race in a time of 3 hours 7 minutes.

Did Gordon meet his target? You **must** show your working.

8   **a**   The nth term of a sequence is $\frac{3}{2}n + 5$

    i   Work out the first three terms of the sequence.

    ii   Is 85 a term in the sequence? Show working to justify your answer.

  b   Work out the nth term of the sequence

    3, 7, 11, 15, 19, ……

D
C

9 Fred has two dogs Misty and Millie.

Misty eats $\frac{1}{3}$ of a tin of dog food twice a day.

Millie eats $\frac{1}{2}$ a tin of the same dog food each day.

Work out how many tins of dog food Fred should buy for a week.

Each tin costs £1.15.

He has a voucher from his local store.

5p off each tin

when you spend over £20

Will he save money if he buys enough dog food for four weeks?
Explain your answer.

C

10 p, q and r are prime numbers.

$1 < p \leqslant 4$

$7 \leqslant q \leqslant 9$

$10 \leqslant r < 15$

$x = pq$ and $y = qr$

Write down **all** the possible values of $x + y$.

11 You are given that $90 = 2 \times 3 \times 3 \times 5$

a Write 63 as the product of prime factors.

b Work out the highest common factor of 90 and 63.

c Write 900 as the product of prime factors.

> **Bump up your grade**
>
> To get a Grade C you need to be able to work out highest common factors.

12 x is an integer such that $-5 < 2x \leqslant 6$.

Write down all the possible values of x.

13 Dave and Debbie want to go out.
They can go to the cinema, an exhibition or a show at a theatre.
If they go to these they will need to travel by taxi each way.

	Distance from home	Ticket price per person
Cinema	8 miles	£8.50
Exhibition	6 miles	£10
Show	5 miles	£15.50

They have a choice of two taxi companies.

	Charge per trip
A2B Cabs	£2.60 per mile
Sapphire Taxis	£1.20 per mile plus £10

Use this information to work out which would be the cheapest option for them.

14 The diagram shows the graph of the equation $ax + by = 12$ where a and b are constants.

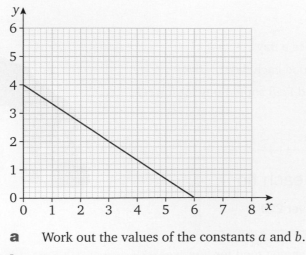

a Work out the values of the constants a and b.

b Work out the gradient of the line.

15 Solve:

   a $6(a - 2) = 2a + 16$

   b $\dfrac{d + 3}{2} - 5 = d$

16 In an experiment, different weights, w, are attached to a spring.

The length of the spring, l, is then measured.

The graph shows the results.

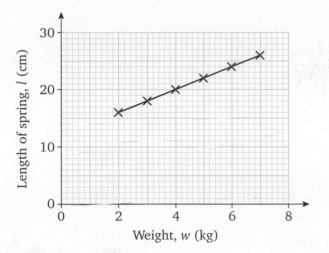

   a   Estimate the length of the spring when no weight is attached.

   b   Use the graph to write a formula to give the length of the spring, l, in terms of the attached weight, w.

   c   What weight is needed to **stretch** the spring by 30 cm?

17 Simplify:

   a $x^2 \times x^3$

   b $x^6 \div x^2$

   c $(x^2)^3$

   d $2x^2 \times 3x^3$

18 **a**   Show that $(x - 3)(x + 3) \equiv x^2 - 9$

   b   Hence simplify $\dfrac{x^2 - 9}{x + 3}$

19 Alfie, Ben, Colin and Dave share some money in the ratio of their ages.

Alfie and Ben together get $\frac{1}{4}$ of the money shared in the ratio 2 : 3

Colin has 40% of what is left.

Dave is 18.

How old are the other three boys?

20 Factorise fully:

   a $10x - 15x^2$

   b $5x^2 - x - 6$

B
A

21 Two lines, L_1 and L_2 intersect at P.

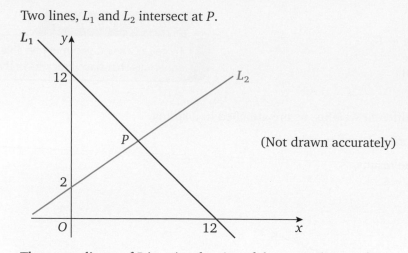

(Not drawn accurately)

The y-coordinate of P is twice the size of the x-coordinate of P.

a Show that the equation of L_1 is $y = 12 - x$

b Work out the equation of L_2.

22 Four friends Alana, Ben, Charlie and Della are playing a game.

During the game they collect red and blue cards.

The table shows the numbers of cards each player collects during the game.

Player	Red cards	Blue cards
Alana	10	8
Ben	11	4
Charlie	13	11
Della	9	2

a Each red card is worth r points.

Each blue card is worth b points.

Write an expression in terms of r and b for the total number of points won by Alana.

b Altogether Alana wins 64 points and Ben wins 80 points.

The player with the greatest total number of points wins the game.

Which of the four players wins the game?

You **must** show your working.

B

23 Solve the following simultaneous equations.

$2x + 5y = 16$

$4x + y = 5$

You **must** show your working.

Do **not** use trial and improvement.

A

24 x and y are integers.

$0 < x < 6$

$0 < y < 5$

$x + y \geqslant 7$

Work out the greatest possible value of $2x - y$.

You **must** show your working to justify your answer.

25 Look at this pattern.

1^3	1	= 1	$= 1^2$	$= 1^2$
$1^3 + 2^3$	1 + 8	= 9	$= (1 + 2)^2$	$= 3^2$
$1^3 + 2^3 + 3^3$	1 + 8 + 27	= 36	$= (1 + 2 + 3)^2$	$= 6^2$

a Copy the pattern of sequences and add the next three lines.

b Describe the sequence of numbers in the middle column.

c Describe the sequence of numbers in the last column.

d Find the differences between successive numbers in the middle column and describe the sequence that they form.

e Use the ideas in the table to write down the value of $(1 + 2 + 3 + 4 + 5 + 6 + 7 + 8 + 9 + 10)^2$.

26 A straight line L is parallel to $y = 4x + 1$. Line L passes through $(2, 3)$.

Find the equation of line L.

27 **a** Here are five numbers.

$$3.6 \times 10^6 \qquad 4 \times 10^{-2} \qquad 0.9 \times 10^4 \qquad 8 \times 10^5 \qquad 8.5 \times 10^{-3}$$

   i Which number is **not** written in standard index form?

   ii Which is the smallest number?

b $a \times 10^b$ and $b \times 10^a$ are both written in standard index form.

When written out in full the number $a \times 10^b$ has twice as many digits as $b \times 10^a$.

Find four possible pairs of values for a and b.

28 You are given that $u = \sqrt{5} + 1$ and $v = \sqrt{5} - 1$

a $u + v = \sqrt{n}$

Work out the value of n.

b Find the value of:

$$\frac{uv}{u - v}$$

29 Make x the subject of the formula:

$$y = \frac{4(2 - 5x)}{2 - 3x}$$

30 Lipin thinks of a number.

She doubles the number and then adds it to the reciprocal of the number.

She gets the answer 3.

Write down and solve an equation to work out the **two** possible numbers that Lipin could be thinking of.

You **must** show your working.

AQA Examination-style questions

1   A shopkeeper uses these formulae to calculate the total
    cost when customers pay by monthly instalments.

    $d = 0.2C$

    $C = d + 24m$

        C is the total cost in pounds.

        d is the deposit in pounds.

        m is the monthly instalment in pounds.

    The total cost of a sofa is £600.

    Work out the value of the monthly instalment.   *(3 marks)*

                                                                      AQA 2009

2   75 scientists are trapped in the Antarctic.

    They have enough food for 30 days on full rations.

    After 16 days on full rations a rescue party of 9 people arrive.

    The rescue party brings enough food to increase existing supplies by 60%

    The weather then gets worse and both the scientist and rescue party are trapped.

    They decide to go on half rations.

    How many more days before the food runs out?   *(4 marks)*

                                                                      AQA 2008

3   a   Work out $\frac{4}{5} \div \frac{6}{7}$

        Give your answer in its simplest form.   *(3 marks)*

    b   Work out $3\frac{3}{4} - 1\frac{2}{5}$ *(3 marks)*

    c   Calculate the reciprocal of 0.5   *(2 marks)*

                                                                      AQA 2008

Glossary

amount – the principal + the interest (i.e. the total you will have in the bank or the total you will owe the bank, at the end of the period of time).

balance – (i) how much money you have in your bank account (ii) how much you owe a shopkeeper after you have paid a deposit.

brackets – these show that the terms inside the brackets should be treated the same, for example,
$3(2x + 1) = 3 \times 2x + 3 \times 1$

coefficient – the number (with its sign) in front of the letter representing the unknown, for example, in $4p - 5$, 4 is the coefficient of p. In $2 - 3p^2, -3$ is the coefficient of p^2.

common factor – factors that two or more numbers have in common, for example,
the factors of 10 are **1**, 2, **5**, 10
the factors of 15 are **1**, 3, **5**, 15
the common factors of 10 and 15 are **1** and **5**

consecutive – in sequence.

constant – a number that does not change, for example, the formula $P = 4l$ states that the perimeter of a square is always four times the length of one side; 4 is a constant and P and l are variables. In the equation $y = 3x + 5$, +5 is the constant.

credit – when you buy goods 'on credit' you do not pay all the cost at once. Instead you make a number of payments at regular intervals, often once a month. NB When your bank account is '**in credit**', this means you have some money in it.

cube number – a cube number is the outcome when a whole number is multiplied by itself then multiplied by itself again; cube numbers are 1, 8, 27, 64, 125, …

cube root – the cube root of a number such as 125 is a number whose outcome is 125 when multiplied by itself then multiplied by itself again.

denominator – the bottom number of a fraction, indicating how many fractional parts the unit has been split into.

deposit – an amount of money you pay towards the cost of an item. The rest of the cost is paid later.

depreciation – a reduction in value (of used cars, for example).

discount – a reduction in the price. Sometimes this is for paying in cash or paying early.

eliminate – to remove one of the unknowns from a pair of simultaneous equations by adding or subtracting like terms; the unknown being eliminated must have a matching coefficient in both equations.

equation – a statement showing that two expressions are equal, for example, $2y - 17 = 15$

equivalent fractions – two or more fractions that have the same value. Equivalent fractions can be made by multiplying or dividing the numerator and denominator of any fraction by the same number.

expand – to remove brackets to create an equivalent expression (expanding is the opposite of factorising).

expression – a mathematical statement written in symbols, for example, $3x + 1$ or $x^2 + 2x$.

factor – a natural number which divides exactly into another number with no remainder, for example, the factors of 18 are 1, 2, 3, 6, 9, 18

factorise – to include brackets by taking common factors (factorising is the opposite of expanding).

formula – a formula shows the relationship between two or more variables, for example, in a rectangle area = length × width, or $A = lw$

gradient – a measure of how steep a line is
$$\text{gradient} = \frac{\text{change in vertical distance}}{\text{change in horizontal distance}}$$

highest common factor (HCF) – the highest factor that two or more numbers have in common, for example,

the factors of 12 are **1**, **2**, 3, **4**, 6, 12
the factors of 20 are **1**, **2**, **4**, 5, 10, 20
the common factors are 1, 2, 4
the highest common factor is 4

identity – two expressions linked by the $\equiv$ sign are true for all values of the variable, for example, $3x + 3 \equiv 3(x + 1)$

improper fraction – a fraction with a numerator greater than its denominator.

index – the index (or power or exponent) tells you how many times the base number is to be multiplied by itself.

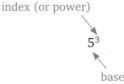

index (or power)

5^3

base

5^3 tells you that 5 (the base number) is to be multiplied by itself 3 times (the index or power).
So $5^3 = 5 \times 5 \times 5$

index notation – when a product such as $2 \times 2 \times 2$ is written as 2^3, the number 3 is the index (plural **indices**).

indices – the plural of index: see **index**.

inequality – statements such as $x < 5, y \geqslant -3$, are inequalities.

integer – any positive or negative whole number or zero, for example, $-2, -1, 0, 1, 2, …$

intercept – the position where a graph crosses the y-axis.

interest – the money paid to you by a bank or building society when you save your money in an account with them.

NB It is also the money you pay for **borrowing** from a bank.

inverse operation – the operation that undoes a previous operation, for example, subtract is the inverse operation to add.

irrational number – a number that is not an integer and cannot be written as a fraction.

$\sqrt{2}, \sqrt{3}, \sqrt{5}, \sqrt{6}, \sqrt{7}, \sqrt{8}, \sqrt{10}, \sqrt{11}, \sqrt{12}, \sqrt{13}, \sqrt{14}, \sqrt{15}, \dots$ are all irrational numbers, but $\sqrt{1} = \frac{1}{1}$ or $\sqrt{4} = \frac{2}{1}$ or $\sqrt{9} = \frac{3}{1}$ or $\sqrt{16} = \frac{4}{1}, \dots$ are all rational numbers. Roots of square numbers are all rational numbers.

least common multiple (LCM) – the least (or lowest) multiple that two or more numbers have in common, for example,

the multiples of 4 are 4, 8, **12**, 16, 20, **24**, 28, 32, **36** …
the multiples of 6 are 6, **12**, 18, **24**, 30, **36** …
the common multiples are 12, 24, 36 …
the least common multiple is 12

linear – describes an equation, expression, graph, etc. where the highest power of a variable is 1; for example, $3x + 2 = 7$ is a linear equation but $3x^2 + 2 = 7$ is not.

linear equation – an equation which can be represented by a straight line graph; the equation will not contain powers of x, such as x^2 or x^3.

linear sequence – in a linear sequence, the differences are all the same.

This is a linear sequence

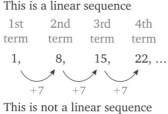

This is not a linear sequence

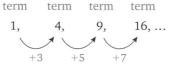

mixed number – a fraction that has both a whole number and a fraction part, for example, $1\frac{4}{7}$, $3\frac{1}{2}$, $5\frac{3}{4}$

multiple – the multiples of a number are the products in its multiplication table, for example,

the multiples of 7 are 7, 14, 21, 28, 35, …

nth term – this phrase is often used to describe a 'general' term in a sequence.

numerator – the top number of a fraction, indicating how many parts there are in the fraction.

operation – a rule for combining two numbers or terms, such as add, subtract, multiply or divide.

percentage – the number of parts per hundred, for example, 15% means $\frac{15}{100}$

power – see **index**.

prime number – a natural number with exactly two factors.

The first 7 prime numbers are:

2	3	5	7	11	13	17
Factors	Factors	Factors	Factors	Factors	Factors	Factors
1 & 2	1 & 3	1 & 5	1 & 7	1 & 11	1 & 13	1 & 17

1 is not a prime number because it has only one factor. 2 is the only even prime number.

principal – the initial amount of money put into the bank (or borrowed from the bank).

product – the result of multiplying two or more numbers, for example, the product of 5 and 7 is 35.

quadratic expression – an expression containing terms where the highest power of the variable is 2.

rate – the percentage at which interest is added.

ratio – a ratio is a means of comparing numbers or quantities. It shows how much bigger one number or quantity is than another.

rational number – a number that can be expressed in the form $\frac{p}{q}$ where p and q are both integers.

for example, 1 $(= \frac{1}{1})$, $2\frac{1}{3}$ $(= \frac{7}{3})$, 0.1 $(= \frac{1}{10})$

reciprocal – any number multiplied by its reciprocal equals 1.

1 divided by a number gives its reciprocal, for example, the reciprocal of 6 is $\frac{1}{6}$ because $6 \times \frac{1}{6} = 1$ or $1 \div 6 = \frac{1}{6}$

region – an area of a graph that has specific lines as its boundaries.

sequence – a sequence is a list of numbers or diagrams which are connected in some way.

significant figures – a digit in a number that is significant in the accuracy of the number. The closer the digit is to the beginning of the number the greater its significance. Zeros can be significant figures but are often in a number just to maintain the correct place value. Examples: The number 30 597 when rounded to three significant figures is 30 600; the first zero is significant but the final two are not. The number 3.0587 rounded to three significant figures is 3.06

simplify – to make simpler by collecting like terms.

simultaneous equations – a pair of equations containing two unknowns where both equations are true at the same time.

solution – the value of the unknown quantity, for example, if the equation is $3y = 6$, the solution is $y = 2$

solve – the instruction to find the value of the unknown, for example, $x = 3$, which is known as the solution of the equation.

speed – speed is the gradient of a line on a distance–time graph.

$$\text{Speed} = \frac{\text{distance travelled}}{\text{time taken}}$$

square number – a square number is the outcome when a number is multiplied by itself; square numbers are 1, 4, 9, 16, 25, …

square root – the square root of a number such as 16 is a number whose outcome is 16 when multiplied by itself.

standard index form – standard index form is a shorthand way of writing very large and very small numbers; standard form numbers are always written as:

A must be at least 1 but less than 10

$$A \times 10^n$$

A power of 10

subject – the subject of the formula $P = 2(l + w)$ is P because the formula starts '$P = \dots$'.

substitute – in order to use a formula to work out the value of one of the variables you replace the letters by numbers. This is called substitution.

substitution – using an expression for one unknown in terms of another, obtained from one of a pair of simultaneous equations, to reduce the second equation to one with a single variable.

sum – the result of adding numbers, for example, the sum of 8 and 2 is 10.

surd – a number involving irrational numbers, for example, $\sqrt{2}$, $3 + 2\sqrt{7}$

term – a number, variable or the product of a number and a variable(s) such as 3, x or $3x$.

term-to-term – the rule which tells you how to move from one term to another.

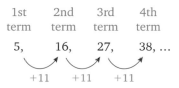

The rule to find the next number in the sequence is +11. The rule is called the term-to-term rule.

unitary method – a way of calculating quantities that are in proportion, for example, if 6 items cost £30 and you want to know the cost of 10 items, you can first find the cost of one item by dividing by 6, then find the cost of 10 by multiplying by 10.

unknown – in the equation $2x - 3 = 8$, x is the unknown.

variable – a symbol representing a quantity that can take different values, such as x, y or z.

VAT (Value Added Tax) – this tax is added on to the price of goods or services.

Index